ANIMAL RIGHTS

A Reference Handbook

ANIMAL RIGHTS

A Reference Handbook

Clifford J. Sherry, Ph.D.

CONTEMPORARY WORLD ISSUES

ABC-CLIO

Santa Barbara, California
Denver, Colorado
Oxford, England

Library of Congress Cataloging-in-Publication Data

Sherry, Clifford J.
Animal Rights : a reference handbook / Clifford J. Sherry
    p. cm.—(Contemporary world issues)
  Includes bibliographical references and index.
    1. Animal rights—United States—Handbooks, manuals, etc.
2. Animal welfare—Law and legislation—United States—Handbooks, manuals, etc. I. Title. II. Series.
  HV4764.S5 1994   179'.3—dc20   94-7168

ISBN 0-87436-733-6

00 99 98 97 96 95   10 9 8 7 6 5 4 3 2

ABC-CLIO, Inc.
130 Cremona Drive, P.O. Box 1911
Santa Barbara, California 93116-1911

This book is printed on acid-free paper ∞ .
Manufactured in the United States of America

*To my wife, Nancy C. Sherry, who is my partner
and best friend, and whose love I cherish most dearly*

Contents

Preface

THE CONTROVERSY SURROUNDING ANIMAL RIGHTS is divisive and potentially volatile. It divides society into three unequally sized groups. The *first* group is comprised of animal activists who believe that all human use of animals should stop immediately. The *second* group is society in general, which may or may not be aware of the controversy and which may or may not have formed an opinion. The *third* group is comprised of the people and industries that work with animals, such as farmers and ranchers, scientific researchers and educators, the entertainment industry (e.g., zoos, circuses, rodeo organizations, and filmmakers), hunters and fishermen, and the fur industry, as well as people who keep animals as pets.

The traditional animal welfare organizations have a long history. For example, the American Society for the Prevention of Cruelty to Animals was organized in 1866 and the American Humane Association was organized in 1877. These organizations sought to prevent cruelty to animals and to promote humane care.

More radical animal rights organizations were organized in the 1970s and 1980s. These organizations tend to focus much of their attention and activities on the use of animals in research, teaching, and product testing. People for the Ethical Treatment of Animals (PETA) is the largest of the new animal rights organizations. PETA was founded in 1980. It conducts rallies and demonstrations to focus attention on the exploitation and abuse of animals in experimentation, the manufacture of fur apparel, and the slaughter of animals for human consumption. PETA has acted as spokesman for the Animal Liberation Front (ALF), an international underground organization that was founded in England. ALF has claimed responsibility for numerous raids and break-ins in the United States beginning in 1979. It reportedly *liberates* animals being used for entertainment, food, clothing, or experimental research. ALF has also allegedly issued personal threats to animal researchers and has allegedly set fires, defaced property, destroyed equipment, planted fake bombs, and stolen research videotapes.

Groups that support the use of animals in research, education, and product testing include Americans for Medical Progress (AMP), the Coalition for Animals and Animal Research (CFAAR), the Foundation for Biomedical Research (FFBM), the Incurably Ill for Animal Research (iiFAR), and Putting People First (PPF). All were organized in the 1980s and 1990s.

It is interesting that two groups of people can use the same set of historical and contemporary information to come to two very different sets of assumptions and beliefs. These opposing assumptions and beliefs are at the core of the controversy. The animal activists, on one hand, argue that animal experimentation should not be done because it is bad science, because one cannot extrapolate from animal models to humans. Further, they say, animal research has not led to any significant improvement in human health, but rather has hurt human health by allowing harmful drugs into the marketplace. They also maintain that much research is unnecessary or duplicative, and that research is often conducted in a cruel and inhumane manner. Finally, they argue that research on animals is morally wrong and should not be done no matter how potentially beneficial the results might be.

The "Saving Lives Coalition-Statement of Support"[1] summarizes many of the assumptions and beliefs of the people who support the use of animals in research, education, and product testing. It says:

> We, the representatives of the undersigned professional and voluntary health organizations, wish to reaffirm our support for the continued humane use of animals in biomedical and behavioral research, testing and education. We ask that the point of view of the patients, the health care provider and the researcher be considered in the public discussion on the use of animals in biomedical research and testing.
>
> We reject the characterization of animal research as unnecessary, for we have seen the life-saving and life-enhancing benefits of such research. We recognize that there is much to be learned from animal experimentation that cannot be achieved in other ways. Thus, we take strong exception to the position of those people who would impede medical progress toward relieving human and animal suffering by halting research with animals.

The abandonment of animal research would be an abrogation of our primary responsibility to try to save human lives and of our responsibilities to save and improve animal lives as well.

Should animal research be lost to the scientific community, the victims would not be the scientists. The victims would be all people; ourselves, our families, our neighbors, our fellow humans. Human life is at stake; human suffering is at issue.

While great strides have been made in the understanding, prevention, and treatment of diseases, there is still much to be learned. Much of that research relies on laboratory animals.

We support only the highest standards of animal care and we encourage the use of all appropriate research methods, including cell and tissue cultures and computer models. However, only one type of research has been under attack consistently. Animal research has been the target of a very public campaign by activists who dismiss its importance to scientific progress.

We call upon all Americans to recognize the importance of the use of animals to continued progress in biomedical research. We ask that the perspective of those of us who suffer from diseases and conditions, those who hope to alleviate that suffering, and those who enjoy good health because of past progress be heard in the public debate on this issue. Our hope for a brighter medical future may well hang in the balance.

Differing beliefs over the animal rights issue are illustrated by the following quotes representing both points of view: For example, sounding the battle cry for animal activists is Ingrid Newkirk, one of the founders of PETA, who said that "[a]nimal liberationists do not separate out the human animal, so there is no rational basis for saying that a human being has special rights. A rat is a pig is a dog is a boy. They are all mammals."[2] Newkirk has also said that "[e]ven if animal research resulted in a cure for AIDS, we'd be against it . . ." and that "[e]ven painless research is fascism, supremacism, because the act of confinement is traumatizing in itself."[3]

Another PETA founder, Alex Pacheco, has said that "[w]e feel that animals have the same rights as a retarded human child."[4]

Kevin Beedy, a political scientist and animal rights activist has said that "[t]en years from now, the animal rights movement could still be grappling with questions of dying human babies being saved because of techniques learned throughout animal experimentation. This argument must be rendered politically useless."[5]

More extreme are the views of two ALF members. Of his opposition, ALF spokesperson Ronnie Lee has said that "[t]hese people are responsible for massive animal suffering. Kill, kill, kill the bastards."[6] ALF member Tim Daley has likened the animal rights struggle to war in which "you have to take up arms and people will get killed."[7]

Conversely, Robert J. White, M.D., a scientist and neurosurgeon states that "[t]here is virtually no major treatment or surgical procedure in modern medicine that could have been developed without animal research. Work with dogs and other animals led to the discovery of insulin and the control of diabetes, to open-heart surgery, the cardiac pacemaker and the whole area of organ transplantation."[8]

Former U.S. Surgeon General C. Everett Koop similarly has stated that "[v]irtually every major medical advance for both humans and animals has been achieved through biomedical research using animal models to study and find a cure for a disease and through animal testing to prove the safety and efficacy of a new treatment."[9]

Dr. Alan M. Goldberg, director of the Center for Alternatives to Animal Testing, Johns Hopkins University, has said that an "integrated approach of clinical, whole animal and *in vitro* studies is currently the best approach to advance science, develop new products and drugs, and treat, cure, and prevent disease."[10]

Sir Peter Medawar, Nobel laureate in immunology, has stressed that "[n]othing but research with animals will provide us with the knowledge that will make it possible for us, one day, to dispense with the use of animals altogether."[11]

Finally, Michael E. DeBakey, M.D., chancellor of Baylor College of Medicine and world renowned cardiovascular surgeon has said that "[i]t is the American public who will decide whether we must tell hundreds of thousands of victims of heart attacks, cancer, AIDS, and other dread diseases that the rights of animals supersede a patient's right to relief from suffering and premature death. Let us hope they reach a decision that is based on facts, reason and good will."[12]

Do animals have rights? Should we continue to use them for food and clothing? For medical research? To test products and drugs to determine if they are safe and effective? Should we keep animals as pets? The answers to these questions will profoundly affect society. Consider, for example, the impact of stopping the use of animals for food. One question that arises is what will happen to the animals that are currently being bred for food. Another is whether the existing technology for growing and harvesting nonanimal foods will support the human population. How do we protect these nonanimal foods from the ravages of insects, rodents, and other mammals that damage or destroy fruits, vegetables, and cereals in the field while they are growing, during harvest, while they are stored, or while they are being processed and distributed for use? Finally, it must be asked whether a diet that does not include animal products is healthy.

It is our responsibility, individually and collectively, to answer these complex questions based on reason, not emotion. This book attempts to provide a balanced overview of the issues involved in this controversy. It offers the reader the tools and information necessary to reach an informed opinion before taking action.

Notes

1. Saving Lives Coalition, Statement of Support. Signed June 1992.

2. Ingrid Newkirk, *Vogue*, September 1989.

3. Ibid., *Washingtonian Magazine*, August 1986.

4. Alex Pacheco, *New York Times*, 14 January 1989.

5. Kevin Beedy, *The Politics of Animal Rights: The Animal's Agenda*, March 1990.

6. Report on National Public Radio, 27 April 1991.

7. Americans for Medical Progress.

8. Dr. Robert J. White, *Reader's Digest*, March 1988.

9. Dr. C. Everett Koop, *Animals: The Vital Link to Health and Safety*, Partners in Discovery.

10. Dr. Alan M. Goldberg, *Animals: The Vital Link to Health and Safety*, Partners in Discovery.

11. Sir Peter Medawar, *Animals: The Vital Link to Health and Safety*, Partners in Discovery.

12. Dr. Michael E. DeBakey, Foundation for Biomedical Research Report.

Acknowledgments

NO BOOK IS THE WORK OF A SINGLE MIND. This book, which deals with a relatively volatile subject, is no exception. I have made every effort to keep my personal views in the background and to provide as balanced a view of the controversy relating to animal rights as possible.

I would like to thank my colleagues, past and present, who have acted as a sounding board for many of the ideas expressed in this book and played the role of devil's advocate. Special thanks go to Drs. Arthur Kling, William R. Klemm, and Thomas J. Walters, and to James T. Merritt.

I would also like to thank my editors at ABC-CLIO, Jeff Serena and Amy Catala, who have been patient, understanding, and supportive.

Several organizations have provided information, data, and insights. They include the following groups:

American Association for Accreditation of Laboratory Animal Care

Animal Care and Welfare Institute

Amimal Welfare Information Center (National Agricultural Library)

Coalition for Animals and Animal Research

Foundation for Biomedical Research

Fur Farm Animal Welfare Coalition

Institute of Laboratory Animal Resources

National Agricultural Library

National Library of Medicine

National Trappers Association and the Sport Fishing Institute

1

Overview

THERE IS MUCH DEBATE GENERATED by the question of whether animals, as well as people, have rights. Regarding the rights of people, the U.S. Declaration of Independence says:

> We hold these truths to be self-evident, that all men are created equal, that they are endowed by their Creator with certain unalienable Rights, that among these are Life, Liberty, and the pursuit of Happiness. That to secure these rights, Governments are instituted among Men, deriving their just Powers from the consent of the governed. . . .

When Thomas Jefferson penned those powerful words, he was propounding the radical idea of liberating humankind from the political oppression and servitude that had been the destiny of most humans from time immemorial and continues to be the fate of most members of our species to this very day. Jefferson and the other Founding Fathers were proposing that men had a right to be free, not because of a ruler's decree or a majority vote, but simply because they were men. This concept is at the very foundation of the United States identity as a nation and gives our moral concerns political force. Its philosophical foundations have been used to endorse a variety of political acts, including violence.

To engage these rights fully, we must liberate ourselves from the ravages of disease and premature death, as well as from ignorance and poverty. Based on this tenet, successive groups of people, such as women and racial, religious, and ethnic minorities, as well as other minorities, such as homosexuals, have appealed for reconsideration of their status.

To establish a government, America's Founding Fathers penned these mighty words as part of the U.S. Constitution:

> We the People of the United States, in Order to form a more perfect Union, establish Justice, insure domestic Tranquillity, provide for the common defense, promote the general Welfare, and secure the Blessings of Liberty to ourselves and our Posterity, do ordain and establish this Constitution for the United States of America.

The Constitution, which is a unique historical document, has survived the test of time. However, as a charter of freedom, it left great gaps in the protection of the individual from the government and popular majorities. This was corrected in 1791 with the ratification of the Bill of Rights, the first ten amendments to the Constitution. The Bill of Rights protects the rights of the individual, which it details as including:

1. Freedom of religion, speech, and assembly and the right to petition the government (Amendment I)
2. The right to keep and bear arms (Amendment II)
3. The right to be secure in their persons, houses, papers, and effects against unreasonable seizures (Amendment IV)
4. The right to not be deprived of life, liberty, or property, without due process of law (Amendment V)
5. The right in criminal prosecutions to a speedy and public trial, to be informed of the nature and cause of accusation, to be confronted with the witnesses against the accused, to have compulsory process for obtaining witness in one's favor, and to have the assistance of counsel for one's defense (Amendment VI)
6. That the enumeration of certain rights in the Constitution shall not be construed to deny or disparage others retained by the people (Amendment IX)
7. That the powers not delegated to the United States by the Constitution, nor prohibited by it to the states, are reserved by the states, respectively, or by the people (Amendment X)

Defining the Idea of Rights

Right in an abstract sense, means justice, ethical correctness, or consonance with the rules of law or the principles of morals.[1] Law in the abstract is considered the foundation for all rights or the complex of underlying moral principles that impart the character of justice to all positive law or give it ethical content. In a concrete sense, a right is a power, privilege, faculty, or demand, inherent in one person and incident upon another. The primal rights pertaining to humankind are: (1) enjoyed by human beings, (2) grounded in human beings purely as such, (3) grounded in the human personality, and (4) antecedent to their recognition by positive law (i.e., a law that was enacted or adopted by a government).

When used as an adjective, the term *right* means just, morally correct, and consonant with ethical principles or rules of positive law. Based on its juristic content, *right* can be defined as a capacity residing in one man of controlling, with the assent and assistance of the state, the action of others.

Natural rights grow out of and conform to humankind's nature (its whole mental, moral, and physical constitution) and depend upon its personality. Natural rights are distinguished from those created by positive laws enacted by government to create an orderly civilized society. Natural rights grow from natural law, which entails the necessary and obligatory rules of human conduct.

In short, humans have rights. The fact that most humans throughout history and currently throughout the world cannot exercise these rights does not alter the fact that they have them. However, do animals have rights? If so, the question is whether we violate these rights when we use animals for our own purposes.

Philosophical Basis of Animal Rights

Two influential books, *Animal Liberation: A New Ethics for Our Treatment of Animals,* by Peter Singer, and *The Case for Animal Rights,* by Thomas Regan, provide the philosophical basis for the modern animal rights movement. Singer and Regan are philosophers who use the methods of analytical ethics. They would argue that ethics are objective and are rooted in reason and the very logic of our language. Both base their positions on modern secular reasons and eschew arguments based on religious suppositions. A central tenet of analytical ethics is universality, which means that any ethical prescription is applicable to everyone in relatively similar circumstances. If a duty can be extended to more people or situations, then analytical ethics demands that it must be extended. Further, if different moral judgments are made in two different cases, analytical ethics demands that one must demonstrate a morally relevant difference between the cases.

Animal Liberation has been called the bible of the animal rights movement. Singer is a utilitarian. As such, he argues that one should act to bring about the best balance of good and bad consequences for everyone affected by an act. Singer's basic moral postulate is that equal consideration of interests is not arbitrarily limited to members of our own species. Singer argues that avoidance of pain is a characteristic of all *sentient* creatures; that is, organisms that are responsive to or conscious of sense impressions. He maintains that humans have ruthlessly and cruelly exploited animals and have inflicted needless suffering on them. Singer says this must be stopped because all sentient beings should be considered as equals with respect to infliction of pain. According to Singer, a difference in species is no more a morally relevant distinction than are other arbitrary characteristics, such as race or sex.

Liberation movements demand an end to prejudice and discrimination based on these arbitrary characteristics. Singer argues that liberation movements force an expansion of moral horizons and cause practices that were previously regarded as natural and inevitable to be seen as the result of unjustifiable prejudice. Further, he argues that since animals cannot speak for themselves, it is our duty to speak for them. He reasons that the very use of the word "animal" to mean "animals other than human beings" sets humans apart from other animals and implies that we are not animals. Singer is heavily indebted to eighteenth-century utilitarian philosopher Jeremy Bentham, who wrote of animals, "The question is not, can they reason? Nor can they talk? But, can they suffer?"

In *The Case for Animal Rights*, Regan, on the other hand, argues that animals have moral rights because of the concept of inherent value; that is, simple nonnatural, unanalyzable properties that are known to us through our moral intuition. He uses the concept of subject of a life as the basis for his argument that animals have rights. Regan develops a cumulative argument for animal consciousness and the complexity of awareness in animals. He maintains that an animal's individual welfare has importance to it, whatever its usefulness to others. Any such creature has inherent value, Regan says, and should be treated as a moral being with moral rights. He argues that the benefits of scientific research are real, but that they are ill gotten because they violate the rights of the individual (animal). This is true, Regan says, even if the research produces the best possible aggregate consequences. Thus, Regan uses the principles of justice and equality to develop a theory of moral rights for humans and animals, based on the inherent value of individuals, which are subjects of life.

Despite their differences, Singer and Regan distinguish between animals and humans and maintain that animals are not equal to humans in all respects. Both authors argue that a normal adult human has more value than an animal. They maintain that if one must choose between the life of an animal and the life of a human, the death of a human would *prima facie* be a greater harm. Both assert that these situations arise only when the life of a human being is in direct conflict with the life of an animal. However, it is important to note that Singer's and Regan's arguments are not rationally reconcilable. Regan faults Singer and Singer faults Regan. Indeed, each shows that the other's ethical model is inconsistent and leads to immoral or irrational outcomes. For example, Regan argues that utilitarianism does not provide any categorical protection against any act, as long as its result provides the greatest good for the greatest number. R. G. Frey, like Singer, is a utilitarian, but Frey uses the same ethical arguments as Singer to defend medical research utilizing animals.[2]

Conversely, Singer uses Regan's lifeboat example to criticize Regan's position. In this example, a group of normal humans and a dog are on an overcrowded lifeboat and the boat is sinking. Someone must be thrown overboard. Who? According to Regan, the dog. Why? Because the magnitude of harm is a function of the number of opportunities for satisfaction available for an individual. The death of a human takes away more possible opportunities for satisfaction than the death of an animal. Regan argues that even in the presence of 1 million dogs, it would still not be right to throw one human overboard. Regan maintains that the intrinsic value of each dog must be determined, one at a time, before each is thrown overboard. Regan also argues that in the lifeboat situation, the humans are permitted to eat a dog to avoid starvation.

Singer asks, if such killing is allowed, where will it stop? Further, intuitionists, like Regan, have difficulty explaining why ethically sophisticated and sensitive people disagree.

Regan holds that the difference between the lifeboat situation and medical research is that in the lifeboat situation, the dog would suffer a risk similar to that of the humans by remaining on board, because presumably the dog got on the lifeboat voluntarily. According to Regan's argument, if the dog were coerced into getting on the lifeboat, then it would be immoral to throw the dog overboard. Animal research is similar to the latter situation; the dog is coercively put at risk, because the animal would not otherwise run the risk.

Others, such as Edwin A. Locke and C. Cohen,[3] maintain that it is not the capacity to suffer, but rather the capacity to reason that should be used as the moral boundary. A moral agent is an entity capable of actions that may be appropriately evaluated as right or wrong. This presupposes an entity who is capable of grasping moral principles; that is, an entity that has free will, is capable of reasoning, possesses self-consciousness, and has a sense of time (one who lives in the present, but possesses a memory of the past and an ability to plan for the future). The holders of rights must have the capacity to comprehend the rules of duty, which govern all, including themselves. As humans pass through childhood and adolescence they are generally seen as becoming increasingly morally responsible for their acts. Rights, as previously indicated, are also a social concept. The purpose is to protect people from the actions of other people. The right of life, as mentioned in the Declaration of Independence means that you have a right to think about what you should do to promote your well-being and to be free to act on your judgment. Since animals do not possess reason, they cannot grasp moral principles. Thus, they cannot act volitionally to direct their actions. In our dealing with animals, humans are bound by an obligation to treat them with decency and concern; that is, humanely.

Statistical Profile of Animal Uses

Drs. Charles S. Nicoll and Sharon M. Russell analyzed 20 important books on animal rights as selected by Dr. Charles R. Magel. (Magel is the author of *Keyguide to Information Sources in Animal*

Rights [see chapter 7].) Nicoll and Russell eliminated five books from Magel's original list and added a title that was not on it.[4] These books contained 4,562 pages. Nicoll and Russell made the following observations: that 2,598 of these pages were concerned with ethical and moral questions regarding the use of animals by humans; that 1,680 pages were critical of the ways in which humans exploit animals; that 216 pages considered the history of the animal rights movement and its current status; and that 68 pages covered the plight of wild animals.

Of the 1,680 pages pertaining to the ways that humans use animals, 63.3 percent dealt with the use of animals in biomedical research and education; 30.6 percent with the use of animals for food; and 6 percent concerned all other uses (2.3 percent for pets and pound animals, 2.3 percent for hunting, 0.8 percent for fur garments, and 0.0 percent for entertainment).

Nicoll and Russell point out that more than 6 billion animals (including only mammals and birds, not fish, amphibians, or reptiles) are used in the United States each year. About 96.5 percent are used for food, while 0.3 percent are used for research and teaching. They concluded that the concern/use ratio—the ratio of pages in animal rights publications to the number of animals used for that purpose—was disproportionate.

The concern/use ratio for animals used for food (30.6 percent pages/96.5 percent use) is 0.32, while the concern/use ratio for research and teaching (63.3 percent/0.3 percent) is 211.00. It is not clear why there is so much focus on the use of animals in research and teaching. The remainder of this chapter discusses the use of animals in this context. It compares and contrasts the arguments of animal activists and scientists.

Animal Research: Pros and Cons

Sensitive, thoughtful people should feel somewhat uncomfortable when considering animal research, just as they should feel uncomfortable when thinking about disease, war, famine, and other suffering. Animal rights activists, society in general, and scientists would like to see an end to using animals in research. Yet they differ as to when this should happen.

Activists would like to see animal research, in fact any use of animals, come to an end immediately. They use two basic arguments to support their view. First, activists argue that animal experimentation should not be done because it is bad science; they argue that one cannot extrapolate from animal models to the human condition and that research with animals can be replaced with alternative methods. Activists also argue that instead of leading to any significant improvement in human health, animal research has positively harmed it by allowing harmful drugs into the marketplace. They also maintain that there is too much unnecessary and duplicative research. Second, a more general argument they propound is that research on animals is morally wrong and should not be done no matter how potentially beneficial the results might be and is often conducted in a cruel and inhumane manner.

The Example of Epilepsy Research

Consider a hypothetical situation: a neurologist is presented with a patient with epilepsy. Epilepsy is an ancient malady. It apparently puzzled and plagued mankind in all parts of the world from the dawn of human existence. In the time of Hippocrates (460–370 B.C.) it was called the "falling sickness" or the "sacred disease." Hippocrates attempted to change the popular notion that epilepsy was a form of demonic possession. He claimed that the dramatic symptoms were caused by natural causes.

John Hughlings Jackson, an English neurologist who excelled in the observation and description of neurological phenomena, said in 1873 that seizures were caused by "occasional, sudden, excessive, rapid, and local discharges of the gray matter." This brilliant insight was not confirmed until 1931, when Hans Berger invented the electroencephalograph and recorded the electrical activity of the brain during an epileptic seizure. It is estimated that 3 to 6 out of every 1,000 humans suffer from epilepsy.

It is hoped that everyone today agrees that epilepsy is not caused by demonic possession. Unfortunately, despite significant progress, especially in the last few decades, we still do not know exactly what causes epilepsy in some individuals. We do know that some people may be predisposed to it due to the following causes: injuries to the brain—prior to, during, or anytime after birth— that were caused by mechanical damage such as blows to the head and penetrating wounds; toxic environmental agents; infections; a high fever; hemorrhages; or asphyxia (decrease or lack of oxygen to the brain). In some cases, however, epilepsy seems to appear without apparent cause and without any obvious lesion in the brain.

Between the time of Hippocrates and the middle of the nineteenth century, the record of attempts to treat epilepsy provides a compendium of humankind's attempts to explain and treat one of our more serious bodily ailments based on minimal knowledge of natural phenomena and their causes. The first major breakthrough in the treatment of epilepsy came 20 centuries after Hippocrates.

In 1857, the English physician, Thomas Laycock, introduced bromides as a treatment for epilepsy. It is interesting to note that Laycock thought that epilepsy had some relationship to the menstrual cycle. In Laycock's time, bromides were considered anaphrodisiacs (something that decreases sexual desire). As sometimes happens in medicine, the idea was wrong but the remedy was right. Although potassium bromide does control seizures, it has significant side effects. It can cause bromide psychosis, which is characterized by the occurrence of delirium, delusions, hallucinations, fear reactions, and mania, as well as weakness, tremors, and incoordination. It also can cause skin lesions and gastrointestinal disturbances, such as anorexia, gastric distress, and constipation.

In adults, the most common form of epilepsy is *grand mal.* Grand mal seizures are characterized by loss of posture and vigorous involuntary movements of the limbs, trunk, and head, often accompanied by a temporary loss of consciousness. Seizures vary in intensity, frequency, and duration. In the worst cases they can occur several times each day and each seizure can last from 60–90 seconds to several minutes.

Petit mal seizures, which are not as violent, are more common in children. Generally, the child freezes (stops what he or she is doing and develops a vacant look), but does not lose posture. These are commonly called absence seizures, because during one, the child is apparently not conscious of or interacting with his environment. In the worst cases, the child can have as many as several hundred seizures in a day. Normally, these are relatively brief, usually less than a minute in duration.

Consider a hypothetical neurologist who is approached by a chemist who says she has just synthesized a new drug that she thinks may have some anti-epileptic properties. The neurologist knows that an ideal anti-epileptic drug would suppress all seizures without causing any unwanted side effects. The neurologist will probably wonder whether this new drug is better, safer, and more effective—with fewer side effects—than existing drugs. What should the neurologist do considering that he doesn't know anything about this drug or how toxic it is? Further, he does not know the appropriate dose level or the best route of administration. Finally, the neurologist does not know what side effects this drug might cause, at what dose level these side effects might appear or if the drug is a carcinogen, teratogen, or mutagen.

Should the neurologist give his patient an injection of this new drug and hope for the best? Probably, at least hopefully, not. Scientists or clinicians who use human subjects for biomedical research are generally required to acknowledge that they are aware of, understand, and ascribe to the two international ethical codes that guide biomedical research with human subjects. One is the Nuremberg Code of Ethics in Medical Research (1948), which was developed by the Allies during the war crimes trials after World War II. The other is the Declaration of Helsinki, which was adopted by the Eighteenth World Medical Assembly in 1964 and was revised at the Twenty-ninth World Medical Assembly in 1975.

The Nuremberg Code was the standard used to judge the practices of the Nazis involved in human experimentation. The Code sets forth what criteria must be met before any experiment using human beings as subjects can be judged morally acceptable. Point Three of the Code says the "experiments should be so designed and based on the results of animal experiments and a knowledge of the natural history of the disease or other problem under study that the anticipated results (will) justify the performance of the experiment."

The revised Declaration of Helsinki, under Point One of its basic principles, says that "[b]iomedical research involving human subjects must conform to generally accepted scientific principles and should be based on adequately performed laboratory and animal experimentation and on a thorough knowledge of the scientific literature."

So ethical issues are probably the major consideration for the neurologist. Fortunately, there are several animal models of grand mal epilepsy. These models have been used in the past to screen a variety of chemical compounds to determine if they had anti-epileptic properties, as well as to answer the other questions outlined above. In 1938, these studies yielded one of the drugs that is most commonly used in the clinical management of epilepsy—phenyltoin, or more specifically, diphenylhydantoin.

Phenyltoin exerts anti-epileptic activity without causing generalized depression of the nervous system. It apparently works by limiting the development of maximal seizure activity and also by preventing the spread of seizure activity from the active focus (the localized site where the seizure activity begins). This drug, either alone or in combination with a close chemical relative, phenobarbital, controls seizure activity in about 50 percent of all adult epileptics. It also decreases the frequency, intensity, and/or duration of seizures in at least an additional 25 percent of adult epileptics.

Now the neurologist is presented with an 8-year-old girl who is having several hundred absence seizures each day. Unfortunately, there is no satisfactory animal model of petit mal epilepsy. This means there is no easy method to screen drugs to determine which is the most effective in dealing with such seizures. However, it is likely that the drug has been screened in an animal model to determine the drug's toxicity, safe dose level, and other characteristics as described above.

So what should the neurologist do when presented with an 8-year-old who is having several hundred absence seizures a day? The doctor would probably start with the lowest potentially effective dose of the least toxic drug and gradually increase the dose level until the child's seizures were controlled. If this drug did not work, the doctor would start with the next least toxic drug and repeat this process. The process would continue until the doctor found a drug and dose level that worked, and it can take weeks or months during which the child would still be having seizures. Unfortunately, some children have seizures that are not controlled by existing drugs.

The Tuskegee Experiment

In 1974, Public Law 93-348 mandated the formation of an Institutional Human Investigation Committee. This law came about, in part, because of what is sometimes called the Tuskegee Scandal. In 1932, the United States Public Health Service set up an experiment involving some poor farmers in Macon County, Alabama, a predominantly black and illiterate area with one of the highest syphilis rates in the nation. The subjects were 412 persons with syphilis, 204 undiseased controls, and 275 individuals that had been cured of syphilis with treatments then in use (heavy metals such as bismuth, mercury, and arsenic).

The experiment was not secret; the data was reported in the medical literature from time to time, as it was acquired. The men with syphilis were not systematically treated, even after penicillin became readily available in the 1940s. Unfortunately, there is no evidence that the subjects understood the experiment. Therefore, they did not give informed consent to be a subject in the experiment. When the story of the experiment became widely known, Edmund C. Casey, M.D., the incoming president of the National Medical Association (an organization of black physicians), reportedly commented on the drug testing as follows: "First you try it in mice, then in rats, and then in blacks—because chimpanzees are too expensive." Dr. Casey's statement brings up an important point. If we do not test drugs and other treatments on animals, then whom do we test them on? There is no simple *in vitro* or computer model of many diseases and disorders that plague human beings. Following are some concrete examples to consider.

How Surgeons Learn Surgery

Surgeons need to know how to perform important operations, such as transplanting organs, removing tumors, reattaching severed limbs, treating wounds from gunshots and other causes, just as they need to know how to perform more mundane procedures, such as removing a malfunctioning appendix or a gall bladder. Surgery is as much an art as it is a science.

The only way people become surgeons is by practicing surgery. Cadavers, human or animal, and models can be used to teach surgeons about basic anatomical structure. Yet the only way to learn surgery is to do it on a living, breathing (anesthetized) subject. That is the only way to obtain the feel of the tissues, blood vessels, nerves, and organs, and to learn to deal with individual variations. It is also the only way to develop new surgical techniques.

The Education of Neurobiologists

The human brain is not particularly impressive looking. Weighing only three pounds, it is small enough to be held in one hand. The cerebrum, which looks very much like a giant wrinkled walnut, makes up 70 percent of the entire nervous system. It is about the size of two fists held together. A fresh, unpreserved brain has the consistency of gelatin and is grayish. Despite its unimpressive look, the human brain is more complex than the largest and fastest man-made computer. It is also more complex than the worldwide telephone network, which is probably our largest and most complicated technological achievement.

The basic building blocks of the nervous system are nerve cells or neurons. Although neurons come in a bewildering number of sizes and shapes, most have three component parts. They are: (1) the nerve cell, which contains the nucleus and the metabolic machinery of the cell; (2) a long, relatively undivided process, the axon; and (3) a treelike process with many branches, the dendrites. Neurons are "hooked together" by specialized junctions called synapses. Each neuron receives as few as 10 to as many as 10,000 synapses.

The cerebral cortex is the outer layer of the cerebrum and is responsible for the wrinkled look. Although it is less than one-fourth inch thick and if unfolded would be about the size of a sheet of a tabloid newspaper, this fragile sheath contains more than 8 billion nerve cells. Each cubic inch of cortical tissue contains more than 10,000 miles of fibers. It is the site of consciousness, speech, creativity, and all the functions that make us human.

The brain is not homogeneous. It consists of concentrations of nerve cells that are called nuclei (singular nucleus) and concentrations of axons that are called tracts (inside the nervous system) and nerves (outside the nervous system). Neurobiologists do not currently understand how neurons arrange themselves into nuclei and axons into tracts. Further, neurobiologists do not understand how nerve cells become interconnected. Since the number of neurons and especially the number of synapses exceed the number of human genes by several orders of magnitude, it appears that the placement of neurons and their interconnections is not under direct genetic control.

Although far from complete, almost everything we know about the brain and how it functions has been via experiments on animals. Early experiments involved making lesions in the nervous system and then observing the animal to determine how the lesion impacted behavior. Other experiments involved stimulating the brain, either electrically or with chemicals or drugs, and determining what happened. The only other source of information is what some early investigators called "experiments of nature"; that is, observing a human born with a specific defect in their brain and, following death, removing the brain to attempt to find the defect. There have been some major breakthroughs in the study of the brain in the last few decades, especially in recording and interpreting the electrical activity of the nervous system, as well as in mapping the connections between neurons. More recently, breakthroughs in imaging, such as positron emission tomography, have allowed neurobiologists to tie specific functions to specific portions of the nervous system. Despite these recent break-throughs, however, there is still much about brain function that we do not understand. For example, neurobiologists do not know where or how memories are stored in the brain. Also, among other things, they do not understand how simple sensations are transformed into perceptions; how movements are initiated; how, why, or where emotions and other feelings are initiated, and what function they serve; and why we sleep. Except on the most basic level, neurobiologists also do not understand how the brain controls such basic functions as eating, drinking, and sex. These are not just questions for scientists in the ivory towers of academia. If we do not understand how the brain works we will not be able to fix it when it does not work. For example, neurobiologists and their clinical colleagues do not understand what causes problems of the nervous system such as mental retardation, mental illness, and diseases such as Alzheimer's or Parkinson's. Except on a rather crude level (tranquilizers for schizophrenia; l DOPA for Parkinson's), these scientists and clinicians do not know how to cure these conditions or how to treat them to eliminate or even minimize their impact.

How can neurobiologists study problems of how the brain works and how to fix it when it does not work? No one has succeeded in modeling the entire nervous system. It is unlikely that anyone will succeed in the near future. Models of small portions of the nervous system, such as the hippocampus (a part of the brain that is important for normal memory function), have been proposed. However, it is unlikely that these models will help answer these important questions. Pseudo models, such as neural networks, also will probably not yield the answers. One of the key differences between electronic computers and biological ones (brains or portions of brains; i.e., groups of interconnected neurons) is that the electronic computers are serial processors. They process information and instructions one at a time, in order. Electric computers can do this very quickly, often several billion steps in a second. In contrast, brains are considerably slower. They are, however, parallel processors, which can process multiple pieces of information or instructions at the same time. Neural networks are computer programs or hard-wired computers that mimic the parallel processing functions of small groups of neurons. Neural networks are used in a variety of applications, such as trying to understand the stock or commodity market, metrology, and other complex systems. Yet since neural networks are not true models of the nervous system, they cannot be used to attempt to answer questions about the brain's function or malfunction.

Except for certain basic questions about receptors, channels, and ion transport, it is unlikely that lower animals, such as amphibians, reptiles, and invertebrates, will be useful in this quest. How and where can neurobiologists and their clinical colleagues attempt to study these complex and important questions?

Testing Potentially Dangerous Substances

How should we test substances to learn whether they are injurious to human health? What are the substances in question? With the exception of nutrients—such as carbohydrates, fats, proteins, minerals, and water, which fuel, build, and maintain our bodies— many of the chemicals in our environment are potentially toxic. They include chemicals that are obviously poisonous, such as pesticides and herbicides, as well as solvents and chemical intermediates that are the building blocks of many of our modern wonders, such as plastics and synthetic fibers. But they also include less obvious substances such as chemicals that are naturally present in our food (alkaloids, glycosides, and tannins), as well as chemicals that are intentionally added (food colors, artificial flavors, antioxidants) or unintentionally added (antibiotic residues). Other potential toxins include antibiotics and drugs that are used to treat the ailments of humans and animals.

Environmental Chemicals/Agents

No one knows precisely how many new chemicals or chemical compounds are added to our environment each year. Best estimates suggest that industry creates 2,000 to 3,000 new chemicals each year. Many are produced in small amounts (a kilogram or less) and involve exposure to a small number of people. Others are produced in multiton quantities and involve the exposure of thousands to millions of people.

If these new chemicals do not have anything to do with food or drugs, the vast majority have not been screened, on even the most basic level, to determine their potential health risks. Toxic chemicals that serve no useful function, such as car exhaust, should be eliminated as soon as possible. Other potentially toxic chemicals, such as pesticides, solvents, and chemical intermediates, serve a useful, often vital, function. They cannot, at least in theory, be replaced by a less toxic substitute.

Some toxins are acute poisons. Exposure to a high enough dose (in some cases, such as organophosphates, as little as a few milligrams) will kill on the spot. Others are poisonous after chronic exposure (one or more exposures may cause only minimal problems, but repeated exposure over a long time period may cause potentially life-threatening problems). Still another group of toxins are more subtle and insidious. The effects of exposure to these substances might not show up until months, years, or decades after exposure. These include mutagens, teratogens, and carcinogens.

So, should new chemicals or chemical compounds be tested to determine if they are safe? What about chemicals that are already in use? Finally, how should these substances be tested?

Mutagens cause mutations—permanent alterations in the molecular structure of the genes (structural changes in DNA, the physical basis for inherited characteristics). *The Metabolic Basis of Inherited Disease,* edited by John B. Stanbury, James B. Wyngaarden, and Donald S. Fredrickson,[5] lists more than 60 classes of inherited diseases. Most cause severe problems and many are life threatening. Should new chemicals and other environmental agents be tested to determine if they are mutagens? If so, how and on whom?

Teratogens cause birth defects. The national March of Dimes Foundation publishes *Birth Defects: Atlas and Compendium,*[6] which lists more than 800 birth defects. Major birth defects are more common than most people realize. At least one out of every 12 live births is born with a birth defect. Teratologists (the scientists who study birth defects and their causes) know the cause of a few of the birth defects described in the compendium. However, they do not know the cause of the majority of birth defects that are described. Some, perhaps most, are caused by exogenous (environmental) agents. Should we test new chemicals to determine if they are teratogens? If so, how and on whom?

Carcinogens cause cancer, which is one of the three leading causes of death after the age of five. In fact, 10 percent of all deaths are caused by cancer of which there are at least 100 different forms.

Whereas normal healthy cells grow, divide, and replace themselves in an orderly manner, cancer cells have lost this orderliness.

ivide and grow rapidly, invading and destroying nearby
. Cancer cells also "metastasize" or spread to other more
: parts of the body where they form new tumors. Many
ɔgists (those who study cancer) think that many forms of
r are caused by environmental agents. These chemicals can
ducers, promoters, or cocarcinogens. For example, many
tists think that the risk of developing lung cancer is ten times
ter for smokers than for nonsmokers. Up to 30 percent of all
er deaths are linked to smoking. However, other chemical and
physical agents, such as X rays, can cause cancer. Once again the
questions arise about whether to test, how to do it, and on whom.

Food Additives

The Food Additives Amendment (72 Stat. 1785) of the federal
Food, Drug, and Cosmetic Act (Public Law 717 52 Stat. 1040)
states that if used prior to 1 January 1958 and shown to be safe
either by scientific procedures or experience based on consumer
use, a substance is not a food additive, but rather a GRAS (generally regarded as safe) substance.

The Panel on Food Safety at the 1969 White House Conference on Food, Nutrition, and Health recommended that the
GRAS substances be systematically reevaluated for safety. They
further suggested that the reevaluations be based on objective
investigations under controlled conditions.[7]

Preclinical Drug Trials

Animals are used extensively in preclinical drug evaluations.
These preclinical trials typically involve several species of animals,
mostly small laboratory rodents that are bred especially for this
purpose, in a number of different types of studies. Normally, the
first step in evaluating a new drug (or environmental chemical) is
to determine the Lethal Dose 50% (LD50). This is the dose that
is required to kill 50 percent of the subjects. This information is
important because it tells the scientists how toxic the drug is. The
next step is to determine the Effective Dose 50% (ED50). The precise test(s) that is/are performed here is determined by the type of
drug that is being evaluated. The best route of administration is
also determined at this time. For example, some drugs cannot be
administered orally because they would be "broken down" in the
digestive system to an inactive form. Or possibly they might not
be absorbed from the digestive system. Knowing the LD50 and the

ED50 allows the scientist to determine the risk-benefit ratio for the drug. For example, if the LD50 and the ED50 are relatively close together and the scientist is evaluating headache remedies, he would probably abandon the drug at this point. The reason is that headaches are usually self-limiting (i.e., they eventually go away without treatment) and are not life threatening, so it would be inappropriate to use a potentially toxic drug to treat them. But, if the scientist is evaluating a drug that is used to treat cancer, he might proceed. In this case the risk is the same, but the potential benefit is increased. That is, many forms of cancer are progressive (i.e., get worse without treatment) and life threatening.

If the risk-benefit ratio is appropriate, then the drug is evaluated to determine if it is a mutagen (i.e., causes mutations), teratogen (i.e., causes birth defects), or carcinogen (i.e., causes cancer). Often, it seems that scientists use very high doses when making these evaluations, doses that are far higher than would be encountered by a human using the drug, and this causes confusion for people who do not understand the underlying principle. Consider a concrete example. Suppose that the scientist thinks that the drug (or environmental chemical) might be a carcinogen and on the average, it might cause cancer in 1 out of every 1,000 individuals that are exposed to it. If 10 million people are exposed to it, this means that on the average about 10,000 people might develop cancer that might not otherwise.

Now the scientist is confronted with a practical problem. If he uses the typical dose and exposes 1,000 animals to that dose, it is possible that no animals will develop tumors or possibly 1 or a few animals will. But, consider the magnitude of the problem. He must purchase 1,000 animals. Then he must house and care for these animals for several months to several years. Then he (and hopefully a dozen colleagues) will have to evaluate these animals. And then, it is possible that none of these animals will develop tumors! This is the reason that scientists use what seems like very high dose levels—so that he can keep the study manageable and still obtain interpretable results.

The studies described above are all acute. That is, they evaluate the effects of a single exposure to a drug (or environmental chemical). One important part of these acute studies is evaluating the effects of the drug (or environmental chemical) on fertility and reproduction. This generally involves a multigenerational study of the effects of the drug. These studies usually take a number of years to complete and continue during the early phases of the clinical trials.

Most people are exposed to most drugs (and environmental chemicals) more than one time. Therefore, an important part of the preclinical trials is evaluating the effects of chronic (multiple) exposure. The evaluation of chronic effects takes several years and also continues during the initial phases of the clinical trials.

Clinical Drug Trials

In 1962, the Harris-Kefauver Amendment (Public Law 87-781 76 Stat. 781) was signed into law. It was enacted primarily in response to the thalidomide crisis (detailed later in this chapter). This amendment requires that in determining the effectiveness and safety of a new drug, extensive pharmacological and toxicological research in animals must occur before a drug can be tested on humans in controlled clinical trials (see above).

Before a clinical trial can begin, its protocol must be approved by the institutional human use committee of the institution(s) where it will be conducted. All subjects must give their informed consent. Before they can participate, subjects must be informed of the potential risks and benefits to themselves (and to society in general) of the trial. Then they must sign a statement signifying that they understand the risks and benefits and can withdraw from the trial at any time.

Clinical trials are generally conducted in four phases. In the *first phase*, the drug is given to a small number of normal volunteers. The purpose of this phase is to determine the biological effects of the drug and how it is metabolized, as well as a safe dose range. In the early part of the *second phase*, the drug is administered to a small number of patients to determine its usefulness and therapeutic dose range. Late in the second phase, the drug is given to a larger pool of patients for a longer time. This helps to refine the dose range and provides more information about the body's elimination of the drug. The first two phases usually take about 46 months to complete.

In the *third phase*, the drug is given to 500–3,000 selected patients. Only a few hundred are treated for more than three to six months. Currently, these trials are usually prospective, controlled, double-blind studies that are randomized. A "prospective" study means that evaluation of the treatment begins when the study starts. In a "controlled" trial, the drug is tested on one group of people and the results are compared to a control group. A formal study plan is used. In a "double-blind" trial, neither the physician nor the patient knows what treatment the patient is receiving. This is especially important when the variables that are measured are subjective, since this eliminates potential bias. A "randomized" trial is one in which the patients with a specific condition in common (e.g., AIDS) are assigned to different treatment groups at random. Generally, one group receives the new (unproved, but promising) treatment, while the other receives the standard treatment (sometimes called a positive [active agent] control) or a placebo (an inert chemical, such as a sugar pill, that has no effect on the condition). FDA regulations also allow for two other control groups: untreated, where the control group does not receive any treatment; or historical, where a patient group treated in the past is compared to the group of patients being treated with the new intervention. This phase usually lasts about 23 months.

In the first part of the *fourth phase,* selected medical centers and physicians are given the drug to administer to selected patients under careful supervision of the physician, who monitors the drug's efficacy. In the second part, physicians who prescribe the drug to the general patient population are asked to monitor their patients to determine the efficacy and potential toxicity of the drug under actual treatment conditions.

It is vital to understand that no drug is free of toxicity or side effects. The *Physicians' Desk Reference (PDR)*,[8] which is issued yearly, provides information that is based largely on the results of the third-phase testing described above. This information is nearly identical to that contained in a drug's package insert.

Drug trials are not without controversy. First, they are time consuming. The four phases described above generally take 98 months to complete. This means that a promising therapy may not reach the general patient population for many years after its discovery. Drug trials are also expensive. These costs are obviously passed on to the patient population. Until a drug is approved, it is generally not eligible for third-party reimbursement (health insurance companies will not pay for experimental treatments). In trials using placebos (or no treatment) in the control population, it means that approximately half the patient population does not receive any therapeutic intervention.

Currently, there are only three treatments for cancer. One is to remove the tumor surgically. This is sometimes made difficult by the tumor's size, placement, or distribution. The other treatments are radiotherapy (X rays) and chemotherapy. The latter uses chemicals to treat the disease without seriously harming the patient. Chemotherapy is often combined with hyperthermia (general or, if possible, localized increase in temperature). There are many new and promising chemotherapy agents. Should we test them? If so, on whom?

Vaccine Development

Although it has apparently been thoroughly eradicated, smallpox was once one of the great scourges of mankind. It was pandemic in Europe in 1614 and epidemic in England in 1666–1675. There also were scattered outbreaks throughout New England during the seventeenth century.

Smallpox has no animal hosts or vectors. It is spread by contact, direct or indirect, with someone, dead or alive, who has the disease. In acute infections, it is characterized by fever and skin eruptions, which pass through the stages of papule, vesicle, and pustule. When these eruptions dry up, they leave permanent scars. At their worst, the scars rob the face of any appearance of humanity.

During the smallpox epidemics, almost everyone exposed to the virus got the disease. In the worst cases, one out of three died. There is still no specific treatment for smallpox, except prevention by vaccination. Edward Jenner, an eighteenth-century English physician, discovered the vaccine by following up on an old wives' tale that people who caught cowpox were protected from smallpox. Reportedly, on 14 May 1796 Jenner found a milkmaid that had cowpox. He collected fluid from a blister on her hand and injected it in a young boy, who got cowpox. Two months later, Jenner injected the boy with smallpox. The boy survived and did not develop smallpox. Jenner became a hero. But consider the consequences for Jenner (or a modern physician who performed the same sort of experiment) if the boy had gotten worse or died.

Although modern techniques for fighting viral infection — such as recombinant DNA and monoclonal antibody techniques — hold much promise, most modern vaccines are still produced by growing viruses on living tissue, such as chick or duck embryos.

This is because viruses do not grow well or live long in simple culture. Some vaccines must be grown on other tissues. For example, poliomyelitis vaccine must be grown on monkey kidney tissue. We are able to hold at bay many other afflictions—ones that were much feared in the past and which killed countless humans—with vaccines that cannot be produced without living tissues of animals. These viruses include measles, mumps, rabies, yellow fever, Rocky Mountain spotted fever, and typhus. It is likely that modern horrors, such as AIDS, genital herpes, and hepatitis, will ultimately be brought under control by vaccines from similar sources. Should immunologists attempt to develop vaccines to prevent these new plagues? If so, how will they be cultured? Finally, how and on whom will they be tested to determine if they are safe and effective?

The Thalidomide Crisis

One event was responsible for a significant increase in the use of animals in product testing. This was the thalidomide crisis of the late 1950s. Thalidomide (Contergan, Distavol, Kevadon) was introduced in 1956 as a remedy against influenza. That same year, it was also recommended for use as a sedative or hypnotic. Thalidomide induces normal, quickly reversible sleep in undisturbed adult subjects. In contrast to other hypnotics, such as barbiturates, thalidomide is remarkably safe. It has a large therapeutic index, which means that the relationship between the effective dose (100–200 gm/kg) and the lethal dose (more than 14,000 mg) is very large. Consequently, it is virtually impossible to commit suicide with thalidomide. Since it was thought to be a safe drug, it was recommended as an antiemetic (a drug that prevents nausea and vomiting) to treat morning sickness, which commonly occurs in early pregnancy.

Between 1956 and 1961, thalidomide's popularity increased, especially in Germany and England. However, during this time, it became clear that the occurrence of a relatively rare birth defect, phocomelia, was increasing and reaching epidemic proportions. Thalidomide is not a safe drug for the developing fetus. A single dose in the first trimester of pregnancy (especially between the twenty-third to the thirty-eighth day of conception) causes a major birth defect, amelia (complete absence of all limbs) or more commonly, phocomelia (deformed upper and, sometimes, lower limbs). It also causes congenital heart disease, as well as ocular, intestinal, and renal abnormalities. Worldwide, it is estimated that more than 7,000 children were deformed by the drug, before the brilliant retrospective epidemiological work by W. Lenz in Germany and W. G. McBride in Australia in 1961 led to the conclusion that thalidomide was the causative agent.

Lenz became concerned about the safety of thalidomide based on his observations of a physician's wife who had taken the drug and delivered a child with multiple birth defects. In November 1961, Lenz said, "From a scientific point of view it seems premature to discuss it. But as a human being and as a citizen, I cannot remain silent about my observations."

Animal activists sometimes use thalidomide as an example of a harmful drug that might have been allowed into the marketplace despite animal testing. The lowest dose of thalidomide that can cause a defect in humans if the drug is taken at the critical time is 0.5 to 1.0 milligrams/kilogram, if the drug is taken for several days. Other animals appear to be less susceptible. For example, the lowest dose that appears effective in lower primates is 5–10 milligrams/kilogram. The lowest dose in mice and rats is 31 and 50 milligrams/kilogram, but it has been reported that the largest dose that a mouse or rat can be exposed to and still not have a malformed fetus is as high as 4,000 milligrams/kilogram. The minimum dose for rabbits is about 30 milligrams/kilogram and the maximum dose at which no abnormalities are seen is 50 milligrams/kilogram. Most investigators agree that the teratogenic effects depend on blood levels of thalidomide. Oral dosing of small animals leads to lower blood levels than the same oral dose in humans. But, intravenous injections of thalidomide leads to similar blood levels. When this occurs, these animals appear to be about as susceptible as humans. It is unlikely that if another drug like thalidomide appears, that it would get beyond the animal trials that now precede human clinical trials.

Because of the thalidomide episode, most physicians are now more cautious about prescribing any drugs to pregnant women or even women of childbearing age.

Recently, it has been suggested that thalidomide can be used to treat lepromatous lepra reactions (painful red lesions over the entire body, as well as fever and malaise). These symptoms occur when some individuals are treated for leprosy (Hansen's disease) with a group of drugs called sulfones. Clinicians that prescribe thalidomide in these circumstances must be very careful when treating females during their childbearing years.

The Literature Search

Applied research attempts to answer a specific question for a specific purpose, such as testing a new drug or chemical to determine what it does and if it is safe, so that it can be marketed. For example, separate experiments might attempt to determine the major effect of the drug; its optimum dose; the best route of administration; the dose at which side effects occur; what the side effects are; whether the drug causes cancer, mutations, or birth defects, and if it does, at what dose level; and any potential interactions with other drugs, foods, and environmental agents.

The first step in applied research is to do a literature search to determine what is already known about a drug, as well as closely related drugs. A variety of hard copy (print) and computerized databases are available (see chapter 8). Researchers studying a new drug might start by searching for the chemical name of the drug, as well as its generic and brand names (if it has any) in a database called Unlisted Drugs. This database provides online information about new drugs including the drug's name, company code, and pharmacological use in addition to its chemical and molecular formulas and citations to the literature.

Other databases include PHARMAPROJECTS, TOXLINE, International Pharmaceutical Abstracts, EMBASE, MEDLINE, BIOSIS Previews, CA Search, and Current Contents Search.

PHARMAPROJECTS provides information about the progress on new pharmaceutical products while TOXLINE covers the adverse effects of chemicals, drugs, and physical agents on living systems. International Pharmaceutical Abstracts and EMBASE provide citations from pharmacological and biomedical journals. More general databases such as MEDLINE, BIOSIS Previews, and CA Search provide worldwide coverage of biological and biomedical sciences, as well as chemistry and its applications. CA Search (CAS) offers a CAS registry, which assigns a unique number to each specific chemical compound. To obtain the most recent information available, a researcher would also search a database called Current Contents Search. This database reproduces the table of contents of each issue of many leading scientific and medical journals. This appears well before the hard copy of the journal gets to the library or the individual subscriber. This allows the investigator to scan the titles for articles of interest. Then he can write to the author of the article and ask for a reprint of the article (and potentially other related articles by the same author). All of these databases could be searched for information about closely related drugs, as well as the main effect of the drug in question, if the effect is known.

The next step would be to find and read the pertinent papers identified by these searches. While reading these articles, the researcher would focus on the methods and procedures that were used in each paper; the drug, dose, and route; the animal species used, including the number of animals, their strain, age, and sex; and the statistical procedures that were used, as well as the results obtained. After identifying the important papers, the researcher would probably seek information from another database called SCISEARCH. This would yield a list of all papers that cited the author's work. SCISEARCH is a valuable tool, as it allows investigators to follow the evolving impact, for example, of a particular idea or technique. If no one cites a particular paper, it may mean that the author's work is having minimal or no impact. If many people cite a paper, it means that the work is having an impact.

The U.S. Department of Agriculture's (USDA) regulations to implement the 1985 amendments to the Animal Welfare Act of 1966 (Public Law 99-198 99 Stat. 1645) require scientists to demonstrate that proposed work does not duplicate studies already performed. The USDA regulations also require scientists to demonstrate that they have refined their experimental techniques to minimize the number of animals required to obtain the needed data and the amount of stress and pain the animals are exposed to. They must also demonstrate that the animals cannot be replaced with an *in vitro,* computer, or statistical model or with an alternate (lower) species, such as fish or invertebrates. So, in addition to the search a researcher does on a specific topic, the researcher would check two other databases: AGRICOLA and BIOETHICSLINE. AGRICOLA provides worldwide coverage of the literature dealing with the welfare of animals used for exhibition, in education, and in research. BIOETHICSLINE provides citations dealing with the ethics of human and animal experimentation.

Designing the Experiment

Following the literature search and analysis, the scientists are ready to design their experiment and write the experimental protocol.

The specific format of the protocol will vary from institution to institution. However, in general, it will contain at least four main sections: introduction/rationale; methods and procedures; literature searches/rationale for animal use; and staffing.

In the introduction, the scientists provide the background for their proposed project based on their own thinking and analysis of the literature. They will also discuss why they think it is important to do the experiment and how they think it will add to the database of information.

In the section on methods and procedures, they will describe how the experiment will be conducted. This includes detailing what species of animals will be used, how many animals will be used in each experiment, the form of the drug that will be administered, how the drug will be applied, what variables will be observed, and how the information gained will be quantified and evaluated. This section will also discuss the statistical techniques that will be used to evaluate the data. For example, if the drug that the scientist is going to evaluate is new or if a new route of administration will be used, the first experiment would probably be to determine the "Lethal Dose 50%" (LD50) for the drug. The LD50 is a statistical technique that allows an experimenter to determine the dose of a drug or chemical that is required to kill 50 percent of the animals exposed to it.

Two different methods are commonly used to determine the LD50: probit analysis and the "staircase" or "up-and-down" analysis. Using probit analysis (or its close mathematical relatives, logistic, angular, or maximum likelihood analysis), groups of animals are exposed to increasing doses of the drug under investigation. To be statistically valid, a dose that kills no animals and a dose that kills 100 percent of the animals must be included, as well as several intermediate doses. The up-and-down method was developed to decrease the number of animals needed to determine the LD50. In this method, a single animal is exposed to a dose of the drug. If the animal does not die, then the next animal is given a higher dose. If the initial animal dies, then the next animal is given a lower dose. Each succeeding animal is tested at one step below the dose used in the preceding animal if the predecessor responded. Or the successor is tested at one step above the dose used in the preceding animal if the predecessor did not respond. This test tells the investigators how toxic the drug or chemical is and allows them to compare the new drug with existing drugs or chemicals.

Another important statistic is the ED50 (Effective Dose 50% or median effective dose), which is the dose of a drug or chemical at which 50 percent of the animals give a particular response. For example, if one were studying anticonvulsants, then the ED50 would be the dose at which 50 percent did not have a convulsion in response to some stimulus that normally would elicit one.

The ratio LD50/ED50 is called the "therapeutic index." As this ratio approaches 1, it means that the effective dose is not very different from the toxic dose, so the margin of safety is relatively small. Given a choice between two drugs, the one with the safer therapeutic index should be chosen, since in therapeutics, the potential benefit must clearly outweigh the potential hazard. Unfortunately, in some cases, such as with many of the drugs used to treat cancer, the therapeutic index is relatively small. In using these drugs, the physician and patient must evaluate the risk of using a relatively toxic drug versus the risk of dying of cancer. Conversely, a drug with a small therapeutic index would not be appropriate for a pill to treat the common cold.

In the next section of the protocol, the experimenters describe what literature searches they did and provide a rationale for their selection of particular animals and why their data could not be collected in an *in vitro* preparation, in a lower animal such as an invertebrate, or by using a computer model. Finally, in the last section of the protocol, the researchers describe the people who will work on the project and provide information about their background and training.

Once the protocol is written, it is likely that the scientists will ask some of their colleagues to be devil's advocates by reading it carefully. These colleagues will look for any potential problems with the proposed experiment's rationale, the statistical analysis, or the design of the study. In some institutions, this local evaluation might be a formal requirement.

Defending the Protocol

Once the experimenters have completed this informational informal (or formal) review, they are ready to submit their protocol to the Institutional Animal Care and Use Committee (IACUC). The IACUC, which is appointed by the chief executive officer of the research facility, represents the general community interests in proper care and treatment of animals. This committee must have at least three members, including a doctor of veterinary medicine. At least one member must not be affiliated with the facility other than as a member of the IACUC.

During the meeting with the IACUC, the experimenters will defend their protocol; that is, they must be prepared to answer any substantive questions posed by the IACUC members. One question that will undoubtedly arise is whether the experimenters considered alternatives to any procedure that is likely to cause pain or distress. In any practice that is likely to cause pain, the experimenters will be directed to consult with a doctor of veterinary medicine to plan the procedure and also to help to plan for the use of tranquilizers, analgesics, and anesthetics. The experimenters will also be questioned about the number of animals that they are proposing to use to determine if the number is adequate but not excessive for the purpose. They will also be asked about the sensitivity of their experimental techniques and statistical procedures.

At the conclusion of the meeting, the IACUC will either sign off on the protocol or request revisions. Once the protocol is approved, the experimenters are responsible for following it in all experiments. During the course of the experiments, if any significant changes in methods/statistics are required, the protocol must be amended to reflect these changes. The amendments must be approved by the IACUC.

Funding the Experiment

Now the scientists are ready to seek funds to do the actual work. Research is funded by three different mechanisms. First, private companies fund applied research and, sometimes, basic research. The purpose of this research is to develop new products and improve existing products. Another purpose is to test the products to determine if they are toxic and, if they are, at what level, and to determine how the toxicity is manifested. For example, a drug company might have its chemists synthesize a new chemical compound. Then the pharmacologists or toxicologists will try to evaluate the new compound's characteristics as described above.

The other two funding mechanisms are contracts and grants. There are several major differences between the two. A *contract* typically defines a specific task or program that someone wants performed. The agencies of the federal government, for example, advertise their wants and needs in the *Commerce and Business Daily*. A federal contract generally starts with a "Request for Proposals" (RFP), that appears as an advertisement in the *CBD*. These ads describe such tasks or programs in varying detail. Individuals or companies respond to the RFP by describing their experience and capabilities, as well as why they think that they can perform the task. This initial response could potentially briefly describe their approach to the task.

Next, the professional staff of the federal agency determines who is qualified to do the work. It provides the applicants that are qualified with a more detailed description of the task, typically called the statement of work. Applicants use this information to design the experiment(s) and to determine what staff and materials will be needed to perform the work. Then they typically develop two proposals: One describes how the experiments will be conducted and evaluated, as well as what staff, material, and facilities will be required to perform the work. The second proposal defines the costs of doing the work.

These two proposals are submitted to the agency, which will evaluate them separately. First, the agency's professional staff will determine, among other things, if the methods and procedures and the staffing are appropriate to the task. Some applicants will be eliminated at this stage. Second, the agency will determine if the costs are realistic. Again, some applicants will be eliminated. Finally, the contract generally is awarded to the group with the best design and price.

Private companies, such as drug companies, also seek contractors to perform needed work. Unfortunately, there is no central clearinghouse that describes the needs and wants of these companies.

Grants are the major mechanism for supporting basic research. The applicant comes up with an idea, does the work described above such as developing a protocol and having it approved, then writes a proposal. The proposal can be submitted to a federal agency, such as the National Science Foundation, one of the branches of the National Institutes of Health, the Environmental Protection Agency, or one of the research offices that serve the Department of Defense, such as the Office of Naval Research. Or the applicant can send the proposal to private agencies that support research, such as the American Heart Association, as well as private foundations, such as the Morris Animal Foundation.

The deadlines for submission and the form that the proposal must take vary from agency to agency, but they contain the major sections mentioned above. The methods for judging the proposal also vary from agency to agency. For example, all applications or proposals submitted to the Public Health Service that involve the care and use of animals must contain the following information:

1. Identification of the species and approximate number of animals to be used
2. The rationale for involving animals and for the appropriateness of the species and numbers to be used
3. A complete description of the proposed use of the animals
4. A description of procedures designed to assure that discomfort and injury to animals will be limited to that which is unavoidable in the conduct of scientifically valuable research, and that analgesic, anesthetic, and tranquilizing drugs will be used where indicated and where appropriate to minimize discomfort and pain to animals
5. A description of any euthanasia method to be used.

Most other granting agencies have similar requirements with respect to animal use. The proposals are subjected to some form of peer review; that is, the grant proposal, with or without its budget, is sent to several impartial experts in the area covered by the grant proposal. These experts are asked to evaluate the proposal and determine if the work proposed is new and unique, if the amount of work that is proposed is appropriate for the staffing and budget, and if the methods and procedures are appropriate. The experts are also asked to provide written comments and to indicate whether they recommend funding the project. Some agencies also request these experts to assign the proposal a numerical score that represents their overall evaluation of the proposal.

In the case of a grant, it might be awarded, but not funded. This occurs because there are experiments that are scientifically sound and that the reviewers believe will provide useful information, but there is not enough money in the budget of the funding agency to provide funds for the project. That is why the numerical score mentioned above is important. It allows the funding agency to rank the proposals. If the grant or contract is funded, the scientist is ready to perform the work. It is important to note that this process, from the inception of the idea to the start of the work, can last a year or longer. While the contract or grant application is being reviewed by a funding agency, there is often little or no feedback. If the contract is not won, there is no recourse but to apply when another RFP appears. If the grant is not funded, there is no recourse except to reapply, trying to take into account the comments made by the reviewers.

After an experiment is completed, the experimenters are generally expected to present their methods, data, and conclusions at a scientific meeting and/or publish them in a refereed scientific journal. This is an important step. First, it tells other scientists what experiment was performed and what results were obtained. This helps minimize needless repetitions of experiments. Publication provides another tier of quality control for science. When a paper is submitted to a refereed scientific journal, the editor sends the paper to two or more referees, who are (theoretically) impartial experts in the area. The experts review the paper in much the same way that the IACUC reviews the protocol. If the experts find some flaw, they return the paper to the author with their comments. The author has an opportunity to correct the flaws and resubmit the paper. This may involve reanalyzing the data, rewriting sections of the paper, or performing additional experiments. If the referees do not find any problems with the paper, it is published in the journal. Once published, it is open for review by the entire scientific community. If anyone finds a flaw with the paper, it will very likely be pointed out in a future publication of the scientist who finds the flaw. A scientist who has difficulty publishing his or her work is unlikely to succeed in obtaining funding.

Competition for funds and journal space is intense. There are several tiers of quality control, including local evaluation of a protocol; evaluation by the IACUC; evaluation by a funding agency; evaluation by the referees prior to publication; and evaluation by the entire scientific community after publication. Also not all repetitions of an experiment are meaningless or wasteful. One way that scientists (and, in fact, society at large) come to trust experimental results is to have the experiment replicated by another laboratory that obtains the same results.

Defining the Experience of Pain

Both Thomas Regan and Peter Singer (and Jeremy Bentham before him) seem to fail to distinguish between the sensation, perception, and the subjective experience of pain. PETA president Ingrid Newkirk is responsible for one of the rallying calls of the animal activists movement: "When it comes to feeling, like pain, hunger, and thirst, a rat is a pig is a dog is a boy." Yet if we consider only sensation or sensory/motor integration, then this statement should probably be extended as follows: a chicken is a snake is a frog is a fish is a cockroach is a squid is a worm is a planaria is a hydra is an ameoba is a bacteria, and (according to some people) is a plant. All of these organisms attempt to avoid certain classes of stimuli. It is not clear if this means that these stimuli are painful.

It is difficult to define pain objectively, yet virtually everyone has experienced it at one time or another, and sometimes intensely. For example, more than 300,000 humans suffer from chronic pain as a result of traumatic injuries. Pain has three important components: sensory, perceptual, and emotional. It is more strongly linked with emotion than any other sensory or perceptual event.

Pain is a protective mechanism. It occurs whenever something biologically harmful is happening, as when tissue is being damaged. Pain is what tells us that we have a bruise, a wound, or a burn and where the damage is located. It also tells us when our internal organs are not functioning normally. Generally, pain causes the individual to react to remove the painful stimulus. In contrast to other senses, pain receptors do not adapt (decrease their sensitivity) over time. There are three major types of pain:

1. Prickling pain occurs when the skin is struck with a needle or when a widespread area of the skin is strongly, but diffusely, irritated.
2. Burning pain occurs when the skin is exposed to excessive heat (or friction).
3. Aching pain is not typically felt on the surface of the body, but deep inside. For example, ischemia (decrease or lack of blood flow to an organ) can cause pain in the organ, as can a muscle spasm. This pain is often "referred" to another part of the body. For example, angina, the pain associated with a decrease in blood flow

to the heart, is "referred" to as a pain "felt" in the left shoulder and arm, not usually in the area where the heart is actually located.

The pain receptors are probably the free nerve endings that are found in the superficial layers of the skin. They are also found in internal tissues, such as the *periosteum* (a thick fibrous membrane that covers the entire surface of a bone except its articular cartilage); arterial walls; joint surfaces; the *falx* (a fold in the *dura mater*, which is the thick fibrous membrane forming the outer envelope of the brain); and the *tentorium* (a thick fold in the dura mater that separates the cerebellum from the cerebral hemispheres). Other internal tissues are more weakly supplied with these fibers, but their activity can summate to form an aching pain. The precise mechanism by which tissue damage stimulates free nerve endings is not clearly known. It is likely that bradykinin, a polypeptide that is released when tissue is damaged, is involved. Or it could be other chemicals, such as prostaglandin, histamine, or serotonin.

The phenomena of tickling and itching are probably caused by very mild stimulation of pain fibers. The itch sensation calls attention to a very mild surface stimulation such as a fly about to bite. This mild stimulation elicits signals that lead to scratching. When the scratch is strong enough to elicit mild painful stimuli, these stimuli block the itch signals.

Prickling pain is carried by small nerve fibers at a rate of 3–20 meters per second, while burning and aching sensations are carried by fibers that have a slower travel rate, between 0.5 and 2 meters per second. The sudden onset of painful stimuli often gives a double pain sensation: a fast prickling pain that is followed a second or so later by a burning pain sensation. The slow burning sensation tends to become more and more painful over a period of time and is what causes the intolerable suffering of pain (see below). Pain fibers enter the spinal cord and synapse (form a connection with) nerve cells located there. It is likely that fibers of these nerve cells synapse on other nerve cells in the spinal cord. Ultimately, they will synapse on nerve cells that have long fibers that cross to the other side of the spinal cord and become two nerve tracts that carry pain sensations. They are the spinothalamic and spinoreticular tracts. The fibers carrying prickling pain sensation go to the thalamus (an intermediate "switching station" in the brain) and from there to the cerebral cortex. The fibers carrying burning or aching sensations form connections with the reticular activating system, which transmits the sensation to virtually all parts of the brain, especially to the thalamus, the hypothalamus (a center for emotions), and the cerebral cortex. These sensations are able to arouse someone who is asleep, to create a state of excitement and urgency, and to cause defense reactions. Burning sensations are poorly localized, perhaps to a major part of the body, such as a limb. The brain itself is insensitive; that is, it does not contain any free nerve endings.

Pain thresholds are fairly similar for humans. For example, a great number of people feel pain when a small area of their skin is heated to 45 degrees and virtually everyone perceives pain before the temperature reaches 47 degrees. The amount of a stimulus that will cause a detectable difference in the degree of pain is called a "just noticeable difference" (JND). Most humans can detect approximately 22 JNDs between the level where no pain can be perceived and the most intense pain a person can distinguish. So, contrary to popular belief, people are neither remarkably sensitive nor insensitive to painful stimuli. However, we do differ, sometimes rather dramatically, in the way we respond to painful stimuli. Overstimulation of the other senses can also be painful. For example, a very loud sound or a very intense light can be painful without stimulating the traditional pain fibers.

As indicated above, from one person to another, the threshold for recognition of pain is similar. Pain causes both reflex motor reactions and psychic reactions. Many of these reflex reactions (such as removing a hand from a hot stove) occur at the level of the spinal cord and are withdrawal reflexes that remove part or all of the body from the noxious stimuli. These reflexes usually do not involve higher centers.

Psychic reactions depend on perception rather than sensation. The psychic reaction to pain varies dramatically among individuals. It is determined in part by past experience with pain and in humans, at least, is dependent on their cultural background. Reactions to pain vary from essentially no reaction at all to anguish, anxiety, crying, depression, nausea, and excess muscular excitability. Many of these reactions are learned. For example, a group of Scottish terriers was reared in isolation. They did not experience the normal bodily abuses that accompany growing up. These puppies endured pin pricks with no evidence of pain or emotion. However, their reflexes were normal and they still would jerk away from the pin.

Theories of Pain Perception

There are three different theories of pain perception: specificity, pattern, and a combination of the two. The *specificity* theory originated with the seventeenth-century philosopher Rene Descartes. Its supporters argue that stimulation of specific pain receptors—the free nerve endings—transmits information directly to a pain center in the brain. When these receptors are stimulated, we feel pain and only pain. This theory fails to account for the many psychological variables that influence the amount of pain different individuals experience. Perception of pain depends on the level of anxiety and attention. There are numerous examples of soldiers who fail to notice severe wounds until the heat of battle has subsided. In one study conducted in the emergency room of a hospital, more than a third of the patients who had suffered substantial damage to their bodies did not report feeling pain. This theory also cannot account for phantom limb pain, which occurs when pain is perceived in an amputated arm or leg. While this pain may be intense, it remains a puzzle as to how someone can experience pain where pain receptors are no longer present.

Proponents of the *pattern* theory of pain perception, which originated in the later half of the nineteenth century, claim that before pain is experienced, particular patterns of stimulation must be produced and this stimulation must reach a threshold. They argue that there are no specific pain receptors.

The third *combination* theory was developed in 1965 by Drs. Ronald Melzack and Patrick Wall. It combines the specificity and pattern theory along with psychological factors. This is commonly called the "gate control" theory. Melzack argues that there are two sets of fibers, one large and the other small, involved in pain sensations. These fibers form connections with two centers in the spinal cord. One of these centers is called the *substantia gelatinosa*. The large fibers stimulate the cells in the substantia gelatinosa, while the small fibers inhibit them. Both the large and small fibers and the output of the substantia gelatinosa project onto a second set of cells in the spinal cord, the transmission cells, which transmit pain sensations to higher centers in the brain. The substantia gelatinosa acts as a gate. When substantial large fiber activity is present, the perception of pain decreases. When substantial small fiber activity is present, pain perception increases. Signals from the higher centers (i.e., the brain) also feed into the transmission and substantia gelatinosa cells, thus modulating the control of pain sensations. Therefore, it is clear that pain perception is more than the simple stimulation of free nerve endings.

However, the story of pain perception is still more complicated. It has been known for centuries that opium and its derivatives are analgesics that decrease or eliminate the effects of pain. More specifically, opiates, like morphine, do not block the physical sensation of pain, but minimize the suffering that arises in our response to pain.

Scientists who have studied opiates have discovered that certain parts of the brain are especially sensitive to their effects. Brain cells in these areas have opiate receptors that work like a lock and key; that is, they respond to chemicals that have the chemical structure of an opiate and not to any other chemicals. Yet opiates are derived from plants; they do not occur in the body. Or do they? The discovery of the brain's opiate receptors sent scientists on a quest to find endogenous opiates (substances resembling opiates, which are produced inside the body). Biochemists and neurobiologists discovered that there are at least two classes of molecules that have significant opium-like analgesic effects. They are the enkephalins and the endorphins.

In addition to the opiates, a variety of exogenous drugs are available to help control pain. They include local anesthetics, such as novocaine, which deaden nerves by apparently increasing their firing threshold. They also include aspirin, which blocks the production and release of endogenous chemicals called prostaglandins that are released when tissue is damaged. Prostaglandins may be one of the chemicals that stimulate the free nerve endings.

So the perception of pain is complex. It is controlled by the magnitude of pain sensation and endogenous chemical regulators, as well as a variety of exogenous drugs and other procedures (e.g., the Lamaze method of breathing to ease childbirth pain).

Pain in Nonhuman Animals

Animals that lack higher brain sites, such as the cerebral cortex (i.e., reptiles, amphibians, fish, and invertebrates) probably experience pain at the level of sensory motor integration; that is, they sense something and respond to it. For animals with more complex brains (ones that have a primitive or well-developed cerebral cortex such as birds and mammals), the experience of pain is more complex. It consists of at least three dimensions. The *first* is the "sensory dimension," which carries the basic sensory information about the pain, such as its location in the body and its sensory quality (piercing, burning, or aching). This system helps humans to locate where we hurt and what the hurt feels like. It is likely that we share this system with other animals, especially those that possess a well-developed cerebral cortex, such as other mammals (e.g., cats, dogs, and primates). The Food Security Act of 1985– Subtitle F Animal Welfare mandates that in any practice that is likely to cause pain to an experimental animal, the scientist must consult a doctor of veterinary medicine to plan for the use of tranquilizers, analgesics, and anesthetics during the experiment. It further states that the withholding of tranquilizers, anesthesia, analgesia, or euthanasia when scientifically necessary may continue for only the necessary period of time.

A 1990 report dealing with the USDA Animal Welfare Enforcement Division, cited in *Animal Research and Human Health: Caring for Laboratory Animals* by the Foundation for Biomedical Research, notes that 58 percent of all animals used in research in 1990 did not experience pain or distress. The report states that in an additional 36 percent, pain was alleviated by appropriate drugs. In 6 percent, pain was not alleviated with drugs because the drugs would have obscured the results of the research. For example, in a study of pain mechanisms, it would be inappropriate to administer drugs.

The *second dimension* of experiencing pain involves the motivational affective system. This system is primarily responsible for the unpleasant feelings that are almost invariably associated with pain. The subjective experience of pain also depends on the level of anxiety that the person is experiencing, the attention devoted to the experience, and suggestion. Consider the methods of the French physician Fernand Lamaze. They are commonly used in helping alleviate the pain associated with childbirth, but they can be used in other areas as well. Try a simple experiment. Have a friend grasp your leg just above the knee. Have the friend squeeze your leg, gently at first, but gradually increasing the pressure until you feel fairly severe pain. This should convince you that this is fairly painful. Now try to do three things at once. First, take in five short breaths in a row, followed by a strong blow outward (i.e., pant, pant, pant, pant, pant, blow). Second, count the breaths (i.e., 1, 2, 3, 4, 5, blow). Third, concentrate your visual attention (look intently at) on some specific object in your visual field. If you have your friend squeeze your knee while you are engaged in these three activities, you should either feel no pain at all or the intensity should be significantly decreased. The physical sensation is clearly still there, but you do not "feel" it.

The *third dimension* is the cognitive evaluative system, which is involved in determining the meaning of the sensory experience of pain. It processes sensory information, compares it to past experiences, and determines the probable outcome of the various methods that can be used to respond to the pain.

It is unlikely that humans share the second and third dimensions with other animals except, possibly, our closest cousins—the great apes—and, possibly, the whales and dolphins (cetacea)—the only organisms whose brain/body ratio approaches (and in some cases exceeds) humans. This is because the second and third dimensions would require a well-developed cerebral cortex, significant cognitive ability, and self-consciousness. Animals other than the great apes and cetacea probably do not possess these characteristics.

What Is Acceptable Pain?

If we accept the arguments of Peter Singer and Jeremy Bentham (i.e., "The question is not, can they reason? Nor can they talk? But, can they suffer?"), then we are ignoring the plight of a significant number of human beings who would ultimately be able to reason and talk, and can certainly suffer.

Tearing apart, beheading, or disemboweling a sentient being are all actions that would be considered painful and repugnant by any civilized human being. Yet several thousand human beings in the United States are subjected to these procedures every day; human beings who have not been convicted of any crime and who have no right of appeal. These unfortunates are human embryos that are up to 16 weeks old and who are subjected to a process called dilation and evacuation. This process is also called vacuum curettage, suction abortion, and STOP (suction termination of pregnancy). It is available on demand virtually anywhere in the United States and in many other places in the world.

Consider the words of Davenport Hooker, one of the fathers of behavioral embryology, in his book *The Origin of Overt Behavior*:

Two prerequisites for motion are muscles and nerves. In the sixth and seventh weeks, nerve and muscle work together for the first time. If the area of the lips, the first to become sensitive to touch, is gently stroked, the baby, who then is still an embryo, responds by bending the upper body to one side and making a quick backward motion with the arms. This is called a total pattern response because it involves most of the body rather than the appropriate local part. Localized and more appropriate reactions, such as swallowing in response to a stroking around the lips, follow only in the third month. By the beginning of this third month, the baby moves spontaneously, without being touched, for the first time. Sometimes, his whole little body swings back and forth for a few moments. A few days later, by the eighth and one-half week, the eyelids and palms of the hands become sensitive to touch. If the eyelid is stroked, the baby now has a localized reaction and squints. If the palm of the hand is touched, the fingers close in a partial fist. . . .

It is unlikely that we can understand the amount of pain and suffering that occurs when the vacuum curettage is inserted into the amniotic sac and begins to suck out the contents. We have no real frame of reference. Clearly, the U.S. Supreme Court (and any other civilized person) would recoil in horror if someone suggested that we subject convicted criminals to procedures this horrendous. It is unlikely that the other standard method used for early abortions, dilation and curettage, causes less pain and suffering. These two methods account for almost half of all abortions in the United States.

Abortions after the sixteenth week are generally induced by removing the amniotic fluid and injecting a concentrated saline solution or prostaglandin. The fetus dies at some unknown time after the injection. Within 6–48 hours, the cervix dilates, contractions begin, and labor occurs. The dead baby and the placenta are expelled.

The salt solution also probably causes significant pain and suffering for the fetus. The salt would burn the eyes, the nose, the mouth, the anus, the respiratory tract, and the genitals. If the baby swallows any of the salt solution, which is likely, the salt would cause pain in the upper gastrointestinal tract and, potentially, cramps. Because fetal skin is delicate, it is likely that the salt solution would cause pain by stimulating nerve endings in the baby's skin.

Prostaglandin causes pain in adults, if it is injected between the layers of the skin. It would also cause pain in the eyes, the nose, the mouth, the upper part of the digestive tract, the anus, the respiratory tract, and the genitals. Some kinds of prostaglandin sensitize the nerve endings of the skin to the effects of chemicals or mechanical stimuli, so it would make other painful stimuli even more painful.

Clearly, analytical ethics should argue that we should not subject any moral agent to these procedures. Yet we routinely subject unborn babies to these procedures, babies who can sense and respond to normal stimuli within six weeks of conception, who can undoubtedly sense painful stimuli even earlier. Further, we are not performing these acts based on arbitrary characteristics, such as race or even species, but rather on circumstance.

Conclusion

We must determine what are and what ought to be the boundaries of our moral community. We need to ask how we define person-hood (see chapter 7). For if we do not extend personhood to the developing human embryo and fetus, who are clearly members of our own species, how can we extend personhood to other species?

Finally, who should decide these matters and what criteria should be used in making the decision? It seems right that all of us, individually and collectively, be involved in the decision because it will have a significant impact on society.

If we are going to test environmental chemicals, intentional and unintentional food additives, cosmetics, and drugs, we must decide on whom we will test them. Humans in general? Poor people? Prisoners? Animals? Can we in good conscience not test?

Notes

1. The following discussion is drawn from *Black's Law Dictionary*, St. Paul, MN: West Publishing, 1979.

2. R. G. Frey, *Rights, Killing, and Suffering: Moral Vegetarianism and Applied Ethics*, New York: Basil Blackwell, 1983; *Interests and Rights: The Case against Animals*, New York: Oxford University Press, 1983.

3. Edwin A. Locke, "The Moral Side of the Animal Rights Issue," *CFAAR Newsletter* 4, no. 2 (1991): 9–11; C. Cohen, "The Case for the Use of Animals in Biomedical Research," *New England Journal of Medicine* 315, no. 14 (1986): 865–870.

4. Nicoll and Russell, in *Endocrinology* 127 (1990), eliminated five books from the original list proposed by Magel. They are: L. Gruen, P. Singer, and D. Hind, *Animal Liberation: A Graphic Guide*, London: Camden Press, 1987; A. Linzey and T. Regan, eds., *The Song of Creation: Poetry in Celebration of Animals*, Basingstoke, Hants: Marshall Pickering, 1989; C. R. Magel, *Keyguide to Information Sources in Animal Rights*, Harrisburg, PA: Mansell/McFarland, 1989; T. Regan and P. Singer, eds., *Animal Rights and Human Obligations*, Englewood Cliffs, NJ: Prentice-Hall, 1989; J. Wynne-Tyson, *The Extended Circle: A Dictionary of Humane Thought*, Fontell, Sussex: Centaur Press, 1985. They also added one book that was not on Magel's list: R. Sharp, *The Cruel Deception*, Wellingborough, England: Thorsens, 1988.

5. John B. Stanbury, James B. Wyngaarden, and Donald S. Fredickson, eds., *The Metabolic Basis of Inherited Disease*, New York: Blackiston Division, McGraw-Hill, 1966.

6. Daniel Bergsma, ed., *Birth Defects: Atlas and Compendium*, Baltimore: Williams and Wilkins, 1973.

7. *See* 21 Code of Federal Regulations 170.20 and 170.22.

8. *Physicians' Desk Reference*, Montvale, NJ: Medical Economics Data, 1993.

2

Chronology

THIS CHRONOLOGY PROVIDES A HISTORICAL OVERVIEW of the relationship between humans and animals. Since animal activists focus much of their attention on the use of animals in education, research, and testing (see chapter 1), this chronology highlights the major events in the history of science as they relate to animal use, such as the formation of organizations related to animals. It also focuses on the historical use of animal research in three important areas: development of vaccines, development of new surgical techniques, and neurobiology. The entries are not meant to be exhaustive, but merely to indicate the important role animal research has played in significant breakthroughs in these three areas of investigation. The choice of focusing on these areas does not imply that the use of animals in other areas of research is not important. It was done, however, to keep the size of the chronology manageable.

10000– 7000 B.C.	Dogs are domesticated in Mesopotamia, goats and sheep in Persia; pigs and water buffalo in eastern Asia, and chickens in southern Asia.
5000 B.C.	Horses are domesticated in the Ukraine.
3000 B.C.	Donkeys and mules are domesticated in Israel, camels in Iran, and elephants in India.
2950 B.C.	Imhotep, an Egyptian physician and architect, is the first scientist to be known by name and the only scientist to ever become a god.

2500 B.C.   Cats are domesticated in Egypt.

600 B.C.   Thales of Miletus, a Greek, founds the Ionian school of natural philosophy. The Ionians believe that people can understand the universe by using reason alone.

520 B.C.   Anaximander, born in Miletus, Turkey, introduces the idea of evolution. Although no work(s) has been discovered, he may have written the earliest scientific book.

500 B.C.   Alcmaeon, a Greek philosopher and physician, dissects a human cadaver for scientific purposes.

400 B.C.   The Greek physician Hippocrates develops the ethical oath named after him.

323 B.C.   The Greek philosopher Aristotle became known as the father of the life sciences, especially embryology, because of his observations about the development of embryos in different species. He is the first to engage in large scale classification of plants and animals. Aristotle also introduces the inductive-deductive method of reasoning.

A.D. 40   Pedanius Dioscorides, a Greek physician, publishes *De Materia Medica*, which describes the medicinal properties of herbs.

A.D. 159   Galen, a Greek medical scientist, is one of the first scientists to perform experiments on living animals.

1140   Roger II, a Norman king, decrees that only physicians with a license from the government can practice medicine.

1193   Albertus Magnus describes his dissection of animals.

1612   Fabricius Abaquapendente, an Italian physician, publishes *De Formatione Ovi et Pulli*, a detailed study of the chick embryo. He also discovers the one-way valves in the veins. He is the teacher of William Harvey.

1620   Bacon, born to a family prominent at the English Court, publishes *Novum Organum* in which he recommends induction and experimentation as the basis of the scientific method.

1628 William Harvey, an English physician, publishes *Exercitatio de Motu Cordis et Janguinis.*

1637 French philosopher and mathematician René Descartes publishes *Discours de la Methode Pour Bien Conduire la Raison et Chercher La Verite Dans les Sciences,* in which he argues for the deductive method in science. As a mechanist, Descartes believes that lower animals lack a pineal gland, which he thinks serves as a channel and valve to regulate the flow of thought. Therefore, he maintains that lower animals are mere living machines.

1651 William Harvey publishes *Exercitationes de Generatione Animalium,* which describes organ differentiation in the developing embryo.

1667 Robert Boyle, an English physicist and chemist, demonstrates that an animal can be kept alive by artificial respiration.

1676 Nehemiah Grew, an English scientist, coins the term comparative anatomy.

1683 Thomas Tryon, an English philosopher, publishes *The Way to Health, Long Life and Happiness,* which is the first book in the English language to use the term "rights" in regard to animals.

1735–1737 Swedish botonist Linnaeus (also known as Carl von Linne) publishes *Systema Naturae* in which he describes the classification of animals and *Genera Plantorem,* his classification of plants. This system is used to this day.

1747 Albrecht von Haller, a Swiss scientist, publishes *Primae Lineae Physiologiae,* the first textbook of physiology.

1761 The first school of veterinary medicine is founded at Lyons, France.

1766 Albrecht von Haller, the father of modern experimental neurology, is the first to show that nerves stimulate muscles.

1775 Sir Percival Potts, an English physician, discovers that environmental factors could cause cancer.

1779   Jeremy Bentham, a utilitarian philosopher, publishes *An Introduction to the Principles of Morals and Legislation* in which he writes of animals: "The question is not, can they reason? Nor can they talk? But, can they suffer?" This statement eventually becomes the battle cry of both the Victorian and modern animal protection movements.

1790   Italian physiologist Luigi Galvani determines the effect of electrical stimulation on frog legs.

French chemist Antoine Lavoisier does experiments on the relationship between maintenance and generation of body heat and oxygen in the air.

1796   British physician Edward Jenner performs the first inoculation against smallpox. This is the beginning of the development of vaccines for the prevention of disease.

1817   The Russian zoologist Christian Pander discovers that there are three different layers that form in the early development of the chick embryo.

1822   Martins' Act is passed by British Parliament. It is the first legislation against cruelty to animals. It seeks to prevent cruel and improper treatment of the horse, mare, gelding, mule, ass, ox, cow, heifer, steer, sheep, and cattle. It does not cover dogs, cats, other mammals, or birds.

1824   Henry Hickman uses carbon dioxide as a general anesthetic in an animal.

The Society for the Prevention of Cruelty to Animals (SPCA) is formed in London with the help of Sir Samuel Romilly and Sir William Wilberforce.

1834   Drugs in common use could be, in the words of American physician Oliver Wendell Holmes, "sunk to the bottom of the sea ..." and "... it would be all the better for mankind—and all the worse for the fishes."

1835   Princess Victoria of England extends patronage to the SPCA and it becomes the Royal Society for the Prevention of Cruelty to Animals.

1839   Jan Evangelista Purkinje, a Czechoslovakian physiologist, becomes the director of the first institute at the University of Breslav for physiology.

1843   Sir David Ferrier, a Scot, uses the brains of living primates and other animals to locate and map motor and sensory regions in the brain.

1852   Hermann Ludwig Ferdinand von Helmholtz, a German physiologist, determines the speed of transmission of a nerve impulse in a frog's nerve cell.

1856   Karl Freidrich William Ludwig, a German physiologist, is the first to keep animal organs alive outside the body.

1859   Englishman Charles Darwin publishes *On the Origin of Species.*

1863   Wilhelm Max Wundt, a German psychologist, publishes *Lectures on the Minds of Men and Animals.*

The National Academy of Sciences is formed in the United States.

1865   French physiologist Claude Bernard publishes *An Introduction to Experimental Medicine.*

Austrian monk Gregor Mendel publishes his theory of genetics.

1866   The American Society for the Prevention of Cruelty to Animals is started by Henry Bergh. The first state charter for an animal protection society is granted in New York.

1866–1869   The U.S. cities of Boston, Philadelphia, and San Francisco incorporate humane societies.

1872   Charles Darwin publishes *The Expression of the Emotions in Man and Animals* in which he argues that the similarity of expression of emotions in man and animals argues for the descent of humans from lower forms of life.

1876   British Parliament passes the Cruelty to Animals Act.

1877   The American Humane Association is formed.

1878   The *Home Chronicler,* a publication of one of the London antivivisectionist societies, publishes a list of marginal seats in the House of Commons held by members who voted against the total abolition of vivisection.

1879   French chemist Louis Pasteur discovers that a weakened cholera organism fails to cause the disease in chickens and that chickens infected with the weakened organism are immune to the disease.

1881   Louis Pasteur creates the first artificially produced vaccine. He does this by heating a preparation of anthrax germs to weaken them and then injecting the germs into sheep. The sheep who are treated in this manner fail to develop anthrax.

1882   The Association for the Advancement of Medicine by Research is formed.

1883   The American Antivivisection Society is formed.

1887   Wolfgang Kohler, an Estonian psychologist, one of the founders of Gestalt psychology, studies chimpanzee problem-solving abilities.

1889   Russian physiologist Ivan Pavlov demonstrates classical conditioning of reflexes in dogs.

Oskar Minkowski and Baron Joseph von Mering discover that the pancreas supplies a hormone (insulin) that is essential for normal glucose metabolism. They do this by removing and experimenting on the pancreases of dogs.

1892   The American Psychological Association is formed.

1901   The U.S. Public Health and Marine Hospital Service is formed. (Its name changes to the Public Health Service in 1912.)

The German bacteriologist Emil Adolf von Behring uses guinea pigs in the development of diphtheria antiserum.

1905   German bacteriologist Robert Koch uses cows and sheep in the study of the pathogenesis of tuberculosis.

1906   Neuroanatomists, such as the Italian Camillo Golgi and Spaniard Ramóny Cajal, study animal brains.

1907   R. G. Harrison demonstrates the *in vitro* growth of living animal tissues.

1910   Paul Ehrlich, German bacteriologist, and Ilya Ilich Metchnikov, a Russian biologist, use fish, birds, and guinea pigs in the study of immune reactions and phagocytes.

1912   French surgeon Alexis Carrel uses dogs to study the rejoining of severed blood vessels. This is the first step in organ transplantation.

1913   Charles Robert Richet, a French physiologist, uses dogs and rabbits to study the mechanism of anaphylaxis.

          John Broadus Watson, an American psychologist, publishes his first paper on behaviorism.

1914   Joseph Goldberger, an Austrian American physician of the U.S. Public Health Service, begins a study of pellagra.

1916   The National Research Council is formed.

1923   Canadian physiologists Sir Frederick Grant Banting, John MacLeod, Jr., and Charles H. Best use dogs, rabbits, and fish in the study of insulin and the mechanism of diabetes.

          Otto Heinrich Warburg, a German biochemist, develops a method for studying respiration in thin slices of tissue.

1924   Dutch physiologist Willem Einthoven develops the electrocardiograph using dogs.

1925   Ronald Aymler Fisher, an English statistician, publishes *Statistical Methods for Research Workers.* A. J. Lotka publishes *Elements of Physical Biology,* which contains simple mathematical models of biological phenomena.

          The Scopes "monkey trial" is held in Dayton, Tennessee, where a high school teacher is prosecuted for teaching evolution.

1926   Hermann Joseph Muller, an American biologist, demonstrates that X rays induce genetic mutations.

American physicians George Richards Minot and William Perry Murphy establish the use of liver as a successful treatment for anemia. This is based on earlier work by George Hoyt Whipple, an American physician, in dogs.

1927   Thomas Hunt Morgan, an American geneticist, publishes *Experimental Embryology*. Ivan Pavlov publishes *Conditioned Reflexes*.

1928   Sir Alexander Fleming, a Scottish bacteriologist, discovers penicillin in molds. (The clinical use of it starts in the 1940s after Sir Howard Walter Florey, an Australian-English pathologist, and Ernest Boris Chain, a German-English biochemist, learn how to manufacture it in quantity and test its curative effects on mice.) The chemical structure of penicillin is studied by X-ray diffraction. It is so complex that an electronic computer is needed to work out the tedious mathematics involved.

1929   The Antivivisection Society is formed in the United States.

The German embryologist W. Vogt publishes the first "fate map" of a vertebrate embryo. He stained individual cells in a frog blastula (early embryo) with a vital dye (i.e., a dye that does not kill the cell) and then watched the cells divide to form the later stages of the embryo. He was able to "map" which cells in the blastula formed which tissues at alter stages of embryonic development.

J. H. Woodger publishes *Biological Principles*—an analysis of theoretical biology.

1930   The U.S. National Institutes of Health are formed.

1931   Ernest Goodpasture demonstrates that viruses can be grown in eggs. This is the first step in the development of vaccines for viral diseases.

1932   Experimental neurologists, Sir Charles Scott Sherrington and Baron Edgar Douglas Adrian, an English neurologist, win the Nobel Prize for their discoveries about the function of neurons in cats and dogs.

1932
(cont.)   German chemist Gerhard Domagk uses mice and rabbits to discover the antibacterial effects of Protosil, the first sulfa drug.

1935   Konrad Lorenz, an Austrian biologist, describes the social life of animals.

The first commercial electron microscope becomes available.

1936   Experimental physiologists, such as English Sir Henry Hallett Dale and German-American Otto Loewi, use cats, frogs, birds, and reptiles to study the chemical transmission of nerve impulses.

Alexis Carrel and American aviator Charles Lindbergh develop an artificial heart that is used during cardiac surgery.

1938   The U.S. Federal Food, Drug, and Cosmetic Act (Public Law 75-717 52 Stat. 1040) is signed into law by President Franklin D. Roosevelt.

B. F. Skinner publishes *The Behavior of Organisms.*

1939   Gerhard Domagk wins the Nobel Prize for his discovery of Protosil.

1940   Karl Landsteiner, an Austrian-American, discovers the Rhesus factor in human blood.

1943   Russian-American Selman Abraham Waksman uses guinea pigs to demonstrate the antibacterial effects of streptomycin, an antibiotic that is effective against gram negative bacteria.

1945   Flemming, Florey, and Chain receive the Nobel Prize for their work on penicillin and its value as a weapon against infectious disease.

1946   The U.S. Office of Naval Research is formed.

1948   The Morris Animal Foundation is formed in the United States.

1949   The American Association for Laboratory Animal Science is formed.

Cole and Marmont invent the voltage clamp for controlling cell membrane potential.

Walter Rudolf Hess, a Swiss physiologist, receives the Nobel Prize for his studies of the midbrain in cats.

1950   The U.S. National Science Foundation is formed.

1952   The Institute of Laboratory Animal Resources is formed in the United States.

Alan Lloyd Hodgkin and Andrew Fieldings Huxley, English physiologists, formulate the theory of excitation of nerves, which is based on changes in sodium and potassium ions. They use neurons from squid and crab in their study.

A polio epidemic affects more than 47,000 people in the United States.

American microbiologist Jonas Salk develops the killed virus vaccine against polio. It comes into wide use in 1954.

1953   Evarts A. Graham and Ernest L. Wydner demonstrate that tars from tobacco smoke cause cancer in mice.

1954   The Humane Society of the United States is formed.

John F. Enders, Thomas H. Weller, and Frederick C. Robbins share the Nobel Prize for their work on growing viruses in tissue culture.

1957   American physician and microbiologist Albert B. Sabin develops the live, weakened virus vaccine for polio.

1959   The National Trappers Association is formed in the United States.

1962   The Harris-Kefauver Amendment to the Federal Pure Food, Drug, and Cosmetic Act (Public Law 87-781 76 Stat. 781) is signed into law. This amendment requires extensive pharmacological and toxicological research before a drug can be tested on humans.

1963   The *Guide for the Care and Use of Laboratory Animals* is published by the National Research Council's Institute of Laboratory Animal Resources. The U.S. Public Health Service begins to require all recipients to adhere to its guidelines.

1965   The American Association for Accreditation of Laboratory Animal Care is formed.

Harry Harlow, an American psychologist, demonstrates that monkeys raised in isolation show emotional impairment for the rest of their lives.

1966   The U.S. Research or Experimentation—Cats and Dogs Act of 1966 (Public Law 89-544 80 Stat. 350) is signed into law.

1970   The U.S. Animal Welfare Act of 1970 (Public Law 91-579 84 Stat. 1560) is signed into law.

1973   The Endangered Species Act of 1973 (Public Law 93-205 87 Stat. 884) is signed into law.

1975   Australian philosopher Peter Singer publishes *Animal Liberation: A New Ethics for Our Treatment of Animals.*

The National Congress of Animal Trainers and Breeders is formed in the United States.

1976   The U.S. Animal Welfare Act Amendments of 1976 (Public Law 94-279 90 Stat. 417) are signed into law.

1979   The Animal Liberation Front claims responsibility for a break-in at an animal research facility.

1980   People for the Ethical Treatment of Animals (PETA) is formed.

1981   The Foundation for Biomedical Research is formed in the United States.

AIDS is officially recognized by the U.S. Centers for Disease Control.

Americans Roger W. Sperry, David H. Hubel, and Torsten N. Wiesel win the Nobel Prize for their demonstration of the organization and functions of discrete brain areas. They use cats in their research.

1983   R. G. Frey, a utilitarian philosopher, like Jeremy Bentham and Peter Singer, defends medical research utilizing animals in his book *Rights, Killing, and Suffering: Moral Vegetarianism and Applied Ethics.*

Thomas Regan publishes *The Case for Animal Rights.*

Scientists demonstrate that a genetically engineered yeast can protect chimpanzees from hepatitis B.

1984   The Laboratory Animal Management Association is formed.

1985   The Food Security Act of 1985—Subtitle F (Public Law 99-198 99 Stat. 1645) is signed into law.

Two U.S. organizations, Incurably Ill for Animal Research (iiFAR) and the National Association for Biomedical Research, are formed.

The Fur Farm Animal Welfare Coalition is formed.

The National Association for Biomedical Research is formed.

1986   Michael A. Fox publishes *The Case for Animal Experimentation: An Evolutionary and Ethical Perspective.*

1990   The Medical Scientist's Legal Defense Fund is formed in the United States.

1991   The Coalition for Animals and Animal Research is formed in the United States.

1992   The U.S. Animal Enterprise Protection Act of 1992 (Public Law 102-346 106 Stat. 928) is signed into law.

3

Biographical Sketches

THE FOLLOWING BIOGRAPHICAL SKETCHES PROFILE individuals involved, in one capacity or another, with the issue of animal rights.
This section is not meant to be comprehensive, rather it is intended only to highlight those prominent people who have had a
profound impact on the philosophies, legislation, and practices
centered around animal rights.

Cleveland Amory

Cleveland Amory was born on 2 September 1917 in Nahant,
Massachusetts. He is a freelance writer, lecturer, and television
commentator. He is the host of a syndicated radio program,
"Curmudgeon at Large" (1967–) and the author of a syndicated
newspaper column, "Animail" (1983–). He is the founding president of the Fund for Animals (1967–), which he says is committed to "litigation, legislation, education, and confrontation." The
Fund is famous for painting the baby seals on the ice floes off the
Magdalene Islands in Canada. They painted the baby seals with
red organic dye that did not harm the baby seals, but made their
coats worthless for the sealers that kill them for their coats. The
Fund is also known for its rescue of the burros in the Grand
Canyon. The Fund owns and runs the Black Beauty Ranch for
abused and injured equines and other animals. Amory is the
author of *The Cat Who Came for Christmas* (1987), which describes
his rescue of his feline companion, Polar Bear, and *Man Kind?:
Our Incredible War on Wildlife* (1974). He is the author and editor of

a number of other books. Amory does not take a salary for his work with the Fund.

Jeremy Bentham

Jeremy Bentham was born on Red Lion Street, Houndsditch, London, on 15 February 1748. He attended Queen's College, Oxford, England. Bentham's first book, *Fragment on Government*, published in 1776, is credited with being the beginnings of philosophic radicalism. In his book published in 1789, *An Introduction to the Principles of Morals and Legislation*, Bentham defined the principle of utility as being "that property in any object whereby it tends to produce pleasure, good, or happiness, or to prevent the happening of mischief, pain, evil, or unhappiness to the party whose interest is considered. . . ."

Bentham claimed that humankind was governed by two sovereign motives, pain and pleasure. His principle of utility recognized this subjection. Bentham argued that humans who are hedonistic (pursue personal pleasure and avoid pain) pursue the general happiness because of sanctions, such as being arrested (political sanction); ostracized (moral or social sanction); or punished in the hereafter (theological sanction). Bentham wrote of animals: "The question is not, can they reason? Nor can they talk? But, can they suffer?"

Bentham maintained that because animals can suffer, they have a right to life, liberty, and the pursuit of happiness. This argument became the central logic and battle cry of both the Victorian and modern animal protection movement. Bentham died in Queens Square on 6 June 1832.

Claude Bernard

Claude Bernard was born on 12 July 1813 in Saint Julien, France. When Bernard entered medical school in 1834, blood letting was still a common treatment for a variety of diseases. Germ theory (that is, that disease could be caused by microorganisms) was not yet established. At that time, the American physician and writer Oliver Wendell Holmes suggested that if the drugs in common use could be "sunk to the bottom of the sea," "it would be all the better for mankind—and all the worse for the fishes." Leading physicians of the day believed that chemistry and physics could advance in the laboratory, but biology and medicine could not.

Bernard worked in the laboratory of Francois Magendie. Magendie was one of the first of the modern animal experimenters. In 1822, he cut the anterior and posterior roots of the spinal cord of living animals and discovered loss of sensation followed. Bernard believed that medical knowledge, like other forms of scientific knowledge, could be won through systematic experimentation. He was the first to state the principle of scientific determinism; that is, identical experiments should yield identical results. The real beginnings of animal research probably date from the publication of his book, *An Introduction to Experimental Medicine* in 1865. This book was translated into English by Henry Copley Green in 1927.

Joseph Sill Clark

Senator Clark (D-PA) was one of the sponsors of Public Law 89-544 in the Senate. He was born in Philadelphia, Pennsylvania, on 21 October 1901. He received a B.A. from Harvard University in 1923 and his law degree from the University of Pennsylvania in 1926. He was admitted to the bar and started a law practice in Philadelphia in 1926. He served with the United States Army Air Corps during World War II and achieved the rank of colonel and acted as the deputy chief of staff, Eastern Air Command. He received the Bronze Star, the Legion of Merit, and the Order of the British Empire. He served as the controller for the city of Philadelphia from 1950 to 1952 and mayor from 1952 to 1956. He was elected to the Senate on 3 January 1957 and served until 3 January 1969, when he was defeated for reelection. After his Senate career, he was the president of World Federalists, U.S.A. and the chairman of the Coalition on National Priorities and Military Policy.

Michael Allen Fox

Michael Allen Fox was born in Cleveland, Ohio, in 1940. He received his B.A. from Cornell University, Ithaca, New York, and his M.A. and Ph.D. from the University of Toronto, Ontario, Canada. He has worked at the University of Toronto as an instructor and is currently a full professor of philosophy at Queen's University, Kingston, Ontario. He is the editor of *Queen's Quarterly*. He published *The Case for Animal Experimentation: An Evolutionary and Ethical Perspective* in 1985.

Michael Wilson Fox

Born in Bolton, England, in 1938, Michael Wilson Fox received his B. Vet. Med. from the Royal Veterinary College in London in 1962; he received his Ph.D. in 1967 and his D.Sc. in 1976, both from the University of London. Fox also received a Ms.T. from the Alpha School of Massage.

Fox came to the United States in 1962. He worked at the Jackson Laboratory, Bar Harbor, Maine; the State Research Hospital, Galesburg, Illinois; and Washington University, St. Louis, Missouri. Since 1976, he has been the director of the Institute for the Study of Animal Problems of the Humane Society of America. He published *Between Man and Animals: The Key to the Kingdom* in 1976 and, in 1980, *Returning to Eden: Animal Rights and Human Responsibility*. In 1977, Fox edited *On the Fifth Day: Animal Rights and Human Obligations*. He is the author of a syndicated newspaper column, *Ask Your Animal Doctor*; the editor of the *International Journal for the Study of Animal Problems*; and a contributing editor to *McCall's*.

Charles (C.) Everett Koop

C. Everett Koop was born in Brooklyn, New York, on 14 October 1916. Koop entered Dartmouth College at 16 years of age and received a B.A. in 1937. He received an M.D. from Cornell University in 1941 and a Sc.D. in medicine from the University of Pennsylvania in 1947. Koop was one of the most well known and controversial U.S. surgeon generals. He was appointed by President Reagan and was sworn in on 21 January 1982. The surgeon general is charged by law to promote and assure the highest level of health attainable for every individual and family in America and to develop cooperation in health projects with other nations. Koop warned Americans about the perils of smoking, which he called the "most important public health issue of our time." In 1988, he issued a report that equated nicotine addiction with cocaine and heroin addiction. He also came out against the fatty diets most Americans enjoy. Koop advocated sex education for elementary school children and the use of condoms for adults to counter the scourge of AIDS. He is a staunch anti-abortionist, coauthor of *Whatever Happened to the Human Race* (with theologian Frances A. Schaeffer), and author of *The Right To Live, The Right To Die*.

Prior to becoming the surgeon general, Koop was appointed surgeon-in-chief at the Philadelphia Children's Hospital in 1948 and was named assistant professor of surgery in 1949, associate professor in 1952, and professor of pediatric surgery in 1959. He is credited with making many improvements in pediatric surgery and started the first neonatal intensive care unit at the Philadelphia Children's Hospital.

James McMillan

Senator James McMillan (R-MI) introduced a bill to regulate vivisection in Washington, D.C., in 1896. The bill was defeated. McMillan was born in Hamilton, Ontario, on 12 May 1838. He was educated in the public schools of Hamilton. He moved to Detroit in 1855 and started the Michigan Car Company. In 1863, he built and was the president of the Duluth, South Shore and Atlantic Railroad. He was a member of the Detroit Board of Park Commissioners and the Board of Estimates. McMillan became a member of the Michigan Republican State Central Committee in 1876 and served as its chairman. He was elected to the Senate and served from 3 March 1889 until his death on 10 August 1902 in Manchester, Massachusetts. While in the Senate, he was the chairman of the Senate Committee on the District of Columbia. He was appointed the chairman of a commission that was to develop a plan to beautify Washington, D.C., during the celebration of the centennial of the city in 1900. McMillan and other members of the commission, Daniel H. Burnham and Charles F. McKim, architects; Augustus Saint-Gaudens, sculptor; and Frederick Law Olmsted, Jr., landscape architect, recommended that railroad tracks and a stone depot be removed from the Mall. This was accomplished and yielded the large landscaped area that is a major attraction for visitors to Washington, D.C., to this day.

Warren Grant Magnuson

Senator Magnuson (D-WA) was one of the sponsors of Public Law 89-544 in the Senate. Magnuson was born in Moorhead, Minnesota, on 12 April 1905. He attended the University of North Dakota at Grand Forks and North Dakota State College, and received a B.A. from the University of Washington in 1926 and his J.D. from their law school in 1929. He was admitted to the bar in 1929 and started a law practice in Seattle. He served in the United States Navy during World War II, attaining the rank of lieutenant commander. He was elected to the House of Representatives on 3 January 1937 and served until 13 December 1944, when he resigned and was appointed to the Senate on 14 December 1944 to fill a vacancy caused by the resignation of Homer T. Bone. Magnuson was elected to the Senate on 3 January 1945 and served until 3 January 1975.

Ingrid Newkirk

Ingrid Newkirk was born in Surrey, England, in 1949. In 1967, she settled in Maryland, where she volunteered in the local animal shelter and worked her way up to director. By 1978, Newkirk was an assertive cruelty investigator for the Humane Society in Washington, D.C. Reading Peter Singer's book *Animal Liberation: A New Ethics for Our Treatment of Animals* changed her life. She and Alex Pacheco formed People for the Ethical Treatment of Animals (PETA). Newkirk maintains that "[h]umans possess enough innovation and compassion to switch away from animal experimentation—whether to test drain cleaner, weapons, or cures for human diseases." PETA would stop meat-eating, fur-wearing, experimentation, and the breeding of cats and dogs. It supports retiring circus animals and closing zoos. If Newkirk and PETA had their way, "companion animals"—a term she coined—would be adopted from shelters and the streets.

Thomas Howard Regan

Thomas Howard Regan was born in Pittsburgh, Pennsylvania, in 1938. He received his B.A. from Thiel College, and his M.A. and Ph.D. from the University of Virginia. Regan was an assistant professor of philosophy at Virginia's Sweet Briar College from 1965–1967. He joined the faculty of North Carolina State University at Raleigh in 1967 and is currently a full professor in the philosophy department.

Joseph Yale Resnick

Joseph Yale Resnick was born in Ellenville, New York, in 1924. Resnick was the founder and chairman of the board of the Channel Master Corporation, which engaged in electronics and plastics research and development. Resnick was a Democrat and was elected to the House of Representatives for the 89th and 90th

Congresses. While a member of the House, Resnick introduced the bill that ultimately became the Research or Experimentation–Cats and Dogs Act of 1966 (Public Law 89-544 80 Stat. 350). Resnick was an unsuccessful candidate for nomination to the United States Senate. He died in 1969 while on a business trip.

Peter Singer

Born in Melbourne, Australia, in 1946, Peter Singer attended the University of Melbourne, where he received his B.A. in history and philosophy and an M.A. in philosophy. Singer then studied at University College, Oxford, England, where he received a B.Phil degree in 1971. Singer remained at the university as the Radcliffe lecturer.

Several of Singer's fellow students at Oxford, including Stanley and Rosalind Godlovitch and John Harris, compiled a series of articles providing information about factory farming and animal experimentation, and calling for the ethical treatment of animals. This resulted in *Animals, Men, and Morals,* which was published in England in 1971. Singer wrote a long review of the American edition in which he combined the views of the contributors together into a single coherent philosophy of animal liberation. This appeared as *Animal Liberation* in the *New York Review of Books.* Singer wrote the book *Animal Liberation: A New Ethics for Our Treatment of Animals* during his last year (1973–1974) at Oxford and during the time he spent as a visiting professor of philosophy at New York University. (The 1990 edition of *Animal Liberation* includes an account of the programs and campaigns that the book inspired. Singer reportedly does not object to illegal measures, such as raiding animal laboratories, when the results cannot be obtained in any other way. However, he stands firmly against violence that harms other people.)

Singer returned to Australia in 1974 and joined La Trobe University in Bundoora, Victoria, as a senior lecturer of philosophy. In 1977, he joined the faculty of Monash University in Clayton, Victoria, as a professor of philosophy and, in 1987, became the director of the university's Center for Human Bioethics.

In 1980, Singer and Jim Mason published *Animal Factories* in which they described the use of animals as biomachines to produce food. Five years later, Singer and Helga Kuhse published *Should the Baby Live? The Problem of Handicapped Infants.* He subsequently received considerable attention from the press when he lectured at several universities in Germany about euthanasia for severely handicapped newborn babies.

Singer is a visiting distinguished humanist at the University of Colorado, distinguished visiting professor at the University of California at Irvine, and Fellow of the Woodrow Wilson International Center for Scholars at the Smithsonian Institution. He has served on the editorial boards of *International Journal for the Study of Animal Problems, Australian Journal of Philosophy,* and *Ethics.* He is the coeditor of *Bioethics.*

Thomas Tryon

Tryon was probably the first author to use the word *right* with regard to animals in *The Way to Health, Long Life and Happiness* (1683) where he said "would fain be an absolute monarch or arbitrary tyrant, making nothing at his pleasure to break the laws of God, and invade and destroy all the rights and privileges of inferior creatures." Tryon was born in Bilbury, England, on 6 September 1634. He attended the village school and acted as a shepherd tending his father's flock. When he was 18, he left Bilbury for London, where he apprenticed himself to a castor-maker (hatter) on Bridewell Dock, Fleet Street. Following the example of his master, he became an Anabaptist (a radical movement within Protestantism that advocated church membership and baptism for adult members only). In 1657, he broke with the Anabaptists and became a vegetarian. In 1682, he began to write and publish his convictions to the world. His writings are described as a curious mixture of mystical philosophy and dietetics. Lewis Gompertz, the founder of the Society for the Prevention of Cruelty to Animals was an admirer of Tryon. Tryon died in Hackney, England, on 21 August 1703.

4

Animal Rights Litigation

COMMON LAW DOES NOT PROVIDE ANY RESTRICTION on the use of animals. Therefore, any discussion of cruelty must be based solely on statutory language (local, state, and federal) and its interpretation in the courts (administrative, civil, and criminal).

In the United States, each of the 50 states has enacted criminal statutes that seek to control the human use and abuse of animals. Most states exempt certain activities from anti-cruelty laws, such as hunting, fishing, trapping, slaughtering, or experimenting. In most states, cruelty to animals is a misdemeanor, which is punishable by a fine and/or no more than one year in jail. Generally, the penalty for animal fighting is more severe (larger fines, longer jail sentences). Enforcement is often left to the Society for the Prevention of Cruelty to Animals and other humane societies, which are privately funded and staffed by volunteers.

Chapter 54 of the United States Code Annotated (54 7 sec. 2131–2147) provides a systematic compilation of Public Laws 89-544, 91-579, 94-279, 98-443, and 99-198, and the Code of Federal Regulations, Title 9—Animal and Animal Products, Chapter 1, Animal and Plant Health Inspection Service, Department of Agriculture, contains the regulations promulgated by the Secretary of Agriculture to ensure the humane handling, care, treatment, and transportation of animals under the authority of these laws. The *Guide for the Care and Use of Laboratory Animals,* issued in 1985 by the National Research Council's Institute of Laboratory Animal Resources, converts these requirements and recommendations, as well as other federal, state, and local laws, regulations, and policies into a practical format that can be used to make day-to-day decisions about the care and use of laboratory animals.

The Animal Enterprise Protection Act of 1992 (Public Law 102-346 106 Stat. 928) amends Title 18 of the United States Code by adding Section 43—Animal Enterprise Terrorism. Section 43 makes it a federal crime for anyone who crosses national or state borders and/or uses the mails to cause a physical disruption in the functioning of an animal enterprise by stealing, damaging, or causing the loss of property (including animals and records) that causes economic damage exceeding $10,000 (see chapter 5).

The Carey Brain-Damage Experiment

The case of neurosurgeon Michael E. Carey, M.D., is unique.[1] Carey is a neurosurgeon who saw action in the Vietnam War and in the Middle East Desert Storm campaign against Iraq. He found that postoperative neurosurgical mortality was 10–12 percent in Vietnam, approximately the same level that was reported in World War II, more than 25 years earlier. On returning from Vietnam, he did a literature search and discovered that worldwide, fewer than 25 papers on brain wounding had appeared in the scientific literature. Based on the results of this search, Carey decided to study this problem in his laboratory. He received a grant from the U.S. Army to study this problem in anesthetized cats.

Carey and his colleagues found that a missile delivered with sufficient energy could cause respiratory difficulties, even though the missile tract was not near the brain stem, which controls respiratory functions. They showed that animals that ultimately died showed a decrease in minute volume, while animals that survived did not. The minute volume is the total amount of new air moved into the respiratory passages each minute. It is equal to the tidal volume (the amount of air inspired and expired with each normal breath) times the respiratory rate. In a normal young male adult, the tidal volume is about 500 milliliters and the respiratory rate is about 12 breaths/minute, so the minute volume is equal to about 6,000 milliliters or 6 liters/minute. They began to try to determine the biological and physiological differences between these two groups. They also began to study a new drug, GMI Ganglioside, which appeared to speed and enhance recovery.

At this point, psychiatrist Neal Barnard and his colleagues from an animal rights organization obtained copies of Carey's experimental protocols and research reports from the Army. Barnard heads the animal activist group, Physicians' Committee for Responsible Research, which conducted an independent review of Carey's work and concluded that it was flawed. They reportedly held a news conference in New Orleans that ultimately led to a story in the *New Orleans Times Picayune* and other newspapers nationwide. The physicians' group also allegedly contacted Representative Robert Livingston (R-LA). Representative Livingston reportedly launched a General Accounting Office (GAO) investigation into Carey's research without talking to Carey or anyone at Louisiana State University. Livingston ultimately placed a rider on the 1989 Defense Appropriation Bill, withholding money for Carey's research. The rider reportedly was attached to the legislation before the GAO report was available and before Carey was informed in writing that anyone was concerned about his research. The GAO team collected information about Carey's research, which it allegedly presented to John Jane, M.D., chairman of neurosurgery at the University of Virginia, and to six other neurosurgeons. Although there was said to be no direct contact between Carey and Jane's committee, the scientists on the committee concluded that Carey's research was valid and should be continued. This conclusion reportedly was shared by the American Association of Neurologic Surgeons, which also investigated Carey's work.

The GAO reportedly did not accept the finding of Jane's committee, but consulted with a group of veterinary anesthesiologists. The veterinarians reportedly had not published a single paper dealing with brain research, while the members of Jane's committee had written more than 350 papers dealing with brain research. Ultimately this consultation led to Carey's research money being withheld. Carey claims to be the first person in history to have his peer-reviewed, federally funded research money shut off legislatively by Congress.

PETA Goes Undercover

In 1981, Dr. Edward Taub, a scientist at the Institute of Behavioral Research in Silver Spring, Maryland, was conducting research on the effects of somatosensory deafferentation with monkeys in which all sensation was surgically abolished from one or both forelimbs.[2]

According to Dr. Taub, in May 1981, Alex Pacheco asked him for a job in his laboratory. Since Taub could not afford to pay him, Pacheco agreed to work as a volunteer. Pacheco worked in Taub's laboratory for five months. During this time, Taub asserts that Pacheco never pointed out any deficiencies in the facilities or questioned any of the procedures used in the laboratory. Without Taub's permission, during the night, Pacheco allegedly took photographs of the conditions in Taub's laboratory and admitted five observers. Each observer ultimately filed an affidavit that was highly critical of the conditions in the laboratory. Pacheco failed to mention to Taub that he was the president and one of the founders of People for the Ethical Treatment of Animals (PETA), an antivivisectionist organization. Pacheco took his photographs and affidavits to the Montgomery County police, who raided Taub's laboratory and seized his research subjects (17 monkeys) and some of his research records.

The search and seizure received major local and national media coverage, which Taub thinks was organized by PETA. The monkeys were placed in PETA's care. When Taub petitioned for their return, the monkeys disappeared. They were reportedly transported to Gainsville, Florida, and then back to the Washington, D.C., area. During this unauthorized transportation, the monkeys allegedly were subjected to considerable stress. Taub filed cruelty to animal charges, but claims that these were never investigated.

Taub was charged with 119 counts of violating the Maryland anti-cruelty statutes (Maryland Code 1957, 1976 Repl. Vol., Article 27 sec. 59). His first trial resulted in the complete dismissal of 113 of the counts. He was found guilty of failing to provide adequate veterinary care by an outside veterinarian to six monkeys (*Taub v. State of Maryland* 463 A.2d 819 (MD 1983)).[3] Taub maintained that it is extremely rare for a veterinarian to have experience with animals with deafferentation and that he is a recognized expert in the treatment of this condition, with more than 25 years of experience.

In his second trial, Taub was cleared of five of the remaining six charges. The sixth charge, which led to conviction, concerned a monkey whose arm was amputated seven weeks after it was removed from his laboratory. The amputation allegedly was necessitated by an infection of the bone (osteomyelitis), which was said to date back to the inadequate care received in Taub's laboratory. A pathology report based on an examination of the arm reported that the animal did not have osteomyelitis. The Maryland Court of Appeals overturned this final conviction on the grounds that the statute did not apply to federally funded research, which is covered by the Federal Animal Welfare Act (see 463 A.2d 822). This act provides for the protection of animals used in research facilities, while at the same time recognizing and preserving the validity of using animals in research. Since Taub was the recipient of a grant from the National Institutes of Health (NIH), the court found that he was also subject to that agency's regulations governing the care and treatment of animals used in research.

During the media uproar over the break-in at Taub's laboratory, NIH decided to suspend and then terminate his grant. Taub appealed the decision to the Department of Health and Human Service Departmental Grant Appeals Board. While the Appeals Board did not reinstate Taub's grant, they did report that they found no evidence of inadequate veterinary care. They also found that Taub was well qualified to treat problems associated with deafferentation. The Ethics Committee of the American Psychological Association, the Animal Care Committee of the Society for Neuroscience, and an *ad hoc* committee of the American Physiological Society all agreed, reportedly by unanimous vote, that Taub was not guilty of any wrongdoing. Taub moved to the Psychology Department of the University of Alabama at Birmingham. He maintains that his work at Silver Springs and Birmingham has led to improved treatment of some patients who have suffered a stroke. The disruption of his work delayed the application of this treatment to patients by about eight years.

Title 9 Lawsuits

Relatively little litigation has occurred as a result of the regulations defined in Title 9 of the Code of Federal Regulations or Public Laws 89–544 and their amendments. The case of the *International Primate Protection League v. Institute for Behavioral Research, Inc. and James V. Stunkard, D.V.M., Defendant* (see 799 F.2d 934) is related to Taub's case. The International Primate

Protection League, People for Ethical Treatment of Animals, Inc., the Animal Law Enforcement Association, and a number of private individuals sought to be named the guardians of Taub's monkeys in the case described above. In this case, the court held that private individuals and organizations do not have a standing to bring suit to be designated as guardians of research animals because these individuals and organizations did not show actual or threatened personal injury as a result of the former owners (i.e., the Institute for Behavioral Research, Inc.) regaining control of the animals. Further, the Animal Welfare Act of 1970 did not authorize private individuals or organizations to seek relief of being named guardians of research animals seized from a medical research institute whose chief was convicted of state animal cruelty statute violations (see above). The court held that "a mere interest in a problem, no matter how long-standing the interest and no matter how qualified the organization is in evaluating the problem, is not sufficient by itself to create standing." In the 1976 case of *Haviland v. Butz* (543 F.2d 169; 50 L. Ed. 2d 97),[4] the court decided that the owner of a professional animal act was in violation of licensing provisions. The court held that a dog and pony show that traveled through a number of states where it appeared before paying audiences and occasionally appeared on commercial television fell within the regulatory compass of Title 9. It further stated that Title 9 regulations apply to activities that take place entirely within one state, as well as those that involve traffic across state lines. The court also held that the definition of "exhibitor" used in Title 9—which includes carnivals, circuses, zoos, and animal acts, but excludes retail pet stores, fairs, rodeos, and purebred dog and cat shows—did not infringe on the equal protection guarantee of Constitutional Amendment 5 of the United States Code Annotated.

The case of *Winkler v. Colorado Dept. of Health* (Colo., 564 P.2d 107 (1977)) was a response to the Colorado Department of Health's 1974 adoption of regulations that prohibit importation of pets for resale from states whose licensing laws and regulations are less stringent than those of Colorado. The plantiffs attacked the validity of these regulations on four grounds: (1) they were adopted in violation of statutory authority; (2) are in excess of the state's police power and violative of due process; (3) are violative of equal protection; and (4) are in conflict with the Commerce Clause of the United States Constitution. The Supreme Court of Colorado found each of these points to be invalid. The court ruled that the doctrine of preemption did not invalidate state regulations that prohibited importation of pets for resale from states with less stringent licensing laws and regulations for commercial pet dealers. The court held that the federal regulations did not indicate preemptive intent, but expressly endorsed state-federal cooperation; as stated in 7 U.S.C. 2131 (1970), they did ". . . cooperate with the officials of the various states . . . in carrying out the purposes of this chapter and of any state, local, or municipal legislation or ordinance on the same subject."

In 1980, while working at the marine laboratory of the University of Hawaii at Kewalo Basin, Honolulu, Mr. Le Vasseur removed two Atlantic bottlenose dolphins from the laboratory and released them into the ocean. In *State v. Le Vasseur* (613 P.2d 1328), the appellant (Le Vasseur) argued that his actions protected the United States by enforcing its policy of protecting dolphins (see Marine Protection Act 16 U.S.C. 1361 and Animal Welfare Act 7 U.S.C.S. 2131 et seq.) and that he chose "theft" of the dolphins as that crime is defined by our statutes as the alternative to the "evil" of the alleged violation of the policy of the United States for the protection of laboratory animals. The court held that removing the dolphins from their tanks and releasing them into the ocean was at least as great an evil as a matter of law as that sought to be prevented. Further, the court held that the protection of Title 9 extended to all warm-blooded animals, including dolphins.

In a 1990 case concerning the Animal Welfare Act, *Kerr v. Kimmell* (740 F. Supp. 1525), the court held that the act does not preempt state regulation of animal welfare.

In another 1990 case, *American Society for the Prevention of Cruelty to Animals v. Board of Trustees of State University of New York, State University of New York at Stony Brook* (N.Y. Sup. 1990, 556 N.Y.S.2d 447), the court held that the (researcher's) name, department, location, and telephone number, as well as the grant number or application number of funding source were exempt from disclosure under the Freedom of Information Law. Further, the court held that the university's Institutional Animal Care and Use Committee was required to respond to questions relating to procedures to be performed on laboratory animals. These questions included whether (1) survival surgery would be performed; (2) controlled or hazardous substances would be used; and (3) animals would be euthanized at the completion of research. The court held that these questions must be answered when they are framed to elicit information concerning care and treatment of animals. The questions cannot, except in general terms, explore the underlying hypothesis of the experimenter, the methods that the experimenter used, the analysis and results, or any trade secrets.

In *Animal Legal Defense Fund v. Youtter* (760 F. Supp. 923), the court held that animal welfare organizations satisfied the injury-in-fact standing requirement to challenge the regulation of the Department of Agriculture for their failure to include birds, rats, and mice as animals within the meaning of the federal Laboratory Animal Welfare Act (7 U.S.C.S. 2131 et seq.). This lack allegedly injured the organization's ability to disseminate to their members information about the treatment and conditions of these animals. The court held, in *Animal Legal Defense Fund v. Madigan* (781 F. Supp. 797), that the Secretary of Agriculture's promulgation of regulations that failed to include birds, rats, and mice as "animals" protected by the act (7 U.S.C.S. 2131 et seq.) was arbitrary and capricious and that the department's refusal to institute rule-making proceedings was arbitrary and capricious.

Finally, in the 1991 case *Cox v. U.S. Department of Agriculture* (C.A.8, 1991, 925 F.2d 1102, certiorari denied 112 S. Ct. 178, 116 L. Ed. 2d 141), the court held that a $12,000 fine and a 90-day suspension of a breeder's license was not an excessive penalty for a breeder with a $1 million gross income. The breeder reportedly refused to allow inspection of its premises and records. It allegedly violated several other sections of the act (7 U.S.C.S. 2131 et seq.). Most notably, it was alleged that the breeder transported under-age dogs, failed to hold dogs for five days after acquisition, and falsified records, and that these acts were willful on the part of the breeder.

A recent ALR survey (see 6 ALR5th 733) analyzed the cases that occurred from 1950 to 1994 to determine what constitutes the offense of cruelty to animals. This survey found a minimum number of cases. For example, New York had only five during this time period, California six, Illinois two, and Texas eight. Many of these cases centered around animal fighting.

The following is a fairly typical case. The sheriff's Department of Hopkins County was informed by an unnamed informant that a dog fight between pitbulls would take place on the property of Rogers. On investigation, the sheriff and several deputies found 15–20 vehicles parked at a barn on the property and when the officers exited their car, Rogers honked the horn of her truck. The officers then saw 20–30 people flee from a wooded area located nearby. They placed Rogers under arrest and a search of the area revealed a dogfighting pit with blood stains on the wood, pit bulldogs, and dogfighting equipment. The jury in this case assessed the punishment at a four-year confinement and a $2,000 fine. The sentence was suspended and the defendant was placed on probation for four years. *Rogers v. State of Texas (see* 760 S.W.2d 669) is an appeal of this conviction. The court held under the "open field doctrine" that fourth amendment protection does not extend to undeveloped areas ouside curtilage (yard within the fence surrounding a building) and so a search warrant is not required.

Notes

1. The discussion that follows is drawn from Michael E. Carey, "Another Battlefield: Animal Extremists Wage War on Brain Wound Research," *CFAAR Newsletter* 5 (1993): 1–7, and on a series of interviews that appeared on a segment of the television show *60 Minutes* that originally aired on 26 January 1993.

2. The discussion that follows is drawn from Daniel S. Moretti, *Animal Rights and the Law,* New York: Oceana Publications, 1984; Karen L. McDonald, "Creating a Private Cause of Action against Abusive Animal Research," *University of Pennsylvania Law Review* 134 (1986): 399–432; and Edward Taub, "The Silver Spring Monkey Incident: The Untold Story," *CFAAR Newsletter* 4 (1991): 1–8.

3. This case is cited in volume 463 of the *Atlantic Reporter,* 2d series, page 819. A reporter provides the full text of the decision of a court. In addition to the text of the decision, the editors of the *Reporter* prepare headnotes, which are brief summaries of rules of law or significant facts as they apply to the case in question. The headnotes allow the reader to grasp the legal issues discussed in the case and help the reader to locate other cases on the same or similar points of law. The headnotes also each contain a "Key Number" that refers the reader to specific articles in the *American Digest.* Our system of law follows the doctrine of *stare decisis* (i.e., to abide by or adhere to decided cases). This means that when a court has once laid down a principle of law that applies to a certain set of facts, it will adhere to that principle and apply it to all future cases where the facts are substantially the same. Thus, the decision of a court sets a precedent that is binding on that court and other courts of equal or lessor rank. The *American Digest* is a subject classification system that takes the decisions that are reported chronologically in the *National Reporter System* and rearranges them by subject. This brings all of the cases bearing on similar points of law together and "digests" (abstracts) the decision. This system divides the subject of law into seven main classes; each class is divided into subclasses; and each subclass into topics. Each topic is assigned a "Key Number." For example, "Cruelty to Animals" is assigned "Key Number" 38.

4. This case was also the subject of a report in the *American Law Reports* (ALR), which are published by the Lawyers Co-Operative Publishing Co. (Rochester, NY) and the Bancroft-Whitney Co. (San Francisco, CA). The ALR is a selective

reporter. It reports mostly appellate court decisions. In addition to a report of the action of the court, ALR provides annotations; that is, encyclopedic essays or memoranda on significant legal topics. The annotation typically cites and summarizes the facts and holding of all previous decisions from all jurisdictions that dealt with this topic. The annotation attempts to cover all sides of every question on the point of law, presents general principles deduced from the cases, and gives their exceptions, qualifications, distinctions, and applications. In the case of the Haviland decision, the annotation (36 ALRFed 615) deals with the validity, construction, and application of the Animal Welfare Act (7 U.S.C.S. 2131 et seq.).

5

Federal Legislation in the United States

Overview of Laws on Animal Rights

Although curiosity about the structure and function of the human body probably predates written history, the publication in 1865 of French scientist Claude Bernard's *Introduction à la médecine expérimentale* marked a major turning point. Bernard provided the philosophical rationale for experimental physiology. He described the techniques still used in the study of the physiological responses of living organisms. While there was considerable anti-vivisectionist sentiment on the Continent (even Bernard's wife and two daughters were ardent supporters of the cause), the British were the first to attempt to regulate painful research with the passage of the Cruelty to Animals Act in 1876.

In the United States, in 1896, Representative James McMillan (R-MI) introduced a bill in Congress to regulate vivisection in the District of Columbia. The bill was defeated. After World War II, there was a rapid growth in research using animal subjects.

According to popular anecdotal accounts, the impetus for modern legislation was based on the case of a family who lost their pet dog. The family thought they saw their dog in a news photo of the holding pens of a large New York dog dealer. The dog dealer refused to let the family look at his dogs. The dog dealer's facility was located in Representative Joseph Y. Resnick's district. The family appealed to Resnick (D-NY), who interceded on their behalf. Resnick was angered by the arrogance of the dog dealer, who refused to cooperate. Consequently, Resnick introduced a bill that eventually became the Research or Experimentation—Cats and Dogs Act in the United States House of Representatives on 9 July 1966. A similar bill was introduced by Senators Warren G. Magnuson (D-WA) and Joseph Clark (D-PA).

Significant Animal Rights Acts

Research or Experimentation—Cats and Dogs Act of 1966

The purposes of the Cats and Dogs Act of 1966 (Public Law 89-544 80 Stat. 350) are: (1) to protect the owners of dogs and cats from the theft of such pets; (2) to prevent the sale or use of stolen dogs or cats for the purpose of research or experimentation; and (3) to establish humane standards for the treatment of dogs, cats, monkeys (nonhuman primates), guinea pigs, hamsters, and rabbits by animal dealers and medical research facilities.

The act achieves its purpose by requiring animal dealers to be licensed by, and research facilities to be registered with, the Secretary of Agriculture. The act also meets its mandate by making it unlawful for a research facility to purchase animals from unlicensed dealers. Research facilities included are any department, agency, or instrumentality of the United States or any school, institution, organization, or person that receives funds under a grant, award, loan, or contract from any department, agency, or instrumentality of the United States and that uses animals for research, tests, or experimentation.

Under the act, no dealer is allowed to sell or dispose of any dog or cat within five business days after acquisition of an animal. Dogs and cats must be marked for identification in some humane manner, and dealers and research facilities must make and maintain records of the sale and purchase of dogs and cats. Licensed dealers and research facilities must permit inspection by legally constituted law enforcement agencies in search of lost animals.

The U.S. Secretary of Agriculture, after consultation with other federal agencies, is directed to promulgate regulations to ensure the humane handling, care, treatment, and transportation of animals by dealers and research facilities, except during actual research or experimentation as determined by the research facility. The act says that the standards should include minimum requirements with respect to housing, feeding, watering, sanitation, ventilation, shelter from extremes of weather and temperature, separation of species, and adequate veterinary care. Inspectors appointed by the Secretary of

Agriculture are allowed to make inspections of dealers and research facilities to determine if they are complying with the provisions of the act. Inspectors are able to confiscate or destroy dealer-held and post-research animals found suffering because of violations of this act.

The act does not authorize the Secretary of Agriculture to promulgate rules, regulations, or orders for the handling, care, treatment, or inspections of animals during actual research or experimentation by a research facility as determined by such research facility. Finally, the act describes civil and criminal procedures and penalties.

Animal Welfare Act of 1970

The Animal Welfare Act of 1970 (Public Law 91-579 84 Stat. 1560) amended the Cats and Dogs Act of 1966 to include under its provisions persons or organizations that hold animals for exhibition and for sale as pets, excluding retail pet stores. Exhibitors include carnivals, road shows, circuses, and zoos. They do not include state or county fairs, livestock shows, rodeos, purebred dog or cat shows, and any other fairs or exhibitions that are intended to advance agricultural arts and sciences.

The 1970 act extends the term animal to include any live or dead dog, cat, monkey (nonhuman primate), guinea pig, hamster, rabbit, and other warm-blooded animal. It does not include horses not used for research purposes or other farm animals such as livestock or poultry that are used as food or fiber or for improving animal nutrition, breeding, management, or production efficiency or for improving the quality of food or fiber.

The act does not authorize the Secretary of Agriculture to promulgate rules, regulations, or orders with regard to the design, outlines, guidelines, or performance of actual research or experimentation. However, each research facility must show that professionally acceptable standards governing the care, treatment, and use of animals during actual research or experimentation are being followed, including the appropriate use of anesthetic, analgesic, and tranquilizing drugs. Finally, the act describes civil and criminal procedures and penalties.

Animal Welfare Act Amendments of 1976

The Animal Welfare Act Amendments of 1976 (Public Law 94-279 90 Stat. 417) amended the Animal Welfare Act of 1970 to include under its provisions persons or organizations that are intermediate handlers (express companies, forwarders, and other persons or facilities that handle live animal shipments) and carriers (airlines, railroads, motor carriers, shipping lines, or other enterprises engaged in the business of transporting any animals for hire). Transportation of any dog, cat, or other animal that is less than eight weeks old (or any other age designated by the Secretary of Agriculture) is prohibited. The amended act requires that, before transportation, a licensed veterinarian's certificate be provided showing that an animal appeared free of infectious disease or physical abnormality that would endanger the animal or other animals or endanger human public health. The act prohibits transportation, on a C.O.D. basis, of animals covered by the act, unless the consignor guarantees the round-trip fare, care, and handling charges for any animal not claimed within 48 hours.

Included under the amended act's provisions are persons or organizations that merely negotiate the purchase of animals covered by the act. Any person who grosses less than $500 from the sale of animals other than wild animals, dogs, and cats, as well as retail pet stores (except stores that sell any animals to a research facility, exhibitor, or dealer) are excluded from the provisions. The amended act extends the definition of the word "animal" to cover all dogs, including ones for hunting, security, or breeding purposes.

Prohibition on Animal Fighting

The amended act makes it unlawful for any person to knowingly sell, buy, transport, or deliver to another person any dog or other animal for the purpose of having the dog or other animal participate in an animal fighting venture or to sponsor or exhibit an animal in any animal fighting venture. (Excluded is the use of one or more animals in hunting another animal or animals, such as in hunting waterfowl, birds, raccoons, or foxes.) The amended act also prohibits the use of the United States Postal Service or any interstate instrumentality to promote or otherwise further an animal fighting venture. The activities prohibited with respect to animal fighting ventures involving live fowl are illegal only if the fight takes place in a state where such activity is prohibited by state law.

Finally, the amended act describes civil and criminal procedures and penalties for infractions covered by the amendment.

Civil Aeronautics Board Sunset Act of 1984

The Civil Aeronautics Board Sunset Act of 1984 (Public Law 98-443 98 Stat. 1708) amends (i) Section 15(a) of the Animal Welfare Act

(7 USC 2145(a)) by striking out the language "civil aeronautics board" and inserting in its place "Secretary of Transportation."

Food Security Act of 1985—Subtitle F Animal Welfare

The Food Security Act of 1985—Subtitle F Animal Welfare (Public Law 99-198 99 Stat. 1645) amends the Animal Welfare Act by extending the minimum standard of care to allow exercise for dogs and by mandating a physical environment that is adequate to promote the psychological well-being of primates. During actual experimentation, animal care, treatment, and practices should ensure that animal pain and distress are minimized, including adequate veterinary care with appropriate use of anesthetic, analgesic, tranquilizing drugs, and euthanasia. Subtitle F directs the principal investigator (PI) to consider alternatives to any procedures that are likely to cause pain or distress. In any practice that is likely to cause pain, the PI is directed to consult with a doctor of veterinary medicine to plan the procedure and to plan the use of tranquilizers, analgesics, and anesthetics for the pre- and postsurgical care in accordance with good veterinary and nursing practice. The use of paralytics without anesthesia is prohibited. The withholding of tranquilizers, anesthesia, analgesia, or euthanasia when scientifically necessary may continue for only the necessary period of time.

Subtitle F also directs that no animal may be used in more than one major operative experiment from which it is allowed to recover except in cases of scientific necessity or other special circumstances as determined by the Secretary of Agriculture. Exceptions to these standards must be specified in detail in a research protocol filed with the Institutional Animal Care and Use Committee (IACUC).

The IACUC is appointed by the chief executive officer of the research facility and must have not fewer than three members. Each member must be able to assess animal care, treatment, and practices in experimental research as determined by the needs of the research facility. The members of the IACUC represent society's concerns regarding the welfare of animal subjects. The committee must have at least one member who is a doctor of veterinary medicine. Also, the committee must have at least one member who: (1) is not affiliated with the facility other than as a member of the IACUC; (2) is not a member of the immediate family of any person affiliated with the facility; and (3) represents the general community interests in proper care and treatment of animals. If the IACUC consists of more than three members, no more than three can be from the same administrative unit of the facility. A quorum is required for all committee actions, including at least semiannual review of the study areas, animal facilities, practices involving pain to animals, and the conditions of the animals in the facility to determine that the facility is in compliance with the provisions of the act.

It is unlawful for any member of the IACUC to release any information that concerns or relates to trade secrets, processes, operations, style of work, or apparatus involved in animal research. Members also may not release any information about the identity, amount, or source of any income, profits, losses, expenditures, or confidential statistical data about the research facility. Finally, it is unlawful for any IACUC members to use or attempt to use to their advantage or reveal to any other person any information that is entitled to protection as confidential.

The IACUC must file a certificate of inspection report at the facility that is signed by the majority of the committee. The report must include an account of any violation of the standards and assurances required by the Animal Welfare Act and its amendments, as well as any deficient conditions of animal care or treatment and any deviation from research practices in the originally approved protocols. The report must also include any minority view of the IACUC and other pertinent information about the activities of the IACUC. It must be kept on file for three years.

The IACUC must report any deficiencies or deviations to the administrative representative of the facility. If these remain uncorrected, the committee must report them, in writing, to the Animal and Plant Health Inspection Service and any federal agency that has provided research funding. Subtitle F directs research facilities to provide training for scientists, animal technicians, and other personnel involved with animal care. The training must include instruction on humane practices of animal maintenance and experimentation, research or testing methods that minimize or eliminate the use of animals or limit the amount of animal pain or distress, and how deficiencies in animal care and treatment can be reported. The National Library of Medicine provides information about employee training, ways to prevent duplication of animal experimentation, and improved methods of animal experimentation that include methods that could reduce or replace animal use or minimize animal pain and distress, such as anesthetic and analgesic procedures. Subtitle F describes civil and criminal procedures and penalties for violations of these regulations.

Animal Enterprise Protection Act of 1992

The Animal Enterprise Protection Act of 1992 (Public Law 102-346 106 Stat. 928) amends Title 18 of the United States Code by adding

Section 43—Animal Enterprise Terrorism. This law makes it a federal crime for anyone who crosses national or state borders and/or uses the mails to cause a physical disruption in the functioning of an animal enterprise. The terrorism provision says that it is illegal to steal, damage, or cause the loss of property, including animals and records, that causes economic damage exceeding $10,000. An animal enterprise is defined as follows:

1. A commercial or academic enterprise that uses animals for food or fiber production, agriculture, research, or testing.
2. A zoo, aquarium, circus, rodeo, or lawful competitive animal event.
3. A fair intended to advance agricultural arts and sciences.

The terrorism provision mandates restitution in the form of the reasonable cost of repeating any experimentation that was interrupted or invalidated as a result of the offense and the loss of food production or farm income attributable to the offense. It also outlines penalties for infractions.

Transportation, Sale, and Handling of Certain Animals

Chapter 54 of the *United States Code Annotated* (USCA Chapter 54 7 sec. 2131–2147) provides a systematic compilation of Public Laws 89-544, 91-579, 94-279, 98-443, and 99-198, which all concern animal welfare. It also provides historical and statutory notes; library references to digests that report court cases in a systematic order; specific decisions; legal encyclopedias such as the *Corpus Juris Secundum,* which provide commentary on the law; and law reviews.

Code of Federal Regulations on Animals and Animal Products

Title 9 of the Code of Federal Regulations concerns animal and animal products. Chapter 1 within Title 9 is related to the Department of Agriculture's Animal and Plant Health Inspection Service. This chapter contains regulations promulgated by the Secretary of Agriculture after consultation with other federal agencies, to ensure the humane handling, care, treatment, and transportation of animals under the authority of Public Laws 89-544, 91-579, 94-279, 98-443, and 99-198. This chapter of the Code of Federal Regulations is divided into numerous subchapters, parts, and subparts.

Subchapter A deals with animal welfare. This subchapter is divided into four parts that define terms, define the regulations, standards, and rules of practice under the Animal Welfare Act and its amendments, respectively. The regulations define how an organization (seller, research facility, etc.) must do business in order to be in compliance with the Animal Welfare Act. The standards describe: the facilities (i.e., physical plant) required to house different species of animals; the training of the staff that deal with the animals; and the day-to-day pattern of activity dealing with animal health and husbandry, such as feeding and watering schedules, and sanitation methods.

Humane Slaughter Act of 1958

The Humane Slaughter Act of 1958 (Public Law 85-765) mandates that the slaughtering and handling of livestock and poultry should be carried out by humane methods that prevent needless suffering. This act specifies the following two acceptable methods of slaughtering and handling livestock:

1. Cattle, calves, horses, mules, sheep, swine, and other livestock must be rendered insensible to pain by a single blow or gunshot or by electrical, chemical, or other means that are rapid and effective before the animal is shackled, hoisted, thrown, cast, or cut.
2. Slaughtering is acceptable when done in accordance with ritual requirements of the Jewish or other religious faith where the animal is rendered unconscious by anemia of the brain caused by severance of the carotid arteries.

The Humane Slaughter Act of 1958 says that all agencies of the federal government shall neither contract for nor procure any livestock products that were not slaughtered or handled in a humane manner. The act authorizes and directs the Secretary of Agriculture to conduct, assist, and foster research for the development of humane methods of slaughter and handling of livestock.

Humane Methods of Slaughter Act of 1978

The Humane Methods of Slaughter Act of 1978 (Public Law 95-445 92 Stat. 1069) amends sections 3, 4, 10, and 20a of the federal Meat Inspection Act (21 U.S.C. 603, 610, 620), which deals with antemortem inspection. The Humane Methods Act mandates that the inspectors appointed to inspect slaughtering establishments determine what methods of handling and slaughter are being used. It gives the Secretary of Agriculture the discretionary authority to suspend inspection temporarily if handling and slaughter are not in accordance with the Humane Slaughter Act of 1958 (Public Law 85-765). The Humane Methods Act also prohibits the importation of carcasses, parts of carcasses, meat, or meat food products that have not been handled and slaughtered in accordance with the Humane Slaughter Act of 1958.

The Humane Methods Act deletes section 3, portions of sections 4b and 4c, and section 5 from the Humane Slaughter Act of 1958. It also makes ritual slaughter exempt for the provisions of the Humane Methods of Slaughter Act of 1978.

Endangered Species Act of 1973

The purpose of the Endangered Species Act (Public Law 93-205 87 Stat. 884) is to provide a program to conserve endangered and threatened species and the ecosystems on which they depend for survival. It also provides a mechanism to allow the nation to meet its international commitments such as the Migratory and Endangered Bird Treaty with Japan, the Convention on Nature Protection and Wildlife Preservation in the Western Hemisphere, the International Convention for the Northwest Atlantic Fisheries, the International Convention for the High Seas Fisheries of the North Pacific Ocean, and the Convention on International Trade in Endangered Species of Wild Fauna and Flora (see amendments to Public Laws 94-325, 94-359, 95-212, 95-632, 96-159, 96-246, 97-79, 97-304, 98-327, 99-659, 100-478, 100-653, 100-707).

Related State Legislation

Common law does not provide any restriction on the use of animals, so any discussion of cruelty must be based solely on statutory language. Each of the 50 states in the United States has enacted criminal statutes aimed at controlling the humane use and abuse of animals. Most of these statutes are a few paragraphs long. Enacted in the latter part of the nineteenth or early part of the twentieth century, these statutes have remained essentially unchanged since.

Some state statutes may define "animals" as being all living creatures except man. Others may provide an enumeration of the animals or class of animals they cover. In the latter case, consideration of offenses is restricted to those animals. Cruelty is generally defined as every act, omission, or neglect that causes unjustifiable (i.e., without legally recognized defense) pain, suffering, or death.

In general, cruelty consists of overworking or underfeeding an animal or of depriving it of proper protection. Most states exempt certain activities, such as hunting, fishing, trapping, slaughtering, or experimenting from anti-cruelty laws.

Since significant pain and suffering occur when humans force animals to fight each other, states seek to control animal fighting under their individual anti-cruelty statutes. Some states also prohibit fights between animals and humans such as bullfights and alligator wrestling.

A few states allow people to be convicted of cruelty to animals if they fail to take notice of a substantial risk; in other words, if they deviate from a reasonable standard of care (criminal negligence) or do not act within a reasonable standard of care (ordinary negligence). Conversely, most states require that some *level of intent* be proven to convict a person of cruelty to animals. By legal definition, one or more of the following elements must exist to prove intent. People act *maliciously,* if they act with evil intent; *willfully,* if they act intentionally and voluntarily to do something the law forbids; *intentionally,* when they desire to cause certain results; *knowingly,* when they are aware that their conduct is practically certain to cause a certain result; or *recklessly,* where they disregard a risk, of which they are aware, in hopes that a certain result may occur.

In most states, cruelty to animals is a misdemeanor, which is punishable by a fine and/or *no more* than one year in jail. In contrast, a felony is usually punishable by a fine and/or *more* than one year in jail. Generally, the penalty for animal fighting is more severe (larger fines, longer jail sentences) than the penalties for general cruelty. Most law enforcement officials, such as police or sheriffs, are more concerned about crimes against humans. Enforcement is often left to the Society for the Prevention of Cruelty to Animals and other humane societies, which are privately funded and staffed by volunteers. Few humans who commit cruelty to animals are ever prosecuted. The few that are usually receive minimal penalties.

6

Organizations

Activists for Protective Animal Legislation (APAL)
P.O. Box 11743
Costa Mesa, CA 92627
(714) 540-0583

Founded in 1980, APAL now has 500 members. It monitors legislation dealing with animal welfare, informs the general public on legislation pertaining to animal welfare, and advises and assists lawmakers who support humane animal legislation.

PUBLICATIONS: APAL publishes the quarterly *Political Watchdog*, as well as bulletins and newsletters.

Actors and Others for Animals (AOA)
5510 Cahuenga Boulevard
North Hollywood, CA 91601
(818) 985-6263

AOA has 3,500 members and was formed in 1971. It is made up of individual members who advocate the following policies: zero pet population growth; the alleviation of animal suffering through direct emergency aid and pet adoption programs; and the protection of endangered species and the importance of wildlife conservation.

PUBLICATION: AOA publishes the annual *Actors and Others Newsletter*.

Alaskan Malamute Protection League (AMPL)
P.O. Box 170
Cedar Crest, NM 87008
(505) 281-3961

AMPL, which was founded in 1986, is a coalition of about 50 owners of Alaskan malamute dogs, malamute rescue groups, and interested individuals. AMPL maintains files on lost, found, and homeless malamutes; functions as a support network; provides clerical assistance to malamute rescue groups; and monitors legislation affecting the breed.

American Antivivisection Society (AAVS)
Noble Plaza, Suite 204
801 Old York Road
Jinkintown, PA 19046
(215) 887-0816

AAVS was founded in 1883 and has 11,000 members. It opposes all types of experiments on living animals, advocates abolition of vivisection, and sponsors research on alternative methods.

American Association for Accreditation of Laboratory Animal Care (AAALAC)
9650 Rockville Pike
Bethesda, MD 20814
(301) 564-5111

AAALAC, which started in 1965, is a coalition of about 30 national education, health, and research organizations that provides an accreditation program for laboratory animal facilities via peer reviewed site visits/evaluations.

PUBLICATION: AAALAC publishes the annual *Activities Report*, which includes a list of accredited facilities.

American Association for Laboratory Animal Science (ALAS)
70 Timber Creek, Suite 5
Cordova, TN 38018
(901) 754-8620

ALAS was founded in 1949 and has 4,500 members. It conducts examinations and certification of animal technicians, as well as acts as a clearinghouse for the collection and exchange of information on all aspects of laboratory animal procurement, care, and management.

PUBLICATIONS: ALAS publishes the bimonthlies *ALAS Bulletin* and *Laboratory Animal Science*, as well as the annual *American Association for Laboratory Animal Science-Membership Directory*.

American Council on Science and Health (ACSH)
1995 Broadway, 16th Floor
New York, NY 10023
(212) 362-7044

ACSH reaffirms the critical need for laboratory animals in biomedical research and endorses animal testing and workable, reasonable guidelines to assure the humane treatment of animals.

American Dog Owners Association (ADOA)
1654 Columbia Turnpike
Castleton, NY 12033
(518) 477-8469

ADOA, which was founded in 1970, seeks to educate the public on the responsibilities of pet ownership and advocates stringent laws applying to vicious dogs and their owners.

American Feline Society (AFS)
204 West 20th Street
New York, NY 10011

AFS started in 1938. It provides information on cat history, care, and feeding to the public. AFS also provides food, supplies, and medical attention to cats cared for and rescued by humanitarians, as well as rescuing stray and unwanted pet cats.

PUBLICATIONS: AFS publishes *Cat Care and Feeding* and a newsletter.

American Fund for Alternatives to Animal Research (AFAAR)
175 West 12th Street, No. 16-G
New York, NY 10011
(212) 989-8073

AFAAR has gained 6,000 members since it was created in 1977. It exerts pressure on government agencies to allocate a greater proportion of funds for developing and using nonanimal research. AFAAR offers grants to develop *in vitro* tests, as well as disseminating reports, results, and abstracts of research using *in vitro* techniques to funding agencies, regulatory agencies, interested scientists, and laypersons. AFAAR also offers courses in tissue culture and provides unfinished *in vitro* experiments and stained cells for high school biology classes.

PUBLICATIONS: AFAAR publishes *AFAAR News Abstracts* (3/year)—a newsletter on nonanimal research and testing methods, which includes book reviews and research reports—and the semiannual *International Animal Action*.

American Humane Association (AHA)
9725 East Hampden Avenue
Denver, CO 80231
(303) 695-0811

AHA is a national federation of concerned individuals and animal care and control agencies that was founded in 1877. It is dedicated to the prevention of cruelty, neglect, abuse, and exploitation of animals. AHA activities include legislative advocacy, providing training programs for animal shelter personnel, monitoring the use of animals in motion pictures, and researching shelters and animal population statistics. AHA also administers the National Hearing Dog Project and an emergency disaster relief fund for animals. It is the parent organization for the American Association for Protecting Children.

PUBLICATIONS: AHA publishes the quarterly *Advocate* and the bimonthly newsletter *Shoptalk*, which are distributed to all animal care and control agencies in the United States. It also publishes pamphlets, flyers, and posters on animal care and animal welfare issues.

American Pet Society (APS)
406 South 1st Avenue
Arcadia, CA 91006
(818) 477-2222

APS promotes responsible pet ownership.

American Society for the Prevention of Cruelty to Animals (ASPCA)
441 East 92nd Street
New York, NY 10128
(212) 876-7700

The ASPCA, which has 400,000 members, was created by a special act of the New York State Legislature in 1866 to prevent cruelty to animals throughout the United States. The ASPCA seeks to enforce all laws for the protection of animals, promote appreciation for and humane treatment of animals, and provide effective means for the prevention of cruelty to animals. The ASPCA conducts educational programs and disseminates animal-related information for children and adults. It campaigns for legislation to improve animal welfare and offers national and international legislative, consulting, and educational programs. The ASPCA maintains a library resource center (books, periodicals, films, and animal-related information).

PUBLICATIONS: The ASPCA produces videotapes on animal issues and publishes *ASPCA Report* three times yearly. Other ASPCA publications include the *Animal Rights Handbook, For Kids Who Love Animals, Traveling with Your Pet,* and various educational brochures.

Americans for Medical Progress (AMP)
Crystal Square Three
1735 Jefferson Davis Highway, Suite 907
Arlington, VA 22202
(703) 486-1411

AMP was established to fight for humanity's right to prevent disease and cure illness via basic and applied research using laboratory animals.

Animal Legal Defense Fund (ALDF)
1363 Lincoln Avenue, No. 7
San Rafael, CA 94901
(415) 459-0885

The ALDF represents about 350 people and organizations working for animal rights and welfare. It was founded in 1979. ALDF maintains a central listing of attorneys throughout the United States who are available for animal-related legal assistance, as well as a library of pleadings and legal decisions involving animal rights and welfare issues.

PUBLICATION: The ALDF publishes the quarterly *Animal Legal Defense Fund-Newsletter.*

Animal Liberation (AL)
319 West 74th Street
New York, NY 10023
(212) 874-1792

Animal Liberation is a coalition of about 300 individuals who are sympathetic to the cause of animal welfare reform and who are opposed to all animal experimentation. AL, which formed in 1971, seeks to educate the general public on the benefits of a vegetarian diet.

Animal Liberation Front (ALF)
Address and phone number not available

ALF (also known as "Urban Gorillas") is an international underground organization that was founded in England to end all forms of exploitation of animals. ALF has claimed responsibility for numerous raids and break-ins in the United States beginning in 1979. ALF reportedly liberates animals being used for entertainment, food, clothing, or experimental research. The group has also allegedly issued personal threats to animal researchers. It has also allegedly set fires, defaced property, destroyed equipment, planted fake bombs, and stolen research videotapes.

Animal Political Action Committee (APAC)
P.O. Box 2706
Washington, DC 20013

Founded in 1982, APAC promotes election and reelection campaigns of legislators committed to acting in the interests of animals by providing contributions and volunteer workers for such campaigns. It also provides a computerized database of voting records on issues that are relevant to animal protection.

Animal Protection Institute of America (APIA)
P.O. Box 22505
Sacramento, CA 95822
(916) 731-5521

APIA has 150,000 members and was formed in 1968. It conducts educational and informational programs to promote humane treatment of animals focusing on animal suffering from leg-hold traps, alleviation of marine mammal depletion, and prevention of dog and cat population surplus. APIA distributes humane-oriented materials, maintains a specialized library and archive of animal rights publications and documents, and produces television documentaries and short subjects. It also manages petition campaigns and other forms of organized protest.

PUBLICATIONS: APIA publications include the quarterlies *APE Vine: Animal Protection Education Newsletter of the Animal Protection Institute*, *Mainstream Magazine*, and *New Paths*, as well as *Emergency Update* (published periodically) and the *Animal Activists' Handbook*.

Animal Rights Information and Education Service (ARIES)
P.O. Box 332
Rowayton, CT 06853
(203) 866-0523

As a means of promoting and monitoring animal rights and welfare, ARIES disseminates information on factory farming and the use of animals in research and product testing. Founded in 1989, it has 600 members. ARIES maintains a computerized database of vegetarian groups and animal rights and welfare organizations.

PUBLICATION: ARIES publishes the monthly *ARIES Newsletter*.

Animal Rights International (ARI)
P.O. Box 214, Planetarium Station
New York, NY 10024
(212) 873-3674

ARI, which was founded in 1985, encourages minimizing tests on animals by utilizing tests that require fewer animals and tests that minimize pain and suffering, or by devising *in vitro* tests. ARI encourages agribusinesses to take into account the well-being of food animals and to lessen the pain and suffering of food animals raised on factory farms. It also encourages the promotion of "nonviolent food." ARI promotes vegetarianism and maintains an archive of materials related to farm and laboratory animal welfare.

Animal Rights League of America (ARLA)
P.O. Box 9566
Richmond, VA 23227
(804) 358-1731

ARLA was founded in 1985. It strives to educate the public on the feeding, spaying, neutering, and care of stray animals.

Animal Rights Mobilization (ARM)
P.O. Box 1553
Williamsport, PA 17703
(717) 302-3252

Founded in 1981, ARM has 30,000 members who promote spaying/neutering, the strengthening of regulations for protection of laboratory animals, exposing specific cases of animal abuse, and seeking redress through persuasive and legal means. ARM protests nonviolently against abuse of animals.

PUBLICATIONS: ARM publishes the quarterly *Movement Magazine,* as well as a newsletter, flyers, leaflets, and educational materials.

Animal Rights Network (ARN)
456 Monroe Turnpike
Monroe, CT 06468
(203) 452-0446

ARN formed in 1979. It strives to inform the public about animal rights issues and provides for the exchange of ideas and information on the subject.

PUBLICATION: ARN publishes *Animals' Agenda* ten times yearly.

Animal Transportation Association (ATA)
P.O. Box 797095
Dallas, TX 75379-7095
(214) 713-9954

ATA strives to improve conditions for safe and humane transportation of animals by air. It promotes cooperation between humane and animal welfare groups, air transport manufacturers, carriers, shippers, forwarders, zoos, circuses, and animal breeders. Formed in 1976, ATA has 300 members.

PUBLICATIONS: ATA publishes the *ATA Resource List* and *Conference Proceedings.*

Animal Welfare Institute (AWI)

P.O. Box 3650, Georgetown Station
Washington, DC 20007
(202) 337-2332

Founded in 1951, AWI has 8,000 members. AWI endeavors to prevent the use of cruel trapping devices, the destruction of endangered species, and the capture of exotic birds for the commercial pet trade. It also is opposed to excessive confinement and deprivation of animals raised for food. AWI attempts to prevent the mistreatment of animals used for experiments and tests.

PUBLICATIONS: AWI publishes the *Animal Welfare Institute-Annual Report,* the *AWI Quarterly,* and books such as: *Facts about Furs; The Bird Business; Comfortable Quarters for Laboratory Animals; Animals and Their Legal Rights; Beyond the Laboratory Door, First Aid and Care of Small Animals* (for primary school teachers); the *Endangered Species Handbook* (for teachers); *Injury, Damage to Health and Cruel Treatment; Physical and Mental Suffering of Experimental Animals;* and *Factory Farming: The Experiment That Failed.*

Associated Humane Societies (AHS)

124 Evergreen Avenue
Newark, NJ 07114
(201) 824-7084

AHS, which was founded in 1906, is a coalition of humane societies seeking to assist wild and domestic animals via legislation supporting animal welfare.

Association for Gnotobiotics (AG)

Roswell Park Institute, Department of Dermatology
666 Elm Street
Buffalo, NY 14263
(716) 845-3105

The Association for Gnotobiotics, which has 415 members, seeks to provide researchers with information about raising animals in germ-free and controlled environments, which can be used in researching cancer and infectious diseases. Gnotobiotics is the study of producing germ-free animals. These animals can be inoculated with known microorganisms to determine the impact of these microorganisms.

Beauty Without Cruelty U.S.A. (BWC)

175 West 12th Street, No. 16-G
New York, NY 10011
(212) 989-8073

BWC has 7,000 members and was established in 1972. It informs the public about the suffering of wild and farmed furbearing animals, the use of animal products in cosmetics, and the use of laboratory animals in the testing of cosmetics. BWC sponsors fashion shows of simulated fur garments to demonstrate the humane alternatives to real fur. It provides information on where to obtain cruelty-free apparel and toiletries, including a database containing a list of stores that provide makeup and cleansers manufactured without harm to animals.

PUBLICATIONS: Three times yearly, BWC publishes *Action Alert* and *The Compassionate Shopper*.

Canine Defense Fund (CDF)
1654 Columbia Turnpike
Castleton, NY 12033
(518) 477-8469

CDF is a coalition of the American Dog Owners Association, American Kennel Club, and the United Kennel Club that formed in 1984 to oppose breed-specific ordinances restricting pet ownership in certain U.S. communities. CDF advocates laws that would hold an owner responsible for personal injury or damage caused by his or her dog.

Citizens to End Animal Suffering Exploitation (CEASE)
P.O. Box 44-456
Somerville, MA 02144
(617) 628-9030

The 5,000 members of CEASE, which was formed in 1979, seek to raise public awareness of animal rights issues through advertising, legislation, protest, and education.

PUBLICATIONS: CEASE publishes the *Cease Newsline* bimonthly, as well as *Animal Rights* (a pamphlet) and the *Guide to Compassionate Living* (a list of manufacturers of personal care and household products that are not tested on animals).

Civitis Publications
Box 26
Swain, NY 14884
(607) 545-6213

Civitis is the United States subsidiary of the Center for Scientific Information on Vivisection, which was founded by Swiss writer Hans Ruesch. It was founded in 1983.

PUBLICATIONS: Civitis published the books *Slaughter of the Innocent* and *Naked Empress*.

Coalition for Animals and Animal Research (CFAAR)
P.O. Box 8060
Berkeley, CA 94707

CFAAR is an organization of professionals and students that formed in 1991 to support the use of animals in biomedical research. CFAAR informs the public about the care and use of animals in research via spokespersons and printed materials.

PUBLICATION: CFAAR publishes the *Coalition for Animals and Animal Research Newsletter.*

Coalition for Non-Violent Food (CNVF)
P.O. Box 214, Planetarium Station
New York, NY 10024
(212) 873-3674

CNVF is a coalition of organizations and individuals, formed in 1986, that advocates eating only nonviolent foods (nonmeat foods). It attempts to foster a reduction in the number of animals used for food by encouraging alternatives to animal food products.

Coalition of Municipalities to Ban Animal Trafficking (COMBAT)
P.O. Box 3189
Fayetteville, AR 72702
(501) 848-3678

Lost and stolen pets are the focus of COMBAT, which formed in 1989 and has 30 municipal members. COMBAT strives to educate the general public about what might happen to a lost or stolen pet. It encourages the use of tags and tattoos to assist in the identification of lost or stolen pets. COMBAT also serves as a network to exchange information on pet theft and animal trafficking and conducts investigations of reputed animal trafficking.

PUBLICATIONS: COMBAT publishes the quarterly *Network News* and *Combat,* which comes out periodically.

Coalition to Abolish Classroom Dissection (CACD)
P.O. Box 214, Planetarium Station
New York, NY 10024
(212) 628-0959

CACD formed in 1984. It seeks to abolish the practice of biological dissection in the classroom.

Coalition to Abolish the Draize Rabbit Blinding Tests (CADRBT)
P.O. Box 214, Planetarium Station
New York, NY 10024
(212) 873-3674

CADRBT, which has 400 members and began in 1979, strives to eliminate the Draize test by conducting boycotts and demonstrations and by encouraging corporate funding to develop innovative, nonanimal testing methods.

Coalition to Abolish the LD50 (CALD-50)
P.O. Box 214, Planetarium Station
New York, NY 10024
(212) 873-3674

CALD-50 is a nonmembership organization that formed in 1981. It is a coalition of animal rights groups that seeks to eliminate the Lethal Dose 50% (LD50) test.

Coalition to Protect Animals in Entertainment (CPAE)
P.O. Box 2448
Riverside, CA 92516
(714) 682-7872

CPAE is a network of organizations interested in protecting animals in the entertainment industry by providing follow-up investigation and action on reported animal abuse cases. It formed in 1987.

PUBLICATION: CPAE publishes the newsletter *Alerts* periodically.

Coalition to Protect Animals in Parks and Refuges (CPAPR)
P.O. Box 26
Swain, NY 14884-0026
(607) 545-6213

CPAPR promotes public awareness of animals killed in parks and refuges. It is comprised of about 500 members and was founded in 1983.

Committee for Humane Legislation (CHL)
1623 Connecticut Avenue, NW
Washington, DC 20009
(202) 483-8998

CHL was founded in 1967 and has 125,000 members. It seeks to encourage legislation at federal and state levels to eliminate sport hunting and recreational trapping of wildlife, discourages the use of animals in experimental research and product testing, and provides increased protection for marine mammals.

PUBLICATION: CHL publishes *Actionline* periodically.

Committee for Responsible Research (CRR)
Harvard Square
P.O. Box 1626
Cambridge, MA 02238
(617) 547-9255

CRR is a citizen advocacy group comprised of about 1,000 members who seek to promote accountability in animal experimentation and research. It was founded in 1986.

PUBLICATIONS: CRR publishes the quarterly *Animals' Advocate*, as well as the pamphlets *The Need for Responsible Research* and *The Blue Ribbon Committee Report: Report on Animals in Laboratories in Cambridge.*

Committee to Abolish Sport Hunting (CASH)
Box 43
White Plains, NY 10605
(914) 428-7523

The 13,120 members of CASH, which formed in 1976, seek to change current government wildlife management programs and to abolish all forms of recreational hunting. They try to achieve this through public education and lobbying.

PUBLICATION: CASH distributes the brochure *Exploring the Abolition of Sport Hunting.*

Compassion for Animals Campaign (CAC)
P.O. Box 52193
Philadelphia, PA 19115
(215) 860-2113

CAC has 10,000 members. It was formed in 1987 to encourage companies to abandon animal testing and to seek alternative testing methods. CAC encourages support for those companies that do not employ animal testing.

PUBLICATIONS: CAC publishes the quarterly *Compassion Campaign*, the semiannual *Directory of Cruelty Free Beauty and Personal Care Companies*, as well as *Be Beautiful, Not Cruel, Compassionate Beauty*, and *Eat Yourself Beautiful.*

Farm Animal Reform Movement (FARM)
P.O. Box 30654
Bethesda, MD 20824
(301) 530-1737

FARM's 12,000 members seek to eliminate abuse of farm animals by holding demonstrations and promoting print, radio, and television interviews. It also promotes the Great American Meatout on 20 March, the national Veal Ban Campaign on Mother's Day, and World Farm Animals Day on 2 October. It was started in 1986.

PUBLICATION: FARM publishes the quarterly *The FARM Report.*

Farm Sanctuary (FS)
P.O. Box 150
Watkins Glen, NY 14891
(607) 583-2225

FS was founded in 1986 and has 5,000 members. It focuses on educating the public about factory farming, promoting alternatives to factory farm products, and ending factory farm animal abuses.

PUBLICATIONS: FS publishes *Farm Sanctuary Annual Report* and the quarterly *Sanctuary News.*

Feline and Canine Friends (FCF)
505 North Bush Street
Anaheim, CA 92805
(714) 635-7975

FCF is a 2,000-member coalition of individuals, clubs, businesses, and churches that provides education about the humane treatment of animals and promotes animal welfare through the prevention of cruelty. It was founded in 1972.

PUBLICATION: FCF periodically publishes *Feline and Canine Times: Reporting on Animal Welfare in Action.*

Foundation for Biomedical Research (FFBR)
818 Connecticut Avenue, NW
Washington, DC 20006
(202) 457-0654

FFBR, which formed in 1981, provides the public with education programs and information about the need for the use of laboratory animals in research and testing.

PUBLICATIONS: FFBR publishes the bimonthly *Foundation for Biomedical Research Newsletter.* It has published two books, *The Use of Animals in Biomedical Research and Testing* and *Caring for Laboratory Animals.* Other FFBR educational materials include the film *Hope!* and two videotapes, *Caring for Life* and *The New Research Environment.*

Friends of Animals (FOA)
Box 1244
Norwalk, CT 06856
(203) 866-5223

FOA has 120,000 members and was founded in 1957. It seeks to protect marine mammals; ban hunting and trapping on wildlife refuges; boycott the use of furs; and eliminate the use of animals for experiments, research, and testing.

PUBLICATION: FOA publishes *Action Line* bimonthly.

Fund for Animals (FFA)
200 West 57th Street
New York, NY 10019
(212) 246-2096

The 200,000-member FFA was founded in 1967. It uses legal action, activism, public education (via books, press releases, articles, meetings, and spots on network television), and lobbying to fight cruelty to animals and to protect wildlife.

Fur Farm Animal Welfare Coalition (FFAWC)
405 Sibley Street, Suite 120
St. Paul, MN 55101
(612) 293-0349

FFAWC, which was founded in 1985 and has 2,000 members, promotes humane care practices for farm animals. It establishes care guidelines and conducts veterinarian inspections.

PUBLICATION: FFAWC publishes the quarterly *American Fur*.

Humane Farming Association (HFA)
1550 California Street, Suite 6
San Francisco, CA 94109
(415) 845-1495

HFA, which formed in 1984, is a coalition of about 70,000 individuals and groups that seek to make the public aware of the inhumane practices used in veal production, factory farming, genetic engineering, and slaughterhouses.

Humane Society of the United States (HSUS)
2100 L Street, NW
Washington, DC 20037
(202) 452-1100

HSUS was founded in 1954 and has 1.4 million members. It is affiliated with the World Society for the Protection of Animals. HSUS maintains nine regional offices from which it promotes public education to foster respect, understanding, and compassion for all creatures. It focuses on reducing the overbreeding of cats and dogs and promoting responsible pet care; eliminating cruelty in hunting and trapping; exposing and eliminating painful uses of animals in research and testing; and eliminating the abuse of animals in movies, television productions, circuses, and competitive events. HSUS also tries to correct inhumane conditions for animals in zoos, menageries, pet shops, puppy mills, and kennels; stop cruelty in the raising, handling, and transporting of animals used for food; address critical environmental issues in terms of their impact on animals and humans; and protect endangered wildlife and marine mammals. HSUS also campaigns for or against legislation affecting animal protection and monitors enforcement of existing animal protection statutes; works with local agencies to establish effective and humane animal control programs; assists local humane societies in improving their administrative, organizational, and sheltering techniques; sponsors the HSUS Animal Control Academy and the National Association for Humane and Environmental Education (see separate entry); and conducts workshops, symposia, and seminars for individuals who work with animals.

PUBLICATIONS: HSUS's publications include the quarterlies *Animal Activist Alert* (animal legislation), *HSUS Close-Up Reports* (critical problems affecting animals), and *HSUS News* (a magazine covering HSUS activities). It also publishes the annual *Kind Teacher,* which contains educational program information and activities for teachers and students, and *Shelter Sense* a newsletter (ten/year) concerning community animal control.

Humans Against Rabbit Exploitation (HARE)
P.O. Box 1553
Williamsport, PA 17703
(717) 322-3252

HARE has 100 members and was founded in 1982. It opposes all forms of exploitation of rabbits, including factory farming and the use of rabbits in product testing. HARE organizes demonstrations and boycotts against stores and restaurants that sell rabbit meat, as well as universities that offer rabbit breeding courses.

PUBLICATIONS: HARE publishes *HARE Lines* quarterly and its *Bulletin* periodically.

In Defense of Animals (IDOA)
816 West Francisco Boulevard
San Rafael, CA 94901
(415) 453-9984

IDOA, which was founded in 1983 and has 30,000 members, conducts demonstrations and protests at experimental laboratories to prevent "cruel treatment in the name of science." It promotes and disseminates information about animal advocacy.

PUBLICATION: IDOA publishes the quarterly *In Defense of Animals.*

Incurably Ill for Animal Research (iiFAR)
P.O. Box 1873
Bridgeview, IL 60455
(708) 598-7787

The 2,500 members of iiFAR, formed in 1985, are persons with health problems who support the use of laboratory animals in biomedical research. It provides education programs to the public.

PUBLICATIONS: iiFAR publishes the monthly *Bulletin* and the quarterly *Newsletter.*

Institute of Laboratory Animal Resources (ILAR)
National Research Council
2101 Constitution Avenue, NW
Washington, DC 20418
(202) 334-2590

A nonmembership organization, ILAR was formed in 1952 to act as an advisor to federal, public, and private agencies. ILAR offers advice on the use of animal models in biomedical research, the location of unique animal colonies, and nonanimal alternatives. Through conferences, ILAR provides a forum for the discussion of issues dealing with the use of laboratory animals in research and testing.

PUBLICATIONS: ILAR publishes *ILAR News* quarterly and *Animals for Research—A Directory of Sources* every three to four years.

International Defenders of Animals (IDA)
Box 112
Urbana, MO 65767

IDA was founded in 1958. It promotes interest in birds and animals, animal welfare, and the abolition of vivisection and hunting. The organization also seeks to provide food, shelter, and protection to animals.

International Foundation for Ethical Research (IFER)
53 West Jackson Boulevard, Suite 1550
Chicago, IL 60604-3703
(312) 427-6025

IFER is a nonmembership organization that formed in 1985 to promote the discovery, development, and implementation of scientifically valid alternatives to the use of live animals in research, testing, and technology. It does this by providing research grants and postdoctoral fellowships, and by sponsoring workshops and seminars.

International Fund for Animal Welfare (IFAW)
P.O. Box 193
Yarmouth Port, MA 02675
(617) 362-4944

IFAW's 600,000 members are dedicated to protecting animal species, preventing cruelty to animals, and mitigating animal suffering. IFAW was founded in 1969.

PUBLICATIONS: In addition to the newsletter IFAW produces ten times yearly, its publications include the books *Seal Song, Savage Luxury,* and *Seasons of the Seal.*

International Network for Religion and Animals (INRA)
c/o Rev. Dr. Marc A. Wessels
P.O. Box 1335
North Wales, PA 19454
(215) 699-6067

INRA was founded in 1985 and now has 1,500 members. It seeks to apply the moral principles of the Christian, Buddhist, Jewish, Hindu, and Moslem religions to human interaction with animals. INRA is especially interested in aiding laboratory animals and animals used for food, clothing, or entertainment purposes.

PUBLICATION: INRA publishes *Inroads* three times yearly.

International Primate Protection League (IPPL)
P.O. Box 766
Summerville, SC 29484
(803) 871-2280

IPPL's 10,000 members want to conserve and protect nonhuman primates by working to protect the native habitat of primates, monitoring and reducing international trade/smuggling, and improving conditions in zoos and laboratories.

PUBLICATION: IPPL publishes the quarterly *International Primate Protection League Newsletter.*

International Society for Animal Rights (ISAR)
421 South State Street
Clarks Summit, PA 18411
(717) 586-2200

ISAR was founded in 1959 and has 38,000 members. It works to prevent exploitation and abuse of animals by providing educational programs; serving as an information resource for the media, writers, and other humane organizations; and drafting legislation.

PUBLICATION: ISAR publishes the quarterly *International Society for Animal Rights-Report* four times yearly.

Jews for Animal Rights (JAR)
255 Humphrey Street
Marblehead, MA 01945
(617) 631-7601

JAR, which was founded in 1985, encourages vegetarianism and preventive medicine to promote animal rights/welfare and the alleviation of animal suffering.

PUBLICATIONS: JAR has published the books *Autobiography of a Revolutionary: Essays on Animal and Human Rights, The Dark Face of Science, Guide to Compassionate Living, In Pity and Anger, Judaism and Vegetarianism, The 6th Day of Creation—A Prose Poem about Vivisection,* as well as calendars, cookbooks, and curriculum guides.

Laboratory Animal Management Association (LAMA)
P.O. Box 1744
Silver Spring, MD 20902
(301) 295-0423

LAMA is a coalition of laboratory animal facility managers that evaluates and updates management practices in that field.

PUBLICATION: LAMA publishes *LAMA Lines* bimonthly.

Medical Scientist's Legal Defense Fund (MSLDF)
P.O. Box 40418
Washington, DC 20016

MSLDF provides legal advice, strategy, and assistance for scientists whose rights are under attack from animal activists. It was founded in 1990.

Millenium Guild (MG)
95 Belden Street, Route 126
Falls Village, CT 06031
(203) 824-0831

A vegetarian organization founded in 1912, MG believes that all creatures have a right to life and should be protected by human beings. MG members oppose the killing of animals for food and the use of animals in medical research. They also oppose the use of furs, feathers from slain birds, maribou, kid, leather, tortoise shell, and ivory.

Morris Animal Foundation (MAF)
45 Inverness Drive, East
Englewood, CO 80112
(303) 790-2345

Founded in 1948, MAF has 3,000 members. The foundation supports research on the diseases and health problems of wildlife, companion animals, and zoo animals as a method to find ways to prevent or cure these diseases.

PUBLICATIONS: Three times yearly, MAF publishes *Companion Animal News* and *Friends and Family*. It also publishes the annual *Morris Animals Foundation Directory*, *Practitioners' Update* (periodically), and the book *Zoo and Wild Animal Medicine*.

National Alliance for Animal Legislation (NAFAL)
P.O. Box 75116
Washington, DC 20013

NAFAL was founded in 1984. It promotes legislation protecting animals and their environment. NAFAL also teaches the public how to use the legislative process to establish laws protecting animals.

PUBLICATIONS: NAFAL publishes the quarterlies *Action Alert Legislative Summary* and *Legislative Cosponsor List,* as well as the annual *Congressional Report Card.*

National Animal Control Association (NACA)
P.O. Box 1600
Indianola, WA 98342
(800) 828-6474

NACA, which has 3,000 members, was founded in 1977. It works to educate and train personnel in the animal care and control professions. NACA also teaches about responsible pet ownership.

PUBLICATIONS: NACA publishes the bimonthly *NACA News* and the *National Animal Control Association Training Guide.*

National Antivivisection Society (NAVS)
53 West Jackson, Suite 1552
Chicago, IL 60604
(312) 427-6065

NAVS has 54,000 members and was founded in 1929. It conducts educational programs and distributes information to teach the methods and means of combating vivisection. NAVS also underwrites research to find alternatives to animal testing techniques.

PUBLICATIONS: NAVS publishes the quarterly *National Antivivisection Society-Bulletin* and the book *Personal Care with Principle.*

National Association for Biomedical Research (NAFBR)
818 Connecticut Avenue, NW, Suite 303
Washington, DC 20006
(202) 857-0540

Founded in 1985, NAFBR is a coalition of 400 universities, research institutes, professional societies, voluntary health organizations, animal breeders/suppliers, and pharmaceutical/chemical/testing companies. It monitors and attempts to influence legislation and regulations on behalf of the humane use of laboratory animals in biomedical research and testing.

PUBLICATIONS: Each year, NAFBR publishes *NAFBR Alert* (6–10/ year) and *NAFBR Update* (18–26/year).

National Association for Humane and Environmental Education (NAHEE)
67 Salem Road
East Haddam, CT 06423
(203) 434-8666

NAHEE was established in 1974. It seeks to improve humane and environmental education programs by providing leadership, practical ideas, materials, and consultation. NAHEE provides these services for local school systems, educational organizations, and humane societies interested in incorporating humane concepts into their educational master plans.

PUBLICATION: During the school year, NAHEE publishes *KIND News* nine times.

National Cat Protection Society (NCPS)
1528 West 17th Street
Long Beach, CA 90813
(213) 436-3162

NCPS, which was founded in 1968, supports campaigns for strong laws that will protect cats and afford them the same rights as other domestic animals. It promotes humane education to enlighten the American public about the need for cat protection. NCPS also seeks to control cat breeding, to institute a program of euthanasia for homeless cats, and to form a group of trained humane officers who will investigate cases of cruelty and neglect.

PUBLICATIONS: NCPS publishes the quarterlies *Feline Defenders* and *Shelter News.*

National Congress of Animal Trainers and Breeders (NCATB)
23675 West Chardon Road
Grayslake, IL 60030
(708) 546-0717

Formed in 1975, the NCATB is a coalition of about 300 animal trainers and breeders of rare animals. It seeks to prevent the extinction of rare animals by opposing endangered species laws and government regulations that prohibit the sale or trade of such animals and thus prevent breeding. NCATB monitors government activities and testifies at government hearings on pending legislation regarding animals.

National Dog Registry (NDR)
Box 116
Woodstock, NY 12498
(914) 679-2355

NDR was founded in 1966. It encourages dog owners to have an identification number tattooed on their pets and to register this number with the NDR to reduce the traffic in stolen pets and to expedite the identification of lost, stray, injured, or dead animals.

PUBLICATIONS: NDR publishes *Rescue Magazine* bimonthly and the *National Dog Registry Product Catalog.*

National Humane Education Society (NHES)
15B Catoctin Circle, SE, Suite 207
Leesburg, VA 22075
(703) 777-8319

Founded in 1948, the NHES now has 200,000 members. It fights for the prevention of cruelty to animals in any form including hunting and fur trapping. It works to protect and conserve wildlife, and to advance programs for humane sterilization of animals to reduce overpopulation. NHES conducts humane education programs.

PUBLICATION: NHES publishes the *NHES Quarterly Journal.*

National Society for Animal Protection (NSAP)
Address and phone number not available

NSAP was organized in 1989. It provides architectural planning services for animal shelters and hospitals, as well as consultative services in areas such as shelter husbandry, cruelty investigation and prosecution, adoption counseling, animal evaluation, euthanasia training, and legal and educational advice. NSAP also engages in legislative and litigative activities to help stop animal suffering.

PUBLICATION: NSAP publishes *Silent Voice* periodically.

National Trappers Association (NTA)
P.O. Box 3667
Bloomington, IL 61702
(309) 829-2422

NTA was founded in 1959 and has 20,000 members. It promotes the harvesting of furbearers for the purpose of wildlife management, animal damage control, outdoor recreation, and as a method of conserving natural resources.

PUBLICATIONS: NTA publishes the *American Trapper* bimonthly, as well as the pamphlets *Facts about Furs, Furbearer Management,* and *Traps Today.*

People for the Ethical Treatment of Animals (PETA)
Box 42516
Washington, DC 20015
(301) 770-7444

PETA has gained 350,000 members since it formed in 1980. It conducts rallies and demonstrations to focus attention on the exploitation and abuse of animals in experimentation, the manufacture of fur apparel, and the slaughter of animals for human consumption. PETA seeks to educate the public against speciesism and human chauvinist attitudes toward animals. It has acted as spokesman for the Animal Liberation Front (see above).

PUBLICATIONS: PETA publishes *Caring Consumer Guide* annually, *People for the Ethical Treatment of Animals-Action Alerts* periodically, and *PETA News* quarterly. It has also published the books *Kids Can Save the Animals* and *Save the Animals! 101 Easy Things You Can Do.*

Pet Pride (PP)
P.O. Box 1055
Pacific Palisades, CA 90272
(213) 836-5427

Founded in 1961, PP now has 45,000 members. It offers public education programs on proper cat care and is the national humane society for cats.

PUBLICATION: PP publishes *Purr-Ress* quarterly.

Political Action Committee for Animal Welfare and Protection (PAW PAC)
P.O. Box 14448
Columbus, OH 43214
(614) 262-0129

PAW PAC was organized in 1986. It focuses on electing legislators who will speak for and work to help animals. It provides candidates with research and speech materials and logistical support.

Political Animal Welfare Action Committee (PAWAC)
P.O. Box 68
San Ramon, CA 94583
(415) 474-4020

California political candidates who have established a record of supporting animal legislation can receive financial assistance and endorsements from PAWAC, which was formed in 1982.

Project Stigma (PS)
P.O. Box 1094
Paris, TX 75461
(903) 784-5922

Project Stigma was founded in 1978. It provides information regarding animal mutilation investigations. It reports to law enforcement and media professionals, and works to clarify the rationale and methodology of animal mutilations in an effort to identify perpetrators.

PUBLICATION: PS publishes *Stigmata* periodically.

Psychologists for the Ethical Treatment of Animals (PFETA)
P.O. Box 1297
Washington Grove, MD 20880
(301) 963-4751

The 550-member PFETA was formed in 1981. It seeks to ensure proper treatment of animals used in psychological research and education. PFETA works to establish procedures that would reduce the number of animals used in experiments and encourages authors of psychology texts to include animal ethics considerations.

PUBLICATIONS: PFETA publishes *Humane Innovations and Alternatives* annually and *PsyETA Bulletin* semiannually.

Putting People First (PPF)
Suite 310-A
4401 Connecticut Avenue, NW
Washington, DC 20008
(202) 364-7277

PPF seeks to represent the average American who drinks milk, eats meat, wears fur, leather, or wool, hunts and fishes, owns a pet, goes to a zoo, and/or benefits from medical research and testing. PPF acts as a clearinghouse for information about the animal rights movement and seeks to influence legislation and public opinion about animal rights and animal welfare.

PUBLICATIONS: PPF publishes a bimonthly newspaper, *People's Agenda,* and an irregularly issued newsletter, *People's Bulletin.*

Retired Greyhounds as Pets (REGAP)
P.O. Box 111
Camby, IN 46113

REGAP formed in 1988 to promote the adoption of retired greyhound racing dogs as pets and to help find homes for them.

Scientists Center for Animal Welfare (SCAW)
4805 South Elmo Avenue
Bethesda, MD 20814
(301) 654-6350

SCAW has 2,000 members and was founded in 1978. It supports responsible and humane research on animals. SCAW provides a forum for the discussion of public accountability and public policy.

PUBLICATIONS: SCAW publishes the *Scientists Center for Animal Welfare Newsletter* quarterly. Its other publications include the following books: *Canine Research Environment, Effective Animal Care and Use Committees, Science and Animals: Addressing Contemporary Issues, Scientific Perspectives on Animal Welfare, Well-Being of Non-Human Primates in Research, Academic Press,* and the *Field Research Guidelines* series on mammalogy, wild birds, live amphibians and reptiles, and fish.

Scientists' Group for Reform of Animal Experimentation (SGRAE)
P.O. Box 1297
Washington Grove, MD 20880
(301) 963-4751

SGRAE, which was founded in 1982, encourages the use of alternatives to animal experimentation, promotes a humane approach to animal experimentation, seeks to prevent cruel and unethical procedures, and opposes pound seizure of animals for experimentation. SGRAE advocates adequate housing and care for experimental animals and encourages experimenters to refine the procedures used in order to minimize stress on the animal (i.e., appropriate anesthesia and pre- and post-surgical tranquilizers and analgesics). It also advocates reduction of the number of animals used and replacement of animal research with other techniques whenever possible.

Simian Society of America (SSA)
3625 Watson Road
St. Louis, MO 63109
(314) 647-6218

The 400-member SSA was founded in 1957. It promotes better husbandry and living conditions for monkeys in captivity by exchanging information about their biological and psychological needs. SSA distributes material on basic monkey care and provides an adoption/relocation service for unwanted simians.

PUBLICATION: SSA publishes the *Simian Newsletter* monthly.

Society Against Vivisection (SAV)
P.O. Box 10206
Costa Mesa, CA 92627
(714) 540-0583

This grass-roots organization seeks to abolish vivisection. SAV subsidizes spaying and neutering of pets and provides animal rescue services.

Society for Animal Protective Legislation (SAPL)
P.O. Box 3719, Georgetown Station
Washington, DC 20007
(202) 337-2334

SAPL has 14,000 members and was founded in 1955. It prepares information for use by members of Congress, their staffs, and other persons interested in the progress of proposed state and federal legislation for the protection of animals.

Sport Fishing Institute (SPI)
1010 Massachusetts Avenue, NW
Washington, DC 20001
(202) 898-0770

Founded in 1949, SPI now has 18,000 members. It is a sport fish conservation organization. SPI believes that fish and wildlife are renewable natural resources that should be managed on a sustainable basis for the benefit of humans.

Student Action Corps for Animals (SACA)
P.O. Box 15588
Washington, DC 20003
(202) 543-8983

SACA was formed in 1981 and has 4,000 members. It encourages youth participation in the animal rights movement by aiding in the organization of local groups and serving as a national network/clearinghouse to enhance awareness of animal rights issues. SACA coordinates a Stop Dissection Campaign and assists students with questions about dissection refusal and vegetarianism. It also provides written overviews on animal rights issues for students and teachers.

PUBLICATIONS: SACA publishes the *SACA News* three times yearly. It has also published the books *Action Alerts* and *101 Non-Animal Biology Lab Methods,* as well as the fold-out poster set *Their Eyes Don't Lie.*

Tatoo-A-Pet (TAP)
1625 Emmons Avenue, Suite 1H
Brooklyn, NY 11235
(718) 646-8200

Tatoo-A-Pet is a for-profit organization that was formed in 1972. It promotes the tattooing of pets for permanent identification to protect against their loss, theft, and laboratory use.

PUBLICATIONS: TAP periodically publishes the *Bulletin* and the *Directory of Tatoo-A-Pet Agents.* It publishes the annual *Directory of U.S. Tatoo Registration Services* and the quarterly *Tatoo-A-Pet News.* TAP also has produced two audio- and videocassettes, *Welcome to Tatoo-A-Pet* and *This Tattoo Means I Love You.*

Unexpected Wildlife Refuge (UWR)
Unexpected Road
P.O. Box 765
Newfield, NJ 08344
(609) 697-3541

The 200-member UWR promotes the education of children about the humane treatment of animals and the study of wildlife in the field. UWR operates a 450-acre wildlife refuge where volunteers plant trees and crops for the animals. Small groups may attend guided tours.

PUBLICATION: UWR publishes *Beaver Defenders* quarterly.

United Action for Animals (UAA)
P.O. Box 2448
Riverside, CA 92516
(212) 983-5315

UAA was formed in 1987 to abolish the fur industry, vivisection, and factory farming. It wants to curb pet overpopulation and works for the passage of animal rights legislation.

United Humanitarians (UH)
P.O. Box 14587
Philadelphia, PA 19115
(212) 750-0171

An organization with 6,000 members, UH was founded in 1961. It seeks to alter the present system of licensing pets with a permit system that would place complete responsibility on owners, who would be cited for violations. This would replace the system of impounding and killing pets found at large. UH seeks to establish a program of mass spaying and neutering of pets to control overpopulation.

PUBLICATION: UH publishes the bimonthly *National Humanitarian*.

Vivisection Investigation League (VIL)
Last Post
95 Belden Street, Route 126
Falls Village, CT 06031
(203) 824-0831

VIL has 10,000 members. Through protests and demonstrations, it opposes laboratory experiments on live animals, especially the LD50 test. VIL offers "last post" havens for pets whose owners have died or have gone into nursing homes and provides assistance to limited-income pet owners. VIL objects to experiments on any human being without that individual's informed consent.

PUBLICATION: VIL publishes *Last Post Report* three to four times yearly.

World Women for Animal Rights/Empowerment Vegetarian Activist Collective (WWAR)
616 6th Street, No. 2
Brooklyn, NY 11215
(718) 788-1362

Founded in 1982, WWAR has sought to heighten women's "sensitivity to nature and ecology" through feminism via the dissemination of information and promotional materials.

7

Selected Print Resources

Alternative Procedures and Methods

The Food Security Act of 1985 (see chapter 5) mandates that the principal investigator in a research project must consider alternatives to any procedures that are likely to cause pain or distress to an animal used in an experiment. This act also mandates that each scientist must consider methods that could reduce or replace animal use or minimize animal pain and distress.

Payne, John W., ed. *In Vitro* **Techniques in Research.** Philadelphia, PA: Open Universities Press, 1989. ISBN 0-335-15885-4.

This book represents the proceedings of a conference dealing with *in vitro* techniques. *In vitro* means "in glass." It refers to experiments using cells or tissues removed from plants, animals, or humans and cultured under controlled conditions. These cells and tissues can theoretically be used to test chemicals and drugs to determine, for example, if they are carcinogens or teratogens. The book also refers to the use of bacteria, such as *Escherichia coli,* and other lower organisms for the same purpose.

Pratt, Dallas. **Alternatives to Pain in Experiments on Animals.** New York, NY: Argus Archives, 1980. ISBN 0-916858-06-5.

Pratt suggests that it is unlikely animals will vanish from the laboratory in the near future, so he proposes methods that will decrease the pain and suffering that lab animals experience. Pratt argues that scientists must be sure that the animals in their experiments are supplied with adequate anesthesia and postoperative analgesia. He examines experiments dealing with behavior, cancer, immunology, radiation, and toxicology testing. Where possible, he describes either alternatives to the use of animals or methods that can minimize the pain and suffering of the animal.

Reines, Brandon. **Cancer Research on Animals: Impact and Alternatives.** Chicago: National Antivivisection Society, 1986.

Reines claims that animal testing does not lead to new anticancer drugs nor to appropriate dose levels of a new drug for early clinical trials in humans.

————. **Heart Research on Animals: A Critique of Animal Models of Cardiovascular Disease.** Jenkintown, PA: American Antivivisection Society, 1985.

Reines maintains that basic research on animals has not led to any advances in the diagnosis or treatment of cardiovascular disease and that the major advances, such as heart transplants, occurred as a result of clinical research in human patients.

Stephens, Martin L. **Alternatives to Current Use of Animals in Research, Safety Testing, and Education.** Washington, DC: Humane Society of the United States, 1986.

Stephens describes human studies (clinical, epidemiological, and postmortem); *in vitro* techniques; mathematical models; use of invertebrates, microorganisms, and plants; and physical/chemical techniques. He stresses that computer-assisted mannequins can be used to simulate the workings of the human or animal body; that computer programs can simulate surgical procedures, drug effects, and metabolic functions; and that human cadavers can be used in virtually all aspects of medical training.

Stratmann, G. C., C. J. Stratmann, and C. L. Paxton. **Animal Experiments and Their Alternatives.** Braunton, England: Merlin Books, 1987. ISBN 0-86303-332-6.

One way to achieve the three Rs—that is, refinement, replacement, and reduction—is by careful examination of existing experimental protocols and good planning when developing new protocols. Replacement means the use of techniques that completely replace the use of animals while still obtaining the desired result. Reduction means the use of fewer animals to achieve the desired results by improving experimental methods and critically examining statistical methods. Refinement means improvement of experimental techniques to reduce the possible suffering and stress of the animal and to avoid poor experimental results due to improper handling and care of the animals.

Turner, Paul. **Animals in Scientific Research: An Effective Substitute for Man?** London: Macmillian Press, 1983. ISBN 0-333-33628-3.

Turner recommends the use of isolated cells and tissues *in vitro* as potential substrates for toxicity testing, testing for mutagenesis, carcinogenesis, and teratogenesis.

Animal Rights

Animal rights activists argue that animal rights is an ethical term and that the issues of animal rights are philosophical ones. The definition of animal, in its broadest sense, is an organism that possesses sensory/motor abilities, can perceive changes in its environment, and can respond to them. By this definition, "animal" includes humans and other primates, as well as mammals, birds, reptiles, amphibians, fish, and many invertebrates. Several themes reoccur in the animal rights literature. For example, animals— human and nonhuman—have sentience (the capacity to enjoy and suffer, to experience pleasure and pain) and their lives have significant value. To mutilate, kill, or obstruct (to cause pain, distress, suffering, misery, or terror to) an animal is to harm it. Animal rights activists argue that we have a duty not to harm animals and that animals have a right not to be harmed by us.

American Humane Association. **American Humane Association Directory for Humane Education Materials.** Denver: American Humane Association, 1982.

This directory lists resources dealing with animal rights/welfare. It is divided into 38 categories about animals ranging from animal control to *zoonoses* (the study of diseases that can be transmitted from animals to man). The directory provides the names and addresses of organizations that can supply information on these topics.

Baird, Robert M., and Stuart E. Rosenbaum, eds. **Animal Experimentation: The Moral Issues.** Buffalo, NY: Prometheus Books, 1991. 175p. ISBN 0-87975-667-5.

Medical and consumer product testing have, on one hand, brought humans greater control over health and appearance. On the other hand, they have caused some degree of suffering for animals. It is likely that few researchers would be willing to forgo this control or give up the prospect of greater control in the future. People with specific maladies, such as those who are infected with the AIDS virus, seek greater and greater support from both public and private sectors for the research necessary to bring these maladies under control. Much of this research will involve animals. This book presents the views of those in favor of animal experimentation and those opposed to it, including essays chosen to introduce the moral controversy about animal experimentation.

Bentham, Jeremy. **An Introduction to the Principles of Morals and Legislation.** Library of Classics No. 6. New York: Hafner, 1970. ISBN 0-02-841200-1 (paperback).

Bentham was a utilitarian philosopher who wrote of animals, "[t]he question is not, can they reason? Nor can they talk? But, can they suffer?" This statement became the battle cry of both the Victorian and modern animal protection movement. He maintained that because they can suffer, animals have a right to life, liberty, and the pursuit of happiness.

Brown, Antony. **Who Cares for Animals?** London: Heinemann, 1974.

This book was written for the 150th anniversary of the Royal Society for the Prevention of Cruelty to Animals. It presents a portrait of the people who work for the Royal Society and the work they do.

Brown, Leslie Melville. **Cruelty to Animals: The Moral Debt.** London: Macmillan Press, 1988. ISBN 0-333-45806-0.

The purpose of this book is to expose and explain unfavorable attitudes toward animals from as detached a moral standpoint as possible. This should help people step outside their humanness and give them a degree of impartiality that is not typical of human beings. Brown presents a historical and contemporary overview of cruelty to animals. He also argues that vertebrates, especially mammals, are part of our moral world. Brown says that animals do not need to be like humans to be considered part of our moral world and that we must understand their nature as animals. He also asserts that we must eliminate animal experimentation, despite the relief from suffering that it has brought about for humans as well as animals.

Carson, Gerald. **Men, Beasts, and Gods: A History of Cruelty and Kindness to Animals.** New York: Charles Scribner's Sons, 1972. ISBN 684-13039-4.

This book describes the relationship between humans and animals and why humans are ambivalent in their attitudes toward animals. Carson claims that humans are the only animals that can (1) choose to kill and torture all forms of sentient life; (2) feel tenderness; (3) weep; and (4) distinguish between good and evil.

Clark, Stephen R. L. **The Nature of the Beast: Are Animals Moral?** New York: Oxford University Press, 1982.

Ethological studies suggest that there is not a sharp gulf between animals and humans. Considering this, Clark asks if animals are moral.

Crowe, Henry. **Zoophilos: Or Considerations on the Moral Treatment of Inferior Animals.** London: Henry Crowe, 1819.

Crowe was critical of mistreatment of animals, including some types of animal experimentation and testing, as well as bullbaiting, cockfighting, and bearbaiting.

Darwin, Charles. **The Descent of Man and Selection in Relation to Sex.** New York: P. F. Collier, 1981. 935p. ISBN 0-691-08278-2.

Darwin argues that animals and humans form a biological and psychological continuum. Further, he claims that there is no fundamental difference between man and other higher mammals.

————. **The Expression of the Emotions in Man and Animals.** London: D. Appleton, 1969. ISBN 0-8371-2291-0.

Darwin argues that the similarity of expression of emotions in man and animals argues for the descent of humans from lower forms of life. Others have used Darwin's views to argue that humans and animals are similar and, thus, if humans have rights, animals must also.

Dawkins, Marian Stamp. **Animal Suffering: The Science of Animal Welfare.** London: Chapman and Hall, 1980. ISBN 0-412-22590-5 (paperback).

This book describes how to recognize animal suffering, particularly when there are no obvious signs of physical ill health or injury. Dawkins asserts that suffering must be recognizable in some objective manner. She says there is no single method by itself, whether based on physiology, behavior, or productivity, that can tell us about the emotional experiences of an animal.

Dodds, W. Jean, and Barbara F. Orlans, eds. **Scientific Perspectives on Animal Welfare.** New York: Academic Press, 1982. ISBN 0-12-219140-4.

This book highlights the four basic stages by which scientists are held accountable for the proper use of animals in experimentation. In the first stage, the researcher develops an idea for an experiment and formalizes the idea as an experimental protocol. In the second stage, the research institution, via its institutional animal care and use committee, determines that the protocol is in compliance with local, state, national, and federal standards of animal welfare. In the third stage, the funding agency determines if the protocol has scientific merit and its experimental procedures are humane. In the fourth stage, the experimenter is expected to publish the results of the experiment in a refereed scientific journal, where it is reviewed to determine if it has scientific merit and if it contains an adequate description of the experimental procedures and results. The book also discusses the principles of refinement, replacement, and reduction; the feasibility of reducing the invasiveness of the experimental procedures; and the economic and ethical costs of animals used in experimental research.

Evans, Peter. **Ourselves and Other Animals: From the TV Series with Gerald and Lee Durrell.** New York: Pantheon Books, 1987.

Some people view animals as machines, powered and controlled by a bundle of instincts with no evidence of human thought processes. Evans suggests that these people are using the wrong yardstick: ourselves. He claims that the science of ethology leads to the conclusion that animals' lives are intricate and that they have abilities just as extensive as our own. Further, he argues that studying ethology forces us to acknowledge that we are animals ourselves. Evans highlights the accomplishments of the great apes, whales, and dolphins, among others.

Fox, Michael A. **The Case for Animal Experimentation: An Evolutionary and Ethical Perspective.** Berkeley, CA: University of California Press, 1986. 278p. ISBN 0-520-05501-2.

Philosopher Michael A. Fox suggests that modern antivivisectionists are presenting a one-sided distorted view of animal welfare issues that often focuses on animal suffering during research. He further asserts that the antivivisectionists fail to mention the efforts to maintain and improve animal care and/or the benefits gained from the research. Fox holds that animals are not the moral equals of human beings and there is no compelling reason for treating them as such. He notes that in both common and scientific discourse, "animal" is defined as any living thing that is not a plant. Thus, the definition includes creatures as simple as sea cucumbers and as complex as humans. Fox asks which of these creatures, if any, should be treated as the moral equivalent of humans?

Fox reasons that much of the attention and energy used to improve the lot of animals would be better directed at ameliorating human need and suffering. This goal deserves more of our dedication, he says, because humans are more important than animals.

Fox maintains that there are three factors that led to the controversy about animals: (1) the speed at which new information is acquired and processed; (2) the rise of ecology as a major scientific field; and (3) the general broadening of moral concern that is the legacy of the 1960s and

1970s counterculture and the civil rights and antiwar movements. Further, because of fairy tales and cartoons, as well as best-sellers such as *Jonathan Livingston Seagull* and *Watership Down*, Fox says that many people have developed a false sense of nature as being peaceful and idyllic along with a false sense of animals' abilities and natures. Fox also contends that existing evidence suggests that humans and their ancestors are natural omnivores.

Fox, Michael W. **Between Man and Animals: The Key to the Kingdom.** New York: Coward, McCann & Geoghegan, 1976. 224p. ISBN 0-89874-827-5.

Michael W. Fox, a veterinarian, says that veterinary school taught him a good deal about diseases and the healing arts, but nothing about normal behavior or animal psychology. When the author began to study wild canids (wolves, coyotes, and foxes), his view of research began changing. At the beginning, he was a scientist studying animals to gain knowledge for knowledge's sake. However, he gradually changed his view toward conservation and human values.

————. **Inhumane Society: The American Way of Exploiting Animals.** New York: St. Martin's Press, 1990. ISBN 0-312-04274-4.

Fox believes that human well-being and animal welfare are intimately related. He asserts that "the degree and extent of animal exploitation, suffering, and environmental desecration are symptomatic of a dysfunctional society." Fox proposes that we give up meat and become vegetarians and that no experiments be performed on animals unless they totally benefit from them. He also feels that his own veterinary profession has failed to alleviate, to any significant degree, the suffering of animals under humanity's domination.

————. **Returning to Eden: Animal Rights and Human Responsibility.** New York: Viking Press, 1980. 300p. ISBN 0-670-12722-1.

Fox describes how we and our social institutions act without feeling toward our fellow creatures, who are so closely related to us that we are all kin in a biological, if not spiritual, sense. He explores and exposes many of the attitudes and values that make our species the most dangerous, destructive, selfish, and unethical on earth. Fox believes that our very existence depends on the liberation of nature from "our selfish treatment" and on "humane consideration."

Frey, R. G. **Rights, Killing, and Suffering: Moral Vegetarianism and Applied Ethics.** New York: Basil Blackwell, 1983. 286p. ISBN 0-631-12684-8.

Although Frey is a utilitarian, similar to Jeremy Bentham and Peter Singer, he defends medical research utilizing animals.

Griffin, Donald R. **The Question of Animal Awareness: Evolutionary Continuity of Mental Experience.** New York: Rockefeller University Press, 1981. 209p. ISBN 0-86576-002-1.

Griffin argues that animals have feelings and wants. He says they act intentionally and that this has significant implications for their moral status.

Guernsey, JoAnn Bren. **Facts about Animal Rights.** New York: Crestwood House, Macmillan, 1990. 48p. ISBN 0-89698-534-7.

Guernesy provides an overview of the thinking of animal rights activists. This book focuses on the use of animals in experimentation and product testing, as well as for food, clothing, and sport.

Guttman, Helene N., and Joy A. Mench, eds. **Science and Animals: Addressing Contemporary Issues.** Bethesda, MD: Scientists Center for Animal Welfare, 1989. 149p. ISBN 0-317-99957-5.

Individual authors in this symposium describe the importance of institutional animal care and use committees. They discuss the issues that they must deal with in both the academic and industrial (drug- and product-testing companies) setting. They also discuss the concept of well-being and what scientists are doing to ensure it in animals.

Hoage, R. J., ed. **Perceptions of Animals in American Culture.** Washington, DC: Smithsonian Institution Press, 1989. 160p. ISBN 0-87474-493-8 (paperback).

Hoage maintains that we must see animals without prejudice or preconceived notions and, especially, without anthropomorphic projections. Anthropomorphized animals range from Mickey Mouse and other cartoon characters to Smokey the Bear. The book notes that many visitors to the National Zoological Park in Washington, D.C., describe the giant panda "as cute, cuddly, and adorable." In reality, the book notes, the giant panda is a relatively large (70–135 kilograms) carnivore that is a close relative of either the raccoons or bears. Why certain creatures, such as the panda—which has a relatively large head, flat face, short limbs, and eyes that appear large—are described as "cute" is a topic that is pursued in this book. Individual authors discuss how humans perceive animals and how these perceptions affect our judgments about animals.

Howard, Walter E. **Animal Rights vs. Nature.** Davis, CA: Dr. Walter E. Howard, 1990. 226p. ISBN 0-9627641-0-8.

Howard distinguishes between animal rights and welfare. He argues that intentional mistreatment of animals without moral or ethical considerations should not be tolerated. As this book makes clear, many animal rightists are deeply affected by anthropomorphic arguments and the "Bambi" syndrome. They fail to realize that animals in the wild do not normally live to a ripe old age even if they are protected from humans. This is because wild animals do not have a safe water supply, abundant food, or the ability to provide a safe indoor or outdoor environment in which to live. The book notes that many animal rightists think that humans should become vegetarians. However, it points out that plants cannot grow untended and still produce grains, vegetables, fibers, and fruits in sufficient quantities to support the human population. Animals, the book asserts, especially insects and mammals, must be controlled in order to allow plants to produce in quantity. If uncontrolled, he says, they will eat the plants meant for humans. Further, the book notes that a number of vitamins, such as cobalamin (vitamin B-12), are only found in animal products.

Lapage, G. **Achievement: Some Contributions of Animal Experiments to the Conquest of Disease.** Cambridge: W. Heffer, 1960.

Lapage provides an overview of the contribution of animal research to medical progress.

Magel, Charles R. **Keyguide to Information Sources in Animal Rights.** London: Mansell Publishing, 1989. 281p. ISBN 0-89950-405-1.

Magel presents an overview of the animal rights literature including an annotated bibliography arranged in chronological order. He also provides a list of animal rights organizations.

Miller, Harlan B., and William H. Williams, eds. **Ethics and Animals.** Clifton, NJ: Humana Press, 1983. 416p. ISBN 0-89603-053-9.

This book deals with the issue of how humans should treat nonhuman animals. Animal behaviorists, scientists, philosophers, economists, psychologists, and animal welfare activists all present their viewpoints. They cite at least six causes for the increase in interest in the status of nonhuman animals. First, they say, at least intellectually, nationalism, chauvinism, colonialism, racism, and sexism have been vanquished. Why not vanquish speciesism? Second, some animals, such as the great apes, appear to have acquired language: one of the hallmarks of humanness. Third, the abortion controversy has forced consideration of personhood. Fourth, they argue, the dualistic concept of mind and body is less and less plausible. Mental life is identical with or an aspect of the activity of the central nervous system. Fifth, ethology and sociobiology suggest that nonhumans can be studied to help understand human society. Sixth, what they cite as potentially most important is the growing interest in holistic health, which increases awareness of nature and humanity's interdependence with other species and with the natural and artificial world.

Moore, J. Howard. **The Universal Kinship.** Chicago: C. H. Kerr, 1906.

Moore argues that there is a physical, mental, and ethical kinship between all animals, human and nonhuman, and that all animals have rights.

Morris, Richard Knowles, and Michael W. Fox, eds. **On the Fifth Day: Animal Rights and Human Ethics.** Washington, DC: Humane Society of the United States, 1978. ISBN 0-87491-196-6.

In this series of essays, the Humane Society seeks to set forth the major scientific, philosophical, and theological foundations for humane attitudes and ethics, especially as they relate to animals. It covers the history and basic doctrines of the humane point of view.

Morse, Mel. **Ordeal of the Animals.** Englewood Cliffs, NJ: Prentice-Hall, 1968.

Morse suggests that cockfights and dogfights are more or less clandestine, but still exist and are more common than most people realize. He also discusses what happens to stolen pets, as well as other ways in which he thinks animals are mistreated.

Mouras, Belton P. **I Care about Animals: Moving from Emotion to Action.** New York: A. S. Barnes, 1977. ISBN 0-498-02113-0.

Mouras presents some specific issues dealing with animal use by humans. In a series of essays, Mouras describes people who have had an impact on animal rights, as well as some of the key issues facing people interested in animal rights.

Newkirk, I. **Save the Animals: 101 Easy Things You Can Do.** New York: Warner Books, 1990. ISBN 0-446-39234-0.

Newkirk, one of the founders of People for the Ethical Treatment of Animals (PETA), maintains that we should not question how animals should be treated within the context of their usefulness or perceived usefulness to us, but whether we have a right to use them at all. She offers 101 ways that anyone can stop using animals. These range from suggesting that everyone become a vegetarian to suggesting avoidance of products made by companies that test their products on animals.

Paterson, David, and Mary Palmer, eds. **The Status of Animals: Ethics, Education, and Welfare.** Wallingford, England: CAB International (for the Humane Education Foundation), 1989. 268p. ISBN 0-85198-650-1.

This book contains the proceedings of a symposium dealing with seven major topics: ethics—our moral obligation to animals, education, farming, experimentation, the role of the veterinarian in animal welfare, and animals and the media.

Paterson, David, and Richard D. Ryder, eds. **Animals' Rights: A Symposium.** London: Centaur Press, 1978. ISBN 0-90000090-2.

The participants at this symposium sought to develop the proposition that there is no absolute division between humans and other animals and that if the concept of rights is appropriate for humans then they must be appropriate for the rest of sentient creation. The participants sought to formulate principles for further action. They said these should entail a full statement of animals' rights and must include consideration of the following: the right to life, the right to be protected from suffering, the right to live free from interference, and the right to live in accordance with one's natural requirements. They claim that the traditional animal welfare organizations appeal to our kindly instincts, but not to our sense of justice or our respect for the rights of others. The participants also proposed and signed a *Declaration against Speciesism.*

Pratt, Dallas. **Animal Films for Humane Education.** New York: Argus Archives, 1986. ISBN 0-916858-07-3.

This book provides an annotated list of films concerning animals and animal rights. It is divided into 16 chapters with topics ranging from attitudes toward animals to zoos.

Regan, Thomas H. **All That Dwell Therein: Animal Rights and Environmental Ethics.** Berkeley, CA: University of California Press, 1982. ISBN 0-520-04571-8.

This book is a collection of Regan's essays and lectures dealing with topics as diverse as vegetarianism, animal experimentation, and whaling. In these essays, he presents his views on human obligations to nonhumans and what an environmental ethic should be like.

————. **Animal Sacrifices: Religious Perspectives on the Use of Animals in Science.** Philadelphia: Temple University Press, 1986. 288p. Library of Congress Catalog No. 85-22093. ISBN 0-87722-511-7.

This book presents an overview of historical and modern Christian, Jewish, Moslem, and Hindu thought on the use of animals in science.

————. **The Case for Animal Rights.** Berkeley, CA: University of California Press, 1983. Library of Congress Catalog No. 83-1087. ISBN 0-520-04904-7.

Regan develops a cumulative argument for animal consciousness and the complexity of awareness in animals. He critiques several philosophical theories including rational egoism, contractarianism, humanity as an end in itself, hedonistic utilitarianism, and preference utilitarianism. Regan uses the principles of justice and equality to develop a theory of moral rights for humans and animals, based on the inherent value of individuals, which are subjects of life. Regan believes that vegetarianism is morally obligatory.

Regan, Thomas H., and Peter Singer, eds. **Animal Rights and Human Obligations.** 2d ed. Englewood Cliffs, NJ: Prentice-Hall, 1989. 288p. ISBN 0-13-036864-4 (paperback).

These readings on animal rights are intended to be used in college-level courses in ethics and humanities. The authors include Aristotle, Henry S. Salt, Peter Singer, and Richard Ryder.

Rohr, Janelle, ed. **Animal Rights: Opposing Viewpoints.** San Diego: Greenhaven Press, 1989. 235p. ISBN 0-89908-440-0.

The editors of the *Opposing Viewpoints* series believe that the best way to become informed about a specific issue is to study the ideas of experts in the area, from mainstream to minority and from radical to reactionary. This book is divided into five sections, each dealing with a specific issue related to animal rights. The section topics are as follows:

1. Do animals have rights?
2. Is animal experimentation justified?
3. Should animals be used as food?
4. Does wildlife need to be protected?
5. How can the animal rights movement improve animal welfare?

Each section contains a preface and a series of differing viewpoints by people who are considered knowledgeable in the area. The viewpoints, which are extracted from speeches, articles, and books, discuss the central issue of the chapter. Each viewpoint is preceded by an introduction that provides a brief background of the author and a series of questions for the reader to consider while reading.

Rollin, Bernard E. **Animal Rights and Human Morality.** Buffalo, NY: Prometheus Books, 1992. 310p. ISBN 0-87975-789-2 (paperback).

The thesis of this book is that animals (and humans) have a right to life and to the kind of life that their nature dictates.

Rollin, Bernard E., and Lynne M. Kesel, eds. **The Experimental Animal in Biomedical Research: Volume I: A Survey of Scientific and Ethical Issues for Investigators.** Boca Raton, FL: CRC Press, 1990. ISBN 0-8493-4981-8.

Rollin and Kesel suggest that two factors are increasingly impacting how researchers view the animals they use. First, animals are sensitive to a wide variety of environmental, psychological, and stress variables that can significantly affect virtually all biological parameters. Many of the papers in this book deal with these issues. Second, society's attitude toward research animals is changing. This has caused a new demand for scientific accountability concerning how and why animals are used in research. Scientists must assimilate a significant volume of information about regulations and laws regarding the use of animals. They must also be prepared to justify their work to the public, particularly as it relates to animal suffering and pain and what they are doing to minimize, mitigate, and control it. The papers concern not only physical but also psychological and emotional pain, distress, anxiety, and boredom. Many of these issues are new to biomedical researchers, so this book provides an overview.

Rood, Ronald. **Animals Nobody Loves.** Brattleboro, VT: Stephen Greene Press, 1987. 215p. ISBN 0-933050-54-2.

Rood describes 12 animals or groups of animals that many people do not like. They include the wolf, rat, flea, mosquito, octopus, bat, snake, spider, vulture, pig, eel, and coyote. He feels that this attitude is based on the way the animal looks or acts.

Rowan, Andrew N. **Animals and People Sharing the World.** Hanover, NH: University Press of New England, 1988. 206p. ISBN 0-87451-449-5.

The authors in this collection of essays describe the emergence of modern pet keeping, pet keeping in other societies, and human and animal interactions, as well as other issues involved in the animal rights/welfare controversy.

―――. **Of Mice, Models, and Men: A Critical Evaluation of Animal Research.** Albany, NY: State University of New York Press, 1984. 323p. ISBN 0-87395-776-8.

Rowan, a biochemist, suggests that the ultimate goal of scientists is to eliminate animal research. Rowan maintains that scientists must continue to seek alternatives to animals. He suggests that institutions that do animal research should establish ethical review committees for review of animal experimentation and ethical training for researchers. The ethical costs of research must be weighed as part of a cost-benefit analysis, he says. Rowan thinks that psychologists, in particular, face an ethical paradox. The more humanlike their animal model, the more restricted its use should be.

Ruesch, Hans. **Slaughter of the Innocent.** New York: Bantam Books, 1978. 446p. ISBN 0-9610016-0-7.

Ruesch maintains that animal experimentation and using animals to test products does humans more harm than good. He presents a long series of individual vignettes about animal research and researchers who use animals in their work.

Ryder, Richard D. **Animal Revolution: Changing Attitudes towards Speciesism.** Cambridge, MA: Basil Blackwell, 1989. 320p. ISBN 0-631-15239-3.

Ryder presents a historical (chiefly British) analysis of the changing relationship between humans and nonhumans (sentients). He believes that when we use the term "human" to describe ourselves and the term "animal" to describe other organisms it is an expression of prejudice, since humans are animals as well. Modern animal rights ideology seeks to conquer suffering and protect nonhuman life universally. Ryder believes that the conclusion that it is illogical and unjust to discriminate on the basis of species arose spontaneously in many people in the 1960s and 1970s. He argues that our primitive ancestors depended on other sentients for food, clothing, and tools. However, modern humans have alternate sources of food, clothing, and power, so it is no longer necessary to depend on other sentients for these items.

Ryder's central tenet is that species alone is not a valid criterion for cruel discrimination, any more than race or sex is. Like race or sex, species denotes physical and other differences that do not nullify the basic similarity between species, their capacity to suffer. This capacity exists because all vertebrate classes possess biochemical substances, such as endorphins, that are known to mediate pain. Ryder asserts that emotive words, such as "pest" or "vermin," are used to stifle compassion. He notes that modern molecular biology techniques will allow the introduction of human genes into nonhuman species, such as the cancer-prone mouse that was recently patented. How many human genes are required to make a creature human in the eyes of the law? Ryder asks.

————. **Victims of Science: The Use of Animals in Research.** London: National Antivivisection Society, 1983. ISBN 0-905225-06-6.

Ryder, who coined the term "speciesism" (discrimination against other species), suggests that a moral dilemma exists: Should we deliberately cause suffering to animals for the benefit of humanity? He argues that the use of animals for research, especially involving vivisection, is morally wrong and scientifically questionable. He reviews the number of animals used in medical and nonmedical research worldwide, then presents alternatives. The text of the 1876 British Cruelty to Animals Act is also included.

Salt, Henry S. **Animals' Rights: Considered in Relation to Social Progress.** Clarks Summit, PA: Society for Animal Rights, 1980. ISBN 0-9602632-0-9.

This is a reprint of a book originally published in 1892. Salt wrote more than 40 books dealing with abuses in schools, prisons, and other institutions. Although not well known, the author influenced friends such as George Bernard Shaw and Gandhi. Salt believed that animals have a fundamental right to live a natural life, which permits individual development. He asserted that the idea that animals are radically different from humans or that animals have no soul or emotional life is wrong. Salt argued that avoidable infliction of pain or suffering is morally wrong.

Seton, Ernest Thompson. **Wild Animals I Have Known.** New York: Charles Scribner's Sons, 1987. 368p. ISBN 0-88739-053-6.

Seton, a well-known naturalist, argued that animals are creatures with wants and feelings. Therefore, he said, they surely have rights.

Singer, Peter. **Animal Liberation: A New Ethics for Our Treatment of Animals.** New York: A New York Review Book, 1991. 352p. ISBN 0-380-71333-0.

Animal Liberation has been called the "bible" of the animal rights movement. Singer's basic moral postulate is that equal consideration of interests is not arbitrarily limited to members of our own species. He maintains that humans have ruthlessly and cruelly exploited animals and inflicted needless suffering on them. This must be stopped, he says. Singer examines the question of how we ought to treat nonhuman animals and exposes the prejudices that, he says, lie behind our present attitudes and behavior. Liberation movements demand an end to prejudice and discrimination based on arbitrary characteristics, such as race or sex. Singer argues that liberation movements force an expansion of moral horizons and cause practices that were previously regarded as natural and inevitable to be seen as the result of unjustifiable prejudice. Further, he argues that since animals cannot speak for themselves, it is our duty to speak for them. He reasons that the very use of the word "animal" to mean "animals other than human beings" sets humans apart from other animals and implies that we are not animals.

————, ed. **In Defense of Animals.** New York: Basil Blackwell, 1986. 256p. ISBN 0-06-97044-8.

This book contains a series of essays that attempt to define the animal liberation movement, which is relatively new—a product of the 1970s. It is distinct from more traditional movements, most of which began in the nineteenth century and which seek to protect animals only when no serious human interest is at stake. Modern animal liberationists, such as Singer, challenge the notion that in the event of conflict, animals' interests must be sacrificed to our own. They argue that membership in the human species is not morally relevant, and that humans overriding other animals' interests is an example of speciesism.

Singer argues that modern western views of animals arise from ancient Greece, where Aristotle, for example, believed there is a hierarchy in nature in which those with less reasoning ability exist for the sake of those with more reasoning ability. In other words, plants exist for animals, animals for humans, and so on. The other wellspring of modern thought was the Judeo-Christian view of animals as expressed in the first chapters of Genesis, where humans are made in the image of God and man is given dominion over animals. Again, the animal liberationists would condemn these ideas as examples of speciesism. Further, they argue that when animals and humans have similar interests, such as avoiding physical pain, those interests must be counted equally.

————. **Practical Ethics.** 2d ed. Cambridge, England: Cambridge University Press, 1993. 416p. ISBN 0-521-43363-0.

Singer argues that the principle of equality applies to both humans and animals. Equal interests should be given equal consideration. If experimentation on sentient animals is justified, he says, then so is experimentation on infants and severely retarded humans. Singer maintains that some animals, such as whales, are persons (aware of themselves as distinct entities existing over time) and that the case against killing them is strong. He says that some animals, such as chickens, are not persons and the case against killing them is weaker.

Sperling, Susan. **Animal Liberators: Research and Morality.** Berkeley, CA: University of California Press, 1988. 220p. ISBN 0-520-06198-5.

Antivivisectionists protest the surgical cutting of living animals for the purpose of experimental research. In general, they protest all painful experiments with animals. This is true of the Victorian antivivisectionists, as well as their modern counterparts. Sperling provides a historical review of antivivisectionism. She also describes modern use of primates.

Sperlinger, David, ed. **Animals in Research: New Perspectives in Animal Experimentation.** New York: John Wiley, 1981. ISBN 0-8357-4628-3.

This book consists of 16 essays by scientists, philosophers, animal welfare activists, and journalists who discuss the concept of the moral status of animals.

Turner, James. **Reckoning with the Beast: Animal Pain and Humanity in the Victorian Mind.** Baltimore: The Johns Hopkins University Press, 1980. ISBN 0-7837-0046-6.

Turner suggests that during the Victorian age, three revolutionary changes in outlook occurred. The first was that humans were not supernatural, but directly descended from beasts. The second was a rising esteem for science as a model of intellectual endeavor and a key to the future of the race. The third was that men and women developed a dread of pain, for self and for others.

Westerlund, Stuart R., ed. **Humane Education and Realms of Humaneness.** Washington, DC: University Press of America, 1982. ISBN 0-8191-2724-6.

This anthology contains articles that appeared in the journals of the National Association for the Advancement of Humane Education. The book is divided into four sections: a general philosophy of humaneness, a general theory of humane education, humane education from theory to practice, and international perspectives on humaneness and human education.

Williams, Jeanne, ed. **Animal Rights and Welfare.** New York: H. W. Wilson, 1991. ISBN 0-8242-9815-3.

This anthology is comprised of articles dealing with animal rights and animal welfare that have appeared in popular magazines and newspapers. The articles deal with the philosophy of rights and responsibilities, animals in research, and the transition of the animal rights movement.

Wood Gush, David G. M., Marian S. Dawkins, and R. Ewbank, eds. **Self Awareness in Domesticated Animals.** Herts Universities Federation for Animal Welfare, 1981. ISBN 0-317-4387-7.

This collection of seven essays deals with the question of self-awareness in animals and the impact of this awareness on animal experimentation.

Young, Thomas. **An Essay on Humanity to Animals.** London: T. Cadell, 1798.

Young argues that animals are capable of pleasure and pain and that cruelty is against God's will. Young opposes animal experimentation that is done "only to gratify curiosity." He argues that a morally sensitive person should not walk on worms or snails and should help flies in distress.

Cetacea: The Whales and Dolphins

Chimpanzees and the other great apes, which are members of the same genus as humans, share up to 99 percent of the same genetic material as humans. However, whales and dolphins (*Cetacea*), are the only organisms other than the great apes whose brain/body ratio approaches and in some cases exceeds humans. The cetaceans are wholly aquatic mammals that are found in all the world's oceans and seas, as well as in certain rivers and lakes. Living cetaceans are divided into 38 genera and approximately 90 species. They vary in length from 1.25 meters to 30 meters and in weight from 23 kilograms to well over 136 metric tons. The blue whale, for example, measures over 90 feet in length, four times longer than a common city bus. It weighs more than 286,000 pounds. Its tongue weighs more than an elephant. Cetaceans can be distinguished from fish in that cetaceans have a tail fluke that is set in a horizontal position, while the tail fin of a fish is vertical.

The Basques, who were apparently the first whalers, began whaling in the twelfth century. The three main genera pursued by commercial whalers were the right whale (species *Balana*), the humpback whale (species *Megaptera*), and the rorquals or finners (species *Balanoptera*). The sperm whale (*Physeter macrocephalus*) and the bottlenose whale were also hunted.

By the middle of the nineteenth century, whaling appeared to be dying out, because the pursued species had been hunted to near extinction. In 1860, a Norwegian sailor, Svend Foyn, invented the harpoon gun. It did not come into common use until the 1880s. The harpoon gun allowed the capture of smaller, more active whales. What they lacked individually in amount of oil, they made up in quantity.

Since 1900 more than 800,000 cetaceans have been killed for meat, blubber, and whale oil. Whale oil, which was rendered from blubber, was used for making fuel for oil lamps and for making soap and candles. Whales were also killed to obtain whale bone or baleen. Baleen, which was used to stiffen corsets, is an elastic horny substance that grows in place of teeth in some whales (suborder *Mysticeti*). It takes the form of thin parallel plates on each side of the palate.

Sperm whales are hunted for *spermaceti* (sometimes called *cetaceum*). Spermaceti is a pearly white, waxy, translucent solid obtained from the oil in the head of a sperm whale. It is used in making cosmetics, especially emollients (lotions or salves to soothe and soften the skin), candles, and as a lubricant, especially in delicate instruments. Sperm whales also produce ambergris, an opaque, ash-colored secretion of the sperm whale intestine that is used in expensive perfumes to fix delicate odors.

Recently, dolphins and porpoises, as well as beluga and killer whales, have begun appearing in zoos, aquaria, and commercial sea parks. Dolphins and porpoises are members of the family *Delphinidae*, which contains 18 genera and approximately 62 species. The term "dolphin" is usually applied to small cetaceans that have a beak like a snout and a slender, streamlined body. "Porpoise," on the other hand, typically refers to small cetaceans with a blunt snout and a short stocky body. Dolphins and porpoises typically range in length from 1.2–4.3 meters and in weight from 23–225 kilograms. The genus *Orcinus* contains only one species, *O. orca*, commonly called the killer whale. Typically black and white in color, they are approximately 6 meters in length and weigh about 850 kilograms. The scientific name for the beluga whale is *Delphinapterus leucas*. Belugas are typically white. They are about 4 meters long and weigh about 500 kilograms. The name "beluga" causes some confusion, because it is also applied to the great white sturgeon (a fish, not a mammal), which is one of the principal sources of caviar.

All of these species can be trained to perform simple tricks, which makes them a popular attraction at zoos, aquariums, and marine parks. Cetaceans also produce a wide variety of sounds. They use some of these sounds to "echolocate" or find their orientation or food, in much the same manner as we use sonar to locate objects in the water. However, scientists think that cetaceans use some of these sounds to communicate with each other. These "songs" are quite complex and beautiful.

Blond, Georges. **The Great Story of Whales.** Garden City, NY: Hanover House, 1955.

"There she blows!" was the cry of whalers long before the time of *Moby Dick*, Herman Melville's classic story of a New England whaling voyage. Blond's book provides an account, in words and pictures, of a real whaling expedition.

Hunter, Robert, and Rex Weyler. **To Save a Whale: The Voyages of Greenpeace.** San Francisco: Chronicle Books, 1978. ISBN 0-87701-114-1.

Hunter's text and Weyler's photographs describe the beginnings and early history of the environmentalist group, Greenpeace, which was originally the name of that organization's ship. The book focuses on Greenpeace's attempts to prevent whalers from killing whales.

Jenkins, J. T. **A History of the Whale Fisheries.** Port Washington, NY: Kennikat Press, 1971. ISBN 0-8046-1112-2.

Jenkins provides a history of whaling from the Basques, who were the first whalers, to the 1920s.

Lilly, John Cunningham. **Man and Dolphin.** Garden City, NY: Doubleday, 1961.

Dolphins produce a wide variety of complex sounds. Lilly describes a series of experiments in which he and his colleagues attempted to develop meaningful communication between a human and a nonhuman intelligence, the bottlenose dolphin (*Tursiops truncatus*). Lilly chose the dolphin because it is approximately the same size as a human and its brain weighs approximately 1,700 grams (the average human brain is approximately 1,450 grams). In many ways Lilly's work is far more daunting than attempts to communicate with chimpanzees (see for example, Kellogg and Linden in the section below dealing with primates). This is because we have a good deal of common life experience with large primates. However, a dolphin's life experience would be very different from a human's or nonhuman primate's experience.

――――. **The Mind of the Dolphin: A Nonhuman Intelligence.** New York: Doubleday, 1967.

Lilly describes additional experiments in his attempt to establish meaningful communication between humans and dolphins. Based on his work with dolphins, Lilly would add the following language to the United Nations charter:

> No matter differences between species, no matter differences of anatomy, no matter differences between media in which they live,

creatures with a brain above a certain size will be considered 'equal' with man.

Sebeck, Thomas A., and Robert Rosenthal, eds. **The Clever Hans Phenomenon: Communication with Horses, Whales, Apes, and People.** New York: The New York Academy of Science, 1981. 331p. ISBN 0-89766-114-1.

Clever Hans was a horse that lived in Berlin, Germany, in the early part of this century. He belonged to a retired schoolteacher, Wilhelm von Osten, who believed that animals could be taught to think, talk, and calculate if instructed by the right method. The method, invented by von Osten, was to assign a number to each letter of the alphabet. The association between the number and the letter was learned by means of a blackboard. The horse used its front foot to tap out numbers. It appeared that the horse could combine letters into words and words into sentences, as well as add, subtract, multiply, divide, and solve problems of musical harmony. However, careful experiments by Oskar Pfungst of the Psychological Institute of the University of Berlin strongly suggest that Clever Hans could not do any of the feats credited to him. It was Pfungst's conclusion that Clever Hans was a careful observer who noted subtle and probably unconscious movements by von Osten when the correct number of knocks had been reached.

Sebeck and Rosenthal suggest that Clever Hans should provide a major lesson in the subtlety of communication, witting or unwitting, between members of different species. Further, they and the other authors in this book suggest that many of the modern "thinking" animals, such as dolphins or chimpanzees, may be subtle examples of the Clever Hans phenomena.

Domestication

The process of domestication—that is, to tame an animal to live and breed in intimate association with and to the advantage of humans—of animals began about 18,000 years ago during the Stone Age. Neolithic man was undoubtedly interested in a general utility animal, one that could serve equally well for carrying loads, for hunting, and, if the need arose, for food. Therefore, they chose hoofed vertebrates, because they were strong, durable, and provided a large amount of meat.

Only a handful of the estimated 45,000 species of mammals have been domesticated. Perhaps the most important contribution of domestic animals is to provide humans with meat. This is furnished by the various species and breeds of cattle, sheep, and pigs, supplemented in some localities by goats, reindeer, and rabbits. Birds, such as chickens, ducks, and geese, as well as fish, such as carp or catfish, also supply substantial amounts of meat. Given the same amount of feed, dairy cattle will supply two to three times as much human food (such as milk, cheese, and yogurt) as beef cattle. Goats, sheep, and camels also produce dairy products. Mammals also provide wool (sheep, goats) and hides (cattle) to make clothing and shelter for humans.

In many parts of the Third World, most human work in draft (pulling loads) and transport (carrying loads) is still done by animals. Eleven species of mammals—horse, donkey, mule, buffalo, ox, dog, elephant, yak, llama, reindeer, and camel—are the primary animals used for this purpose.

It is estimated that there are more than 700,000 species of insects. Of these, only the honeybee, the silkworm, and two species of scale insects (used to produce *lac,* which helps make shellac and cochineal [a dye]) have been quasi-domesticated. Although the honey and beeswax that bees produce are important products, the bee's most important contribution to human well-being is as a pollinator. Indeed, some species of food and decorative plants could not exist without bees. Unfortunately, many species of insects, such as flies, fleas, ticks, lice, mosquitoes, moths, grasshoppers, and locusts, are considered pests. They are important vectors for human and animal diseases and/or contaminate or consume food that would otherwise be used by humans.

Barloy, J. J. **Les animaux domestiques (Man and Animals: 100 Centuries of Friendship.** Translated by Henry Fox. London: Gordon & Cremonesi Publishers, 1974. ISBN 0-86033-012-5.

Barloy discusses the process of domestication and its effects on animals and humans.

Clutton-Brock, Juliet. **A Natural History of Domesticated Mammals.** Austin, TX: University of Texas Press, 1989. 208p. ISBN 0-292-75540-6.

Clutton-Brock describes the way humans have manipulated and changed mammals. Her account begins in the Ice Age, 10,000 years ago, and ends at the time of the Roman Empire, when the common domestic mammals were well established as discrete breeding populations that were isolated from their wild parent species. Humans, unlike other living primates, evolved as carnivorous predators that had to depend on their mental and physical prowess to hunt and kill other animals.

The author shows how change in domestic animals occurs as a result of artificial selection by humans rather than in response to reproductive isolation or conditions such as environment and climate. Most mammals can be tamed if they are taken from their mothers early in life and reared by a human. Relative tameness as an adult depends on innate social patterns; that is, whether an animal is solitary (cats, except for the African lion) or social (wolves).

Humans began associating with the wolf during the last Ice Age, more than 125,000 years ago. Clutton-Brock claims that man and wolf developed similar hunting skills based on complex social behavior during the hunt. However, wolves typically killed weak, sick, old, or young animals. Paleolithic humans, on the other hand, killed more randomly because they had access to fire and weapons. Even at this early stage, it is likely that humans enjoyed killing for its own sake.

Clutton-Brock quotes Sir Francis Galton's essay about human domination and manipulation of the animal kingdom. She restates the six conditions that Galton thought were required to allow an animal to become domesticated. According to Galton, these animals should be hardy, have an inborn liking for man, be comfort loving, be useful to savages, breed freely, and be easy to tend.

The author divides domestic animals into four large categories:

1. "Man-made" animals, which include dogs, sheep, goats, cattle, pigs, horses, asses, and mules.
2. Exploited captives, which include cats, elephants, camels, llamas, reindeer, and Asiatic cattle.
3. Small mammals, which include rabbits, ferrets, rodents, and carnivores that are exploited for their fur.
4. Animals that are used in game ranching, such as deer and bovids. Clutton-Brock discusses the process of domestication for each group. She also provides a discussion of the ungulates (hoofed mammals) that were exploited by pre-Neolithic humans.

———, ed. **The Walking Larder: Patterns of Domestication, Pastoralism, and Predation.** London: Unwin Hyman, 1989. 384p. ISBN 0-685-46017-7.

This book contains essays by various authors who describe the manifold relationships between humans and animals, both in the past and the present, and how these relationships have affected domestication. For example, early humans were constantly on the move, trying to expand their territory and find new resources. As with modern humans, early humans needed a source of protein. They found it in the wild animals that they followed and hunted, as well as in the domestic animals that accompanied their travels and which they used as a store of meat on the hoof.

The book describes the development of pastoralism (how humans became shepherds and herdsmen) in Europe, Asia, and Africa. Finally, it also describes the effect of human predation on shellfish, fish, and birds, as well as the impact of predators on humans, who were both competitors and potential prey.

Hemmer, Helmut. **Domestikation (Domestication: The Decline of Environmental Appreciation.** Translated by Niel Beckhaus. New York: Cambridge University Press, 1990. 250p. ISBN 0-521-34178-7.

Hemmer provides an overview of the domestic animal and the process of domestication. This is important because the domestic animal is an essential element in the development of human civilization. Hemmer says that understanding the process may help humans develop new and distinct kinds of domestic animals. These animals may help (1) improve food production for people throughout the world who live at subsistence level; (2) develop alternate methods of land use; (3) provide new breeds that will lend themselves to intensive husbandry; and (4) develop new laboratory animals that might help solve some of today's most complex medical mysteries. Hemmer notes that one central issue in grasping the process of domestication is understanding the behavior of an animal and how it differs in the wild. The discussion of this issue includes the role of reactions to stress and psychological tolerance, behavioral flexibility, activity and intensity of action, aptitude for life in social groups, sexual and aggressive reactions, and pigmentation and body development.

Mason, Ian L., ed. **Evolution of Domesticated Animals.** New York: Longham, 1984. ISBN 0-582-46046-8.

This book presents an account of the origin and history of domestic animals. It defines domestic animals as follows:

1. Those whose breeding is under human control.
2. Those who provide a product or service that is useful to humans.
3. Those that are tame.
4. Those that have genetically changed from the wild genotype. Mammals, birds, reptiles, amphibians, fish, insects, crustaceans, and mollusks are included in the list of domesticated animals.

Entertainment

The first time an animal was used to amuse and entertain a human being predates written history. The number of species used by different parts of the modern entertainment industry varies. The rodeo industry typically uses just two species: horses and cattle. The circus generally uses horses, elephants, large wild cats, and domestic dogs. More rarely, the circus uses bears, primates (especially chimpanzees), seals and sea lions, and birds (especially parrots and macaws). The motion picture and television industries use a wide variety of domestic and wild animals. Public and private zoos and aquaria generally have the largest number of species of wild animals.

Animal Fighting

Every effort is being made in the United States to stamp out one form of entertainment involving animals: animal fighting, such as dog- and cockfights. Local and state laws against animal fighting (especially dogfighting) have apparently had some impact, but the practice continues to flourish in some locales. The 1976 amendments to the Animal Welfare Act (see chapter 5) set civil and criminal penalties for (1) using the U.S. Postal Service or any interstate instrumentality to promote or otherwise further an animal fighting venture and/or (2) to knowingly sell, buy, transport, or deliver to another person any dog or other animal for the purpose of having the dog or other animal participate in an animal fighting venture or for the purpose of sponsoring or exhibiting an animal in any animal fighting venture. The 1976 amendments apparently do not apply to animal fighting ventures involving live fowl unless the fight takes place in a state where cockfighting would be in violation of state or local laws. Outside the United States, animal baiting, such as bullfighting, continues to be popular in some countries.

The Circus

The one-ring circus has been in existence for at least 2,500 years. The Romans called them "circulators." They consisted of troupes of jugglers and mountebanks who made their living by performing acrobatics and magic, and by exhibiting trained animals. The Romans apparently liked elephant acts, including one in which an elephant could walk a tightrope. The circus was a way in which people could experience exotic animals, either as performers or in the menagerie.

The modern circus was born in the 1770s in Great Britain. Acrobats, clowning, and animal training did not appear until the end of the eighteenth century. Animals have been a popular part of the circus tradition for centuries. It is likely that as long as the circus exists, animals will be a part of it.

Ballantine, Bill. **Wild Tigers and Tame Fleas.** New York: Rinehart, 1958.

Ballantine provides an interesting behind-the-scenes look at the circus and its animals.

Bouissae, Paul. **Circus and Culture: A Semiotic Approach.** Bloomington, IN: Indiana University Press, 1976. ISBN 0-253-31354-6.

Bouissae provides a brief history of the circus, then describes its culture. He devotes several chapters to the interrelationship between animals and their trainers. He describes how a trainer teaches a horse to perform in a standard horse act—a process that is similar in training any performing animal. Bouissae says the first step in training an animal is to establish rapport. This is done by presenting the animal with pleasurable rewards such as food and by scratching or patting the animal while speaking in a pleasant voice. Incorrect behavior is punished with light blows and a disapproving voice. Gradually, the animal learns to recognize the trainer and treats the trainer with attachment and respect, in much the same manner as the animal would treat a higher ranking member of its own species. The animal gradually learns to respond to the trainer's hand and body signals.

Bouissae notes that the balancing of rewards and punishment is a delicate task. He says the goal is not to break the animal's spirit, but to get it to remain near the trainer and follow his or her movements. For example, the horse can be trained to start and stop pawing the ground depending on subtle movements by the trainer. These movements should be subtle enough that an observer is unaware of them. These cues are what circus trainers call the "keys" to training.

Horse Racing

Horse racing is undoubtedly one of the oldest diversions of humans, probably starting soon after the domestication of horses. Kikkuli, an expert in the employ of a Hittite king, may have written the first treatise dealing with the breeding and training of horses in about 1500 B.C. The 23d Olympiad (about 624 B.C.)

probably had races involving mounted horses. England's Jockey Club, which exercises control over racing and breeding in that country, was formed around 1750. The stallions and mares that provided the foundation for American thoroughbred breeding were imported during the 1700s.

Betting on the outcome of a horse race is probably almost as old as horse racing itself. Until recently, offtrack betting was illegal in the United States. Illegal gambling has caused law enforcement considerable difficulty and has been the source of graft and corruption.

Horse racing actually consists of three distinct sports. In *thoroughbred* racing, the jockey is mounted on the horse's back and the horses race around an oval-shaped, dirt track that is usually about a mile long. In *steeplechasing*, the jockey once again sits on the horse's back. The horse must run a complex course that contains a variety of obstacles that must be jumped over. The steeplechase racecourse, which can contain as many as 30 jumps, tends to be longer than the thoroughbred racecourse. In *harness* racing, the driver sits in a sulky, which is a two-wheeled vehicle of the lightest possible construction, with two pneumatic tires. Most harness racetracks are about one-half mile long. The horses are trained to trot or pace.

Helm, Mike. **A Breed Apart: The Horses and the Players.** New York: Henry Holt, 1991. 320p. ISBN 0-8050-1326-1.

Helm gives a behind-the-scenes look into the world of thoroughbred racehorses, the trainers, jockeys, and players.

Hunting and Fishing

Our primitive ancestors, as early·as the Cro-Magnon race, were hunters who apparently held their animal prey in almost mystical regard. The earliest paintings, which were made in late Paleolithic times, such as those in the caves of Lascaux near Dordogne, France, were of animals such as bulls, horses, and deer. The earliest engravings, reliefs, and sculptures were also of animal subjects. Archaeologists believe that these artworks were used in magico-religious rites bound up in the hunting culture. In many parts of the world today, hunting and fishing are still required for survival. However, this is not typically the case in the industrialized countries where hunting and fishing are usually pursued as sports.

Many modern sportsmen apparently have the same regard for the animals they hunt as did our primitive ancestors.

Modern sportsmen argue that no species of animal has become extinct because of sport hunting or fishing. They assert that game species and their habitats are often better protected than nongame species because of the sportsmen's work. With or without the presence of sportsmen, the fate of most wild animals is death by starvation, disease, or predation.

It was Theodore Roosevelt, an ardent sportsman, who made conservation a household word. For Roosevelt and others of his generation, conservation was a reform movement that relied on political and legal methods to obtain the wise use of limited resources. The Boone and Crockett Club, started by Roosevelt and other prominent sportsmen in 1887, was the first private organization to deal with conservation issues on a national scale. The Sierra Club, started by John Muir, represents the opposite viewpoint.

Countless books and magazine articles have been written about hunting and fishing. The following list contains some good examples.

Capstick, Peter Hathaway. **Death in a Lonely Land: More Hunting, Fishing, and Shooting on Five Continents.** New York: St. Martin's Press, 1990. ISBN 0-312-13810-0.

Capstick, who describes himself as "a full time professional small boy," is also a columnist for *Outdoor Life*. In all probability, he may be the best-selling writer of outdoor books of all time. Capstick transcends the field of outdoor journalism. His books have received favorable comment in *The New York Times* and *Sports Illustrated*. Like our primitive ancestors and many modern hunters, Capstick apparently holds the animals he hunts in almost mystical regard and is able to convey this feeling to his readers. This book is an anthology of a number of magazine articles published during the 1970s.

McIntyre, Thomas. **The Way of the Hunter: The Art and the Spirit of Modern Hunting.** New York: E. P. Dutton, 1988. 256p. ISBN 0-525-24718-1.

McIntyre discusses modern-day hunting. He describes hunters as having "an insatiable hunger to set off, in spite of the lack of experience, the lack of familiarity with the land, and the abundance of reproach in pursuit of animals, to locate them on their native grounds and on their own terms, to take them (capturing their flesh as they capture our souls as fair a trade off as there ever was), and to partake once more of a feast as old as every hill and every hunter, whether naked and carrying a spear or down jacketed and packing an '06, who ever crept over a ridge crest to look for wildlife and to live the wildlife. It is one of the finest mysteries our species retains from our primitive past."

Reiger, John F. **American Sportsmen and the Origins of Conservation.** Norman, OK: University of Oklahoma Press, 1986. 320p. ISBN 0-8061-2021-5.

Reiger presents a historical review of the conservation movement and its early leaders, such as Theodore Roosevelt. He also discusses the institutions associated with the conservation movement, such as Theodore Roosevelt's Boone and Crockett Club and the magazine *American Sportsman.*

Trueblood, Ted. **The Ted Trueblood Hunting Treasury.** New York: David McKay, 1978. ISBN 0-679-50802-3.

Trueblood writes for magazines such as *Field and Stream* and *The Elks Magazine.* This book presents an anthology of his articles dealing with hunting and camping.

Moving Pictures and Television

Animals have been part of the motion picture industry since its beginnings. The first commercial movie was D. W. Griffith's *The Great Train Robbery* (1903), which was a western that used horses. Some animals have been stars in their own right, far more famous than their trainers or in some cases even their human co-stars. Many human co-stars complain about being upstaged by their animal co-stars. Lassie (reportedly portrayed by several generations of male collies) and Rin Tin Tin were well known dog stars. Among horses that appeared on film, Trigger and Champion had almost as much name recognition as their human owners Roy Rogers and Gene Autry. In the early days, some trainers used fear and violence to control an animal's behavior. However, these techniques have been replaced by more rational training methods based on affection training.

Helfer, Ralph. **The Beauty and the Beast: Tales of Hollywood's Wild Animal Stars.** Los Angeles: Jeremy P. Tacher, 1990. ISBN 0-87477-516-7.

Helfer is an animal trainer who has provided trained animals for more than 5,000 movies and television shows. In this book, he highlights his methods for training animals.

Pets

Dogs were domesticated by Neolithic man about 18,000 years ago. They were used to help humans hunt, to carry and pull loads, and to help control herds of hoofed stock. When necessary, they were used for food. However, dogs also provided early and modern man with companionship. More recently, in the nineteenth and twentieth centuries, a variety of species of small mammals, including birds, reptiles, amphibians, and fish, have been quasi-domesticated and kept as pets.

Anchel, Marjorie, ed. **Overpopulation of Cats and Dogs: Causes, Effects, and Prevention.** New York: Fordham University Press, 1990. 250p. ISBN 0-8232-1296-3.

This book represents the proceedings of a conference sponsored by the New York Humane Association. It provides an overview of the problems associated with surplus animals, especially unwanted cats and dogs. It also considers potential solutions, such as neutering (castration or spaying) and euthanasia. The book discusses who is responsible for pet overpopulation; how animals are controlled in rural, urban, and metropolitan areas; and the role of animal shelters and pounds. The importance of education and appropriate legislation in preventing pet overpopulation is stressed.

Benning, Lee E. **The Pet Profiteer$: The Exploitation of Pet Owners and Pets in America.** New York: Quadrangle/The New York Times Book Co., 1976. ISBN 0-8129-0622-5.

Benning points out the magnitude of the pet overpopulation problem. He estimates (based on 1975 figures) that approximately 2,000–3,000 cats and dogs are born every hour in the United States Benning says that to maintain current pet populations approximately 60,000 cats and dogs must die or be euthanized each day. That's more than 22.9 million each year. Benning puts most of the responsibility for pet overpopulation at the door of the puppy or kitten mill, backyard breeders, and commercial private breeders, as well as irresponsible owners who do not have their pets spayed or neutered. He is also critical of irresponsible pet owners who simply abandon their unwanted pets to fend for themselves, which few pets can do. Many die a slow death from starvation, while others succumb to a cruel and agonizing end from disease. However, Benning says it is most common for abandoned pets to be killed by automobiles. He does not mention a fourth cause of death, that of being picked up by the local animal control agency, which euthanizes many stray animals. The responsibility for euthanizing more than 13 million unwanted pets a year falls to humane society shelters and public pounds.

Benning reports that purebred dogs are more likely to be adopted than mongrels. During prosperous times, dogs that are expensive to feed and/or groom are popular. These include the Great Dane, St. Bernard, borzoi (Russian wolfhound), miniature and toy poodles, Lhasa apso, cocker spaniel, Afghan, English sheepdog, and standard French poodle. During bad times, these dogs are the ones that end up in shelters. Moving, allergies, and especially lack of interest (typically caused by the loss of puppy or kitten cuteness) are also reasons given for turning animals in to shelters.

In fiscal year 1974, it cost Bide-A-Wee, a pet adoption agency, approximately $96.46 per animal to find acceptable homes for 13,749 animals. This represented about 0.001 percent of all the animals available for adoption that year. At that rate, it would have cost about $1.3 billion to adopt out all of the animals available that year.

Gentry, Christine. **When Dogs Run Wild: The Sociology of Feral Dogs and Wildlife.** Jefferson, NC: McFarland, 1983. ISBN 0-89950-062-5.

Gentry suggests that the first primitive wolves appeared on earth about 40,000 years ago. Soon humans acquired wolves and by selective breeding transformed them into the doglike animals that could be accepted into the human world.

It is estimated that there are between 50 and 100 million dogs living in the United States. Gentry notes that approximately one-quarter of these animals are stray or unwanted pets and another quarter may be lost or roaming at will. Many of these animals ultimately find their way to woods or forests, where they live and reproduce feral young or breed with wild canids to produce new species. These feral dogs or hybrids hunt large and small game. They may also pose some threat to humans, especially children.

Gentry says that packs of six to eight dogs form and last for a few weeks, then disperse and form new packs. The leader is usually a large dog such as a German shepherd or shepherd cross, and other pack members are generally mongrels, many with collie or hound ancestry. The packs can cover up to six miles per day, and their primary sources of food were dumpsters and trash cans, carrion, such as road kills, and cottontail rabbits. Their home range can include more than 2,000 acres.

Nowell, Iris. **The Dog Crisis.** New York: St. Martin's Press, 1979. ISBN 0-312-21613-0.

Is the dog really man's best friend? In answering this question, Nowell raises some troubling statistics. Dogs have a different culture than humans. Unlike humans, she says, dogs use their teeth for play and to assert dominance. Nowell further notes that they use feces and urine to mark their territory and to communicate with other dogs.

To fit into our culture, Nowell says, dogs need constant supervision. Unfortunately, they do not always receive it. Here are some of the strikes against dogs that Nowell cites:

1. Nearly 2 percent of all children between five and nine years of age are bitten by dogs.
2. Dogs deposit more than 4,000 tons of feces in our streets each year.
3. The grain and food by-products that the pet food industry puts into pet food could potentially be used by humans.
4. Dogs also can transmit a number of diseases, such as rabies, to unwary humans. Typically, a free-running dog is bitten by a rabid fox or skunk and then bites a human. Rocky Mountain spotted fever and *Leptospira* are also diseases that can be transmitted to humans.

Nowell discusses why people want pets and what benefit they derive from their pets, as well as the monetary and social costs of having a pet. She also provides an overview of the pet and pet food industry.

The Rodeo

Rodeo is a popular sport in the United States and Canada. The Professional Rodeo Cowboys Association and the International Rodeo Association together sanction more than 1,000 annual rodeos that are attended by more than 14 million paying spectators. However, many communities and organizations, such as 4-H, Little Britches, and the Girls Rodeo Association, also sponsor rodeos throughout the year.

Rodeo traces its origin back to two diverse sources. The first is the sports and contests of the early working cowboys that they pursued for their own amusement. The second is the uniquely American outdoor entertainment, the Wild West Show, which was started by William Frederick ("Buffalo Bill") Cody in the summer of 1882 in North Platte, Nebraska. This show included performances called "Cowboy Fun," which included attempts to ride wild broncos and mules, steer wrestling, and other skills of the range. In contrast to their modern counterparts, these early cowboys were paid performers. Modern rodeo cowboys only get paid if they win.

Lawrence, Elizabeth A. **Rodeo: An Anthropologist Looks at the Wild and the Tame.** Chicago: University of Chicago Press, 1984. 288p. ISBN 0-226-46955-7.

Modern professional rodeo is almost totally a man's world. Women are typically not allowed to participate as contestants or officials. The typical rodeo is divided into rough stock and timed events.

The *rough stock* events include saddle bronco riding, bareback bronco riding, and bull riding. Saddle bronco riding is often considered the classic rodeo event, because it is perceived as being directly related to the era of cattle drives and open-range ranching. In this event, the bronco (an unbroken wild range horse) is provided with a trimmed-down version of a standard western saddle, a halter, and a single rein. The cowboy's task is to remain on the bronco's back for eight seconds, while holding on to the rein with one hand and rhythmically spurring the horse from the horse's shoulders to the candle of the saddle.

Bareback bronco riding is a relatively new event that was added to rodeo events in the last 30 years. The horse is supplied with a *riggin,* which consists of a leather circingle fitted around the horse's body just behind the withers (the ridge between the shoulder bones) of the horse. The riggin has a handhold similar to a suitcase handle. The cowboy grips the handhold with one hand and must remain on the bucking horse's back for eight seconds.

A bucking strap is used to encourage the horse to buck. It consists of a leather strap covered with sheepskin that is placed around the horse's flank just before the animal is released from the chute. The strap is released after the ride is completed and the horse stops bucking. Rodeo advocates claim the bucking strap is merely annoying, not painful. In bull riding, the bucking strap is replaced by a rope.

Bull riding is the most dangerous of the rough stock events. The riggin is a rope passed around the body of the bull, just behind the hump. The cowboy must grip a loop in the rope and remain on the bull's back for eight seconds.

Timed rodeo events include calf roping, steer wrestling, team roping, and steer roping. The goal of the calf event is to rope a running calf from horseback. The cowboy then secures the rope to the saddle horn, dismounts, runs the calf down, throws it on its side, and ties three of its legs together with a short piece of rope called the piggin string. A skilled cowboy can do this in less than ten seconds.

Steer wrestling or bulldogging is a rodeo event that has little application in ranching. The bulldogger must leap from his horse when it is running at full speed, grab one horn and the jaw of the running steer, stop the steer, then throw it to the ground so that its four feet and head are straight. A skilled cowboy can do this in ten seconds or less.

Steer roping (sometimes called steer jerking or steer tripping) is not allowed in some states. The cowboy ropes the steer around the horns, pitches the slack of his rope over the steer's right hip, and turns his horse off to the left, hitting the steer with the rope and making him fall to the ground. The cowboy then dismounts and ties the steer's feet together.

Two cowboys work together in team roping. One cowboy catches the steer by the head and the second, called the "heeler," catches the hind legs. The clock stops when both ropes are tight around their saddle horns and the two horses are facing the steer.

There are a number of newer events that are included in some rodeos. These include the wild horse and chuckwagon races. In the wild horse race, two cowboys called "muggers" attempt to hold a wild horse long enough to saddle it, then allow a third cowboy to mount and ride the horse. In one version of the wild horse race that is not allowed in some rodeos, one of the muggers grabs one of the broncos' ears and bites it until the pain causes the horse to stand still and allow itself to be saddled. In the chuckwagon race, one team member must throw a 50-pound cookstove, some tent poles, and canvas into the back of the chuckwagon. Then the chuckwagon, which is pulled by four thoroughbred horses, must race around a figure-eight course demarcated by barrels and race around a track to the finish line. Two or three mounted men, commonly called "outriders," must also complete the same course.

The only event in the standard rodeo that women are allowed to enter is the barrel race. This is a timed event, where the horse races in a cloverleaf pattern around a series of barrels and then races out of the arena.

Zoos and Aquaria

Menageries have existed since ancient times in Egypt, Rome, and China. Modern zookeeping dates from the founding of the Imperial Menagerie at the Schönbrunn Palace in Vienna in 1752. It opened to the public in 1765 and is still in operation. The Zoological Society of London established its collection in Regents Park in 1828. This zoo was one of the first to replace its traditional cages with more natural habitats. The first "zoological garden" was established in the United States in Philadelphia in 1874.

Today, virtually every major city in the United States has a zoological garden. Several cities, such as Chicago and New York, have more than one. In the past, zoological gardens housed one or two members of each species in small cages with iron bars across the front. Today, these cages are being replaced by larger, more natural habitats. Recently, drive-through nature parks have become popular. In these parks, the humans remain in the car and the animals are allowed to roam free. In the United States these parks generally contain exotic hoofed stock and large birds, such as ostrich and emu.

Many zoological gardens are attempting to set up breeding populations of specific species. Young produced by these breeding populations can help replenish a zoo's own collection and provide animals to other zoos. Such breeding programs are especially important for species that are endangered in their natural habitat, such as the great apes and the large carnivores.

Bendiner, Robert. **The Fall of the Wild, the Rise of the Zoo.** New York: E. P Dutton, 1981. 256p. ISBN 0-525-10270-1.

Bendiner says that more people visit zoos each year than attend professional major league baseball and football games. He argues that if it were not for zoos, the Siberian tiger, the one-horned rhino, the green turtle, and the orangutan would soon join the dodo, the woolly mammoth, and the passenger pigeon in the vast zoological burial ground. Since life first appeared on earth, species have come into being, lived their allotted time, and died out. While humans have contributed to the extinction of certain species, such as the passenger pigeon, Bendiner notes that the process of extinction was going on long before humans appeared. However, he says, humans can help preserve species by establishing breeding populations in zoos. To do this, Bendiner says, the zoo must provide animals with adequate space and privacy. The zoo must also take into account the animal's "flight distance" when designing cages. This is necessary because animals will allow strangers to get within only a certain distance and then they will try to flee. This flight distance varies from species to species. If a cage is made too small, zoo visitors can approach the animal too closely, causing the animal constant stress.

Elgin, Robert. **Man in a Cage.** Ames, IA: Iowa State University Press, 1972. ISBN 0-8138-1020-5.

Elgin is the director of the Des Moines Children's Zoo. He describes the joys and sorrows of being in charge of several hundred animals and countless human visitors.

Hahn, E. **Animal Gardens: Zoos around the World.** Garden City, NY: Doubleday, 1967. 367p. ISBN 0-941062-3.

Hahn begins her book with the statement, "I like zoos," a sentiment shared by many. In this book, she describes some of the world's most famous zoos.

Farm Animals

Prior to World War II, there were about 6 million farms in the United States with approximately 1,061 million acres of farmland. While the amount of farmland has remained relatively constant, the number of farms has dropped steadily. By 1981, the number of farms had dropped to about 2.4 million. This means that the average size of a farm increased over the same time. So by 1978, 45.5 percent of all farmland was in farms of 2,000 or more acres. This change was due, at least in part, to a decrease in the number of people who wanted to farm. As the number of people decreased, the costs of farm labor increased. This caused an increased dependence on mechanization, including the adoption of intensive industrialized husbandry methods and techniques for cattle, pigs, and poultry.

No one knows exactly how many farm animals there are in the United States. The best estimates suggest that there are about 100 million head of beef cattle, 9.9 million dairy cattle, 57 million swine, 10.8 million sheep, and over a billion chickens. Each year, approximately 34 million head of beef cattle are slaughtered as are 2.7 million head of veal calves, 5.7 million sheep (mostly lambs), and 97 million swine.

Baxter, S. H., M. R. Baxter, and J. A. D. MacCormak, eds. **Farm Animal Housing and Welfare.** Boston: Martinus Nijhoff Publishers, 1983. ISBN 0-89838-597-0.

This book represents the proceeding of a seminar sponsored by the Commission of the European Communities (CEC), Directorate General for Agriculture. It focuses on the relationship between animal housing and animal welfare. One feature of man's use of animals is to place spatial restrictions on their freedom. It has been suggested that agricultural animals suffer unnecessarily due to poorly designed housing and equipment. Human concern about animals and their welfare seems to be based on empathy. This book says that this concern is based on the tacit, but generally untested, assumption that animals (1) have the neural structures required to support self-consciousness; (2) have a mental representation of their physical state; and (3) can mentally experience pain, suffering, distress, and anguish due to this representation. Typically, the study of animal welfare falls into two broad classes: First, researchers allow an animal to choose freely between two or more housing conditions. Second, they measure an animal's nonspecific biological responses that accompany stress. In the latter case, it is assumed that if these responses are not present, the animal is not being stressed. Most of the papers from the CEC symposium focus on evaluating the current housing conditions of cattle and poultry and determining how to improve these conditions to minimize stress.

Copland, J. W., ed. **Draught Animal Power for Production.** Canberra: Australian Centre for International Agricultural Research, 1985. 170p. ISBN 0-685-63250-4.

A large part of the population in Third World countries depends on draught animals as a source of power for the production and distribution of food. This book, which contains the proceedings of an international workshop, provides an overview of the physiology and nutritional requirements of draught animals. It discusses how to improve reproductive success and health of these animals, and how to use modern genetic principles for their improvement.

Fox, Michael W. **Farm Animals: Husbandry, Behavior, and Veterinary Practice (Viewpoints of a Critic).** Baltimore: University Park Press, 1984. ISBN 0-8391-1769-8.

Fox describes the introduction and adoption of new industrialized husbandry methods and techniques for cattle, pigs, and poultry that have occurred since the 1950s. He argues that modern farm animal science is flawed because it makes productivity the sole criterion of sound husbandry practice. Fox thinks that if the animals' physiological, emotional, and behavioral well-being are incorporated into husbandry, then the animals will be healthier and more productive. He questions the notion that animal productivity and feed conversion efficiency are good indicators of animal well-being. Fox focuses on the three Rs of animal welfare: reduction (decreasing the total livestock and poultry population); replacement (eating rice and beans instead of pork and beans); and, especially, refinement (improving husbandry systems and practices).

Gillies, M. T. **Animal Feeds from Waste Materials.** Park Ridge, NJ: Noyes Data Corp., 1978. ISBN 0-8155-0699-6.

Humans face two somewhat related problems: providing food for an increasing population and disposing of the waste this population produces. In the United States the primary source of protein is from animals. Most people prefer the taste of meat to other sources of protein. Also, the amino acid composition of meat is of higher quality than protein obtained from any other source. However, ruminants (cattle, sheep, and goats) utilize only about 35 percent of the feed they consume. If they eat food that humans could consume, such as grain, the amount they consume could feed many more people than the meat they produce. On the other hand, ruminants could potentially be fed wastes, such as molasses, which is a by-product of sugar manufacture. Molasses is generally considered to be a waste product. Disposing of it is a problem, so it can become a pollutant. Since humans do not consume large amounts of molasses, animals that eat it are not competing for a human food as is the case with grain. Also, if livestock are fed molasses, it is no longer a potential pollutant.

Gillies also mentions the potential use of high cellulose wastes, such as straw and wood; oilseed meals; citrus and beet pulps; brewery by-products; cattle and poultry manure, sewage, and other animal waste; and whey. The bulk of information contained in this book was obtained from U.S. patents, as well as federally funded studies and conferences.

Harrison, Ruth. **Animal Machines: The New Factory Farming Industry.** New York: Ballantine Books, 1964.

Harrison describes mechanized factory farming in Great Britain as it is applied to broiler chickens, laying chickens, veal calves, rabbits, and pigs. She argues that "more does not always mean better." Harrison notes that to improve livestock growth rates, farmers add small amounts of antibiotics, such as penicillin, Aureomycin, or Terramycin, and/or synthetic estrogens to the feed of animals. However, Harrison asserts that this use of antibiotics will ultimately lead to the development of strains of bacteria that are resistant to the antibiotics and that the synthetic estrogens are contaminating the meat of these animals.

Hoffmann, D., J. Nari, and R. J. Petheram, eds. **Draught Animals in Rural Development.** Canberra: Australian Centre for International Agricultural Research, 1989. 347p. ISBN 1-86320-003-7.

It is estimated that there are over 1 billion draught animals being used in the developing world for power, transport, milk, meat, and security. This book looks at the magnitude of the use of draught animals. It also provides details about the physiology and nutrition; reproduction, breeding, and selection; health, training, and management; engineering; and economics of draught animal power.

Mason, Jim, and Peter Singer. **Animal Factories**. New York: Crown Publishers, 1990. ISBN 0-517-57751-8.

Mason and Singer describe the change in farming that occurred in the 1970s and that led to the development of the factory farm. Herdsmen and milkmaids were replaced by automated feeders, computers, closed circuit television, and vacuum pumps. Farmers began to raise animals in large buildings, the authors assert, where health and productivity came from syringes and additive-laced feed. They argue that the meat and eggs produced by factory farms may not be as good as that produced by more traditional farming methods. They also argue that there are moral and ethical objections to raising animals under factory-like conditions.

Muller, Z. O. **Feed from Animal Wastes: State of Knowledge.** Rome, Italy: Food and Agriculture Organization of the United Nations, 1980. 201p. ISBN 92-5-100946-5.

More than 1 billion tons of animal waste is produced each year worldwide. Traditionally, this waste was spread back on the land because of its excellent fertilizing properties. This use decreased with the development of chemical fertilizers. Muller describes the results of feeding livestock waste to cattle, pigs, and other animals including fish. The methods used to treat the waste are described in detail, as are the methods used to prevent the accumulation of minerals, antibiotics, pesticides, mycotoxins, and hormonal residues. Industrial conversion of wastes by aerobic, anaerobic, thermophilic, and other processes are also described, as are the photosynthetic recovery of nutrients by plants.

Preston, Thomas R., and M. B. Willis. **Intensive Beef Production.** Oxford, England: Pergamon Press, 1974. ISBN 0-08-018980-6.

Intensive beef production means growing and/or feeding cattle in confinement where the feed is carried to the animals. The authors argue that the amount of available land for grazing cattle is decreasing and that cereals can be grown more efficiently than grass. Preston and Willis also assert that intensive beef production allows the use of industrial type feeds and by-products such as molasses.

This book is divided into four parts. The *first* part describes the market and other factors that control the quality of producing beef. The *second* part describes the raw materials available, such as the type of animals raised, their genetic makeup, and the nutritional principles that determine the extent to which the animals can be exploited. The *third* part describes production, which includes details about growth and fattening, as well as how to deal with disease and waste products. The *last* section deals with the future. It focuses on economic trends and areas of investigation that might improve efficiency.

Sainsbury, David. **Farm Animal Welfare: Cattle, Pigs and Poultry.** London: William Collins Sons, 1986. ISBN 0-00-383157-4.

Sainsbury argues that it is a flawed notion that intensification of meat production is bad and free range is good. He says that free-range animals can suffer harm and stress from bad weather; predators; disease, especially parasitism; and poor diet. Sainsbury suggests that there is some middle ground that exists that should not significantly increase production costs, but will allow animals more freedom than factory settings. For example, he says, laying birds can be kept in straw yards or on deep litter rather than being closely confined in cages. He also suggests that "small really is beautiful." Thus, he says, livestock units should be designed so that they can be completely emptied and cleaned. Sainsbury claims that smaller units give the best productivity by providing a more favorable food conversion efficiency, the lowest incidence of disease, and more manageable methods of dealing with waste.

Sims, John A., and Leslie E. Johnson. **Animals in the American Economy.** Ames, IA: Iowa State University Press, 1972. ISBN 0-8357-6755-8.

The real beginnings of civilization began when early man discovered that a planted field and tended herd required less labor to yield more food than nature on its own. Breeds are animals within a species that have discernible traits that characterize them and make them unique. These include body conformation, color, and markings. Robert Blakewell (1725–1795) established the methods used in improving animals and establishing breeds. His breeding principles were as follows: select the best type based on usefulness, breed best to best, remember that like tends to beget like, and inbreed to fix characteristics and bring refinement.

The authors provide separate chapters dealing with cattle, swine, sheep, goats, horses, poultry, arctic livestock, llamas and alpacas, dogs, cats, and small stock.

Universities Federation for Animal Welfare. **Management and Welfare of Farm Animals.** London: Bailliere Tindall, 1989. ISBN 0-7020-1316-1.

This multi-authored handbook defines animal welfare as a state of complete mental and physical health where the animal is in harmony with its environment and is housed according to its physiological and ethological needs. For example, if an animal is denied its ethological needs, it will lead to intentional movements, such as pacing, for example, and inappropriate or overtly abnormal behaviors. Many people consider these responses to be signs of frustration and a possible form of emotional distress. This handbook suggests that "an animal must have at least sufficient freedom of movement to be able without difficulty, to turn around, groom itself, get up, lie down and stretch its limbs." In addition, the book states that farm animals should be provided with freedom from thirst, hunger, and malnutrition; appropriate comfort and shelter; freedom to display most normal patterns of behavior; and freedom from fear. Housing conditions should also allow prevention or rapid diagnosis and treatment of injury and disease.

The book describes signs for determining if an animal or group of animals is in a state of well-being. These include physical appearance, behavior, productivity, and the state of their environment. All are described in individual chapters. The species covered include dairy cattle, beef cattle and veal calves, sheep, goats, pigs, rabbits, laying hens, broiler chickens, turkeys, and ducks.

Wilkinson, J. M. **Milk and Meat from Grass.** London: Granada Technical Books, 1984. ISBN 0-246-12290-0.

Wilkinson writes about ruminants and how they transform grass into milk and meat.

Zayan, Rene, ed. **Social Space for Domestic Animals.** Dordrecht: Martinus Nijhoff Publishers, 1985. ISBN 0-7923-0615-5.

This book discusses the spatial needs of laying hens in battery cages, as well as the spatial needs of pigs, dairy cattle, and sheep. It focuses on the relationship between spatial measures (group size and floor space per animal) and social behavior.

Zayan, Rene, and R. Dantzer, eds. **Social Stress in Domestic Animals.** Dordrecht: Kluwer Academic Publishers, 1990.

The papers in this volume deal with animal population density and its impact on aggression, productivity, and health.

Fiction

In contrast to other movements, the animal rights movement has yielded relatively little fiction or poetry about the movement. However, R. J. Hoage and Walter E. Howard, among others, would argue that anthropomorphic projections, such as the ability to talk, are common in fiction. This fiction would include ancient and modern fables, cartoons (both still and animated), and live action films (for example, in the 1960s a U.S. television show featured a fictional talking horse, Mr. Ed, who was often wiser than his inept human master).

Fraser, Antonia. **Your Royal Hostage.** New York: Bantam Books, 1989. ISBN 1-553-28019-8.

Fraser is an author who specializes in historical biographies and mysteries. This book is a mystery that features a series character, Jemima Shore, who is a television news anchorwoman in Great Britain. Shore is covering a royal wedding that is disrupted by a radical animal rights group called Innoright. The members of this group give themselves code names based on animals. The novel describes the interactions between the Innoright members, the royals, and Shore.

Linzey, Andrew, and Thomas Regan, eds. **The Song of Creation: Poetry in Celebration of Animals.** Basingstoke, Hants: Marshall Pickering, 1988.

This book consists of poems about animals. It is intended to increase the understanding of the moral status of animals.

Fur Farming/Trapping

Fur farmers maintain that natural fur is an environmentally *green* alternative, because it is an infinitely renewable biodegradable natural fiber. In contrast, synthetics are made from nonrenewable resources. More than 4.5 million mink are raised per year on more than 2,000 family-owned fur farms. Besides the fur, the fat between the skin and the carcass is used to make mink oil, which is an ingredient in hypoallergenic cosmetics and conditioners for fine leather. The mink carcass is sold to feed companies, which combine it with other meat, fish, and poultry products to make feed for pets and livestock.

Fur Farm Animal Welfare Coalition. **Fur Farming in North America.** St. Paul, MN: Fur Farm Animal Welfare Coalition.

This brochure provides an overview of fur farming in North America. It focuses on the interrelationship of fur farming and other agricultural activities. It also highlights the humane efforts of fur farmers.

National Trappers Association. **Facts about Furs.** Bloomington, IL: National Trappers Association.

This booklet, which describes trapping and fur farming, includes a discussion of traps and trapping procedures.

U.S. Government Publications

Animal Care and Welfare Institute. **Animal Care and Welfare Institute Newsletter.** Beltsville, MD: National Agricultural Library.

This free newsletter is published quarterly and distributed by the National Agricultural Library. It provides current information on all aspects of animal welfare to scientists, technicians, administrators, and the public.

―――――. **List of Publications.** Beltsville, MD: National Agricultural Library.

This is a list of the publications of the Animal Care and Welfare Institute, including *Quick Bibliographies,* which are bibliographies generated by computerized searches of the Agricola database; *Special Reference Briefs,* which are bibliographies generated by computerized searches of multiple databases; the *AWIC Series,* which are information products researched and produced by the staff of the National Agricultural Library; and *AWIC Fact Sheets,* which provide information about the products and services of the National Agricultural Library and the Animal Welfare Information Center.

―――――. **Serials at the National Agricultural Library Relating to Animal Care, Use, and Welfare.** Beltsville, MD: National Agricultural Library, 1990. AWIC Series #5.

This is a list of the scientific journals, dealing with animal care, welfare, and experimentation, in the collection of the National Agricultural Library.

Berry, D'Anna. **Audio-Visuals Relating to Animal Care, Use and Welfare.** Beltsville, MD: National Agricultural Library, 1991. AWIC Series #7.

This book provides an annotated list of videocassettes, films, slides, and audiocassettes that deal with animal rights, welfare, and experimentation. The content of these audiovisual programs varies. Some provide panel discussions of the animal rights debate, while others are designed to provide training for students and professionals who are trying to learn a new experimental technique or how to care for a laboratory animal. The potential audience for these audiovisuals varies from the general public to students to professionals. (See chapter 8 for more information about specific audiovisual programs.)

Berry, D'Anna J. **Reference Materials for Members of Animal Care and Use Committees.** Beltsville, MD: National Agricultural Library, 1991. AWIC Series #10.

The chief executive officer of any U.S. institution receiving federal funds that is engaged in animal research must appoint an Institutional

Animal Care and Use Committee (IACUC) to oversee animal care and welfare. This is a requirement of the U.S. Department of Agriculture's regulations to implement the amendments to the Animal Welfare Act of 1966 (see chapter 5). D'Anna's book provides members of IACUCs with an annotated bibliography of books contained in the National Agricultural Library's collection. These listings deal with subjects including laboratory and surgical procedures; analgesia, anesthesia, euthanasia, and pharmacology; anatomy and physiology; pain assessment; humane care and use of animals in research; animal models; alternatives to animal models; ethics and morals; law, legislation, and regulations; laboratory and farm animals; primates; toxicology; animal behavior and thinking; and disease and pathology.

Berry, D'Anna, and Kathryn L. Bielenberg. **Databases for Biomedical, Veterinary and Animal Science Resources.** Beltsville, MD: National Agriculture Library, 1992. AWIC Factsheet.

This is an annotated list of the databases available from the National Agricultural Library. They include AGRICOLA (Agricultural OnLine Access), AGRIS, BIOETHICSLINE; BIOSIS Previews, CRIS (Current Research Information System [U.S. Department of Agriculture]), CRISP (Computer Retrieval of Information on Scientific Projects), EMBASE, the Federal Register, LEGI-SLATE, Life Sciences Collection, MEDLINE, PNI (Pharmaceutical News Index), Philosopher's Index, Primate Information Center, PsychINFO, TOXNET, and Zoological Record Online. (See chapter 8 for a discussion of selected databases and the methods used to search them.)

Clingerman, Karen. **Animal Care and Use Committees.** Beltsville, MD: National Agricultural Library, 1990. Special Reference Brief 90-06.

Clingerman provides an annotated bibliography of articles that have appeared in scientific journals and meeting abstracts dealing with institutional animal care and use committees.

————. **The LD50 (Median Lethal Dose) and LC50 (Median Lethal Concentration) Toxicity Test.** Beltsville, MD: National Agricultural Library, 1990. Special Reference Brief 90-12.

Clingerman details the two different methods that are commonly used to determine the LD50 and the ED50. These are probit analysis and the up-and-down analysis.

The brief also explains the *therapeutic index,* which is the ratio LD50/ED50, and how it is used to evaluate the risk of using a drug to treat a particular illness. (See chapter 1 for a longer discussion.)

Clingerman, Karen, Carol Dowling, and Janice Swanson. **Searching AGRICOLA for ... Animal Welfare.** Beltsville, MD: Animal Welfare Information Center, National Agricultural Library, 1990. Search Tips Series: STS-03.

The U.S. Department of Agriculture's regulations to implement the 1985 amendments to the Animal Welfare Act of 1966 require a series of literature searches, using databases such as AGRICOLA (Agricultural OnLine Access). These databases are designed to help minimize the number of animals that are used in research and testing (see chapters 5 and 8 for more information).

This book focuses on AGRICOLA, a database provided by the National Agricultural Library. It contains bibliographic information on the care and welfare of laboratory, zoo, and farm animals. The book covers topics such as animal care and handling, humane treatment, animal rights, alternatives to animal testing, and laws and regulations relating to animals. The authors offer suggestions on how to search AGRICOLA to satisfy the requirements of the 1985 amendments, including a list of terms that can be used to make these searches.

Engler, Kevin P. **Animal-Related Computer Simulation Programs for Use in Education and Research.** Beltsville, MD: National Agricultural Library, 1989. AWIC Series #1.

The U.S. Department of Agriculture's regulations to implement the 1985 amendments to the Animal Welfare Act of 1966 (see chapter 5) require scientists to reduce the number of animals used in research, testing, and teaching. The amendments suggest that this be done by replacing animal research with *in vitro* tests, using alternate (lower) species, or creating computer or statistical models. This book provides an annotated list of computer simulation programs that are designed to run on desktop personal computers. The continued development of these computers, as well as high density storage devices (e.g., CD-ROM and videodiscs) and powerful software allow simulation designers to add animated computer graphics, audio and visual recordings, digitized photographs, and 3-D graphics to simulations. Individual programs are designed for audiences ranging from elementary school students to graduate or professional students learning sophisticated subjects such as neuroanatomy or pharmakokinetics (the study of how drugs are absorbed, distributed, and eliminated from the body). Some are designed for professionals, such as scientists and clinicians, who are trying to learn a new experimental or clinical technique. (See chapter 8 for more information about computer simulations.)

Institute of Laboratory Animal Resources, National Research Council. **Guide for the Care and Use of Laboratory Animals.** National Institutes of Health, 1985. 93p. Publication number 86-23. ISBN 0-16-0025-40-0.

The Institute of Laboratory Animal Resources (ILAR) was founded in the United States in 1952 to act as a national and international clearing-house for information on laboratory animal resources and for promoting high-quality, humane care of laboratory animals in the United States ILAR published the first edition of *The Guide for Laboratory Animal Facilities and Care* in 1963. The publication was revised in 1965 and 1968. In 1972, it was revised again and given its current title. It was revised again under that title in 1978. The current edition, which has a slightly different name, is widely accepted by scientific institutions as the primary reference on animal care and use.

The *Guide* places the requirements and recommendations of the Animal Welfare Act and its amendments—as well as other federal, state, and local laws, regulations, and policies—into a practical format that can be used to make day-to-day decisions about the care and use of laboratory animals.

The *Guide* describes the qualifications necessary for personnel who work with animals. Its longest chapter, which deals with laboratory animal husbandry, discusses space recommendations for laboratory animals. These recommendations take into consideration issues such as opportunities for social interactions, temperature, humidity, ventilation, illumination, noise levels, food, bedding, water, sanitation, and waste disposal. They also focus on the control of vermin (pests such as cockroaches, flies, and wild rodents). The book discusses veterinary care, such as observing all animals daily to assess their health and welfare; using appropriate methods to prevent, control, diagnose, and treat diseases and injuries; monitoring surgical programs and postsurgical care; and providing scientists and other animal users with guidance on the handling and restraint of animals, as well as the use of anesthesia, analgesia, and euthanasia.

Physical plant requirements for animal research are also detailed. This includes concerns such as appropriate building materials for floors, walls, and ceilings; the placement of drains; the size and placement of doors and windows; how an aseptic surgery should be set up and run; and the methods to use to control hazardous agents, such as chemical carcinogens. Each chapter has a detailed bibliography. In addition, the following appendices are provided:

1. A detailed bibliography of books and journal articles dealing with laboratory animal care and use
2. A description of the professional organizations that deal with laboratory animals, as well as the organizations that certify personnel that work with animals
3. A brief summary of the laws that deal with laboratory animals

National Agricultural Library. **Guide to the Services of the National Agricultural Library.** Beltsville, MD: National Agricultural Library, 1991.

This publication provides an overview of the National Agricultural Library and its products and services. It describes how potential users may gain access to them.

National Library of Medicine. **A Catalog of Publications, Audiovisuals, & Software.** Bethesda, MD: National Library of Medicine, 1993.

This catalog lists the services and products of the National Library of Medicine, such as software, CD-ROM products, bibliographies, and audiovisuals.

————. **MEDLINE Pocket Card.** Bethesda, MD: National Library of Medicine, 1992.

This contains a brief description of the commands that can be used when searching the MEDLINE database. (See chapter 8 for a detailed discussion of MEDLINE.)

————. **NLM Online Databases and Databanks Fact Sheet.** Bethesda, MD: National Library of Medicine, 1993.

This fact sheet offers an annotated list of the online databases and databanks available from the National Library of Medicine, such as BIOETHICSLINE and MEDLINE (see chapter 8 for more information about these sources).

Office of Protection from Research Risks (OPRR), National Institutes of Health. **Public Health Service Policy on Humane Care and Use of Laboratory Animals.** Bethesda, MD: National Institutes of Health, 1986.

This policy statement of the Public Health Service is aimed at scientists and others who have grants and contracts with one of the National Institutes of Health or any of the other branches of the Public Health Service. It is intended to help them implement the regulations and recommendations contained in the Animal Welfare Act, its amendments, and other federal statutes. It also seeks to help them implement the *U.S. Government Principles for the Utilization and Care of Vertebrate Animals Used in Testing, Research, and Training* that was developed by the Interagency Research Animal Committee.

In this policy statement, OPRR focuses primarily on the constituency and responsibilities of the Institutional Animal Care and Use Committee (IACUC). When a grant proposal or contract is submitted to the Public Health Service, it must be accompanied by a verification letter from the

IACUC stating that it has reviewed the proposal and found that it complied with all of the requirements of the Animal Welfare Act and its amendments, as well as other federal statutes dealing with animals and their use. (See chapter 1 for a detailed explanation of the IACUC.)

Swanson, Janice. **The Draize Eye-Irritancy Test.** Beltsville, MD: National Agricultural Library, 1988. Special Reference Brief 89-02.

The eye-irritancy test was developed by J. H. Draize, G. Woodward, and H. O. Calvery ("Methods for the Study of Irritation and Toxicity of Substances Applied Topically to the Skin and Mucous Membranes," *Journal of Pharmacology and Experimental Therapeutics* 82 [1944]: 377–390). The test was designed to assess the potential eye irritation caused by products such as drugs applied to the eye, cosmetics and toiletries, household detergents and chemicals, and industrial chemicals. A small amount of the potential irritant is instilled into one eye each of four to six rabbits. The other eye serves as a control. Tissue changes in the iris, cornea, and conjunctiva are noted as they occur. Rabbit eyes are more sensitive than human eyes, so if a chemical does not cause irritation in the rabbit, it is unlikely to cause irritation in humans.

The Draize test is controversial. Its proponents claim that the Draize (1) provides quantitative and qualitative information about the type and level of irritation; (2) allows the testing of complete products or component chemicals; and (3) allows observation of the recovery and healing processes. Opponents, mainly members of the animal rights community, claim that (1) there is a lack of reproducibility from different laboratories; (2) the scoring procedures are subjective; and (3) the test is ethically unacceptable. The book details a number of *in vitro* tests now under development that might provide an alternative to the Draize test. However, it notes that no single *in vitro* test provides as comprehensive an evaluation of irritation potential as the Draize test.

Thompson, Rebecca, and Karl Schneider. **ALF (Agricultural Library Forum): The National Agricultural Library's Electronic Bulletin Board System.** Beltsville, MD: National Agricultural Library, 1992.

This guide provides an introduction to the National Agricultural Library's electronic bulletin board, ALF, which allows individual users and groups of users to interact and share information about animal care and welfare. (See chapter 8 for a more detailed description of ALF.)

Van Sluyters, Richard C., and Michael D. Oberdorfer, eds. **Preparation and Maintenance of Higher Mammals during Neuroscience Experiments.** Bethesda, MD: National Institutes of Health, 1991. Publication number 91-3207.

This book provides scientists and members of institutional animal care and use committees with the background needed to write and evaluate grant proposals and experimental protocols dealing with neuroscience experiments. It covers survival and nonsurvival surgical preparations, the methods that should be used to evaluate and maintain physiological state, methods of physical restraint, anesthesia and analgesia, and the training and supervision of people involved in neuroscience research.

Law Books

American Law Book Company. **Corpus Juris Secundum (CJS).** St. Paul, MN: West Publishing.

CJS is a multi-volume treatise or commentary on the law. It analyzes federal, state, and local statutes and regulations, as well as case law (federal and state court decisions) dealing with a wide variety of issues including animals and cruelty to animals.

Animal Welfare Institute. **Animals and Their Legal Rights.** Washington, DC: Animal Welfare Institute, 1978.

This book provides a survey of the animal protection laws in the United States from 1641 to 1978.

Favre, David S., and Murray Loring. **Animal Law.** Westport, CT: Quorum Books, 1983. 253p. ISBN 0-89930-021-9.

Favre and Loring provide a detailed analysis of the animal welfare laws concerning humane care, cruelty, and duty to provide care, including a comparison of individual state statutes. They also discuss the powers and duties of the Society for the Prevention of Cruelty to Animals. Individual chapters cover animal ownership, limitations of ownership, and animal bailment, sale, medical care, and recovery. These chapters contain detailed bibliographies.

Moretti, Daniel S. **Animal Rights and the Law.** New York: Oceana Publications, 1984. 147p. ISBN 0-379-11147-0.

This book introduces the general public to their legal rights and responsibilities with respect to animals. Moretti presents an overview of anti-cruelty, animal fighting, humane slaughter, and transportation regulations on a state-by-state basis, including the citations needed to find the official text of the law. State and federal laws concerning wildlife protection and animal trapping are discussed. Moretti also covers the 1983 case of *Edward Taub v. State of Maryland,* also known as the Silver

Spring "Monkey Case" (see chapters 2–4). Taub was the first scientist to be convicted of violating a state's anti-cruelty statute.

United States Code (USC). Washington, DC: Government Printing Office.

This is the official multi-volume compilation of the U.S. statutes. Two volumes of the USC are especially useful. They are (1) the general index, which lists key words that can be used to find statutes dealing with specific topics, such as animals, and (2) the index of popular names of specific statutes. For example, by using the latter index, it is possible to determine that the Research or Experimentation—Cats and Dogs Act (the first federal statute dealing with animal experimentation) is Public Law 89-543. Knowing a statute's number can help locate the text of the statute, its legislative history, and other information. For example, this index would also provide the citation for the statute (80 Stat. 350) in *Statutes at Large*, which is a multi-volume chronological compilation of laws.

United States Code Annotated (USCA). St. Paul, MN: West Publishing.

This is a multi-volume, unofficial compilation of federal statutes and their amendments, which are arranged by topic. In addition to the text of the statute, USCA presents historical footnotes, annotations to law review articles, and cases construing various statutory provisions. It is updated annually with pocket pieces and paperbound advance sheets.

United States Code Congressional and Administrative News. St. Paul, MN: West Publishing.

This is an unofficial chronological (arranged by congressional session) compilation of federal statutes. The text of a statute is presented along with its legislative history, which includes an opening statement, a statement of the statute's purpose, a summary of the outcome of congressional hearings, and a listing of the committees that worked on the statute and their reports. It also includes a chronological record of the actions of the U.S. House of Representatives and Senate with regard to the initial bill and its passage.

U.S. Federal Agencies. **Code of Federal Regulations.** Washington, DC: Office of the Federal Register, 1992.

This official multi-volume compilation of regulations and their amendments is arranged so that regulations covering the same topic are printed in the same section of the book. Federal regulations are published chronologically in the *Federal Register*, then codified in the *Code of Federal*

Regulations (CFR). Within the CFR, federal regulations dealing with animal welfare are found in subchapter A (Animal Welfare) of chapter 1 (Animal and Plant Health Inspection Service, Department of Agriculture) of Title 9 (Animals and Animal Products).

Primates

The great classifier Carl von Linne (better known by the Latinized version of his name, Linnaeus) placed the human species, which he named *Homo sapiens* (translated literally "man wise") into the same order as the monkeys and apes. He named this order primates. It consists of 11 families, 60 genera, and approximately 191 species. Recent research suggests that the African apes (the gorillas and chimpanzees) and humans split off from a common ancestor about 4 million years ago. Modern geneticists tell us that humans and chimpanzees share 99 percent of the same genes.

In recent decades, there have been reports of remarkably humanlike behaviors such as fashioning and using simple tools (J. Goodall, *In the Shadow of Man*, Boston: Houghton Mifflin, 1983); learning and even inventing new signs in American Sign Language; and learning to manipulate tokens in a synthetic language (Eugene Linden, *Apes, Men, and Language*, New York: Penguin Books, 1976). These discoveries suggest that we might have to reevaluate our ethical and moral stand with regard to chimpanzees and the other great apes.

The Food Security Act of 1985–Subtitle F Animal Welfare amends the Animal Welfare Act of 1966. It extends the minimum standard of care to provide a physical environment that is adequate to promote the psychological well-being of primates.

Goodall, Jane. **In the Shadow of Man.** Boston: Houghton Mifflin, 1983. 384p. ISBN 0-395-33145-5.

Goodall was one of the first humans to spend a significant amount of time observing chimpanzees in their natural habitat. She provides what is probably the first description of toolmaking and use by chimpanzees. Goodall describes how a chimpanzee strips the leaves off a small branch and inserts it into a termite mound to extract termites. Toolmaking and language (see Linden, below) are two hallmarks of humanness—the characteristics that separate humans from the rest of the animals.

————. **Through a Window: My Thirty Years with the Chimpanzees of Gombe.** Boston: Houghton Mifflin, 1990. 33p. ISBN 0-395-50081-8.

Goodall has spent most of her adult life studying and living with chimpanzees in their natural habitat, and being treated as almost one of their number. She eloquently makes the point that chimpanzees are more like us than any other living creature. This book reads like a novel describing the day-to-day life of the chimpanzees of the Gombe Research Station.

Kellogg, W. N., and L. A. Kellogg. **The Ape and the Child.** New York: McGraw-Hill, 1933.

In one of the first attempts to establish meaningful communication between a chimpanzee and a human, the Kelloggs took a female chimpanzee, Gua, from its mother at the age of seven and one-half months. They raised Gua alongside their own nine-month-old son, Donald. The Kelloggs compare and contrast the growth and development of the two infants.

Kirkwood, James A., and K. Stathatos. **Biology, Rearing, and Care of Young Primates.** Oxford: Oxford University Press, 1992. 168p. ISBN 0-19-854733-1.

In the past, nonhuman primates were taken from their natural habitats for use in research, in zoos, and as pets. This is no longer possible because many nonhuman primates, including all of the great apes, are endangered species. Therefore, Kirkwood and Stathatos say, it is vital that we develop the methods and procedures needed to breed and maintain primates in captivity. This is especially true since it is likely that populations of many species of primates, especially the great apes, will continue to decrease in their natural habitat because of poaching and habitat destruction. It is vital that we maintain sufficient numbers of selected primates to maintain genetic diversity for the future.

The authors provide basic information about the appropriate sex ratio, gestation period, breeding season, and longevity of 18 species of primates. These species include representatives from 9 of the 11 primate families. Also described are details on infant management, accommodation, and how to reintegrate artificially reared infants into peer or family groups. Finally, the authors provide important information about energy intake throughout growth and development.

Linden, Eugene. **Apes, Men, and Language.** New York: Penguin Books, 1976. ISBN 0-14-021896-3.

Although chimpanzees are relatively close relatives of human beings, their vocal tract is relatively short and poorly controlled. Therefore it is unlikely that they could produce human speech. However, this does not mean that they cannot acquire language. Robert M. Yerkes, a pioneer primatologist (see Yerkes, below), was one of the first scientists to suggest that the great apes could be taught a language based on gesture rather than vocalizations.

Linden provides a popular overview of the primatology work of R. Allen and Beatrice Gardner in their attempt to teach a chimpanzee, named Washoe, American Sign Language or *Ameslan*. Ameslan, which is a language developed to help deaf people communicate, is based on a series of hand and arm gestures that signify words or concepts. Ameslan gestures can be supplemented with finger spelling to convey ideas for which there are no gestures. While still controversial, the Gardners and their associate, Roger Fouts, claim that Washoe uses Ameslan in a very humanlike manner.

Linden also provides an overview of the work of primatologist David Premack and the chimpanzee Sarah. The *language* that Sarah is learning is very different from Ameslan. It consists of a series of arbitrarily shaped and colored plastic tokens, which represent specific concepts. Premack and Sarah communicate by arranging these tokens into messages written from top to bottom.

Novak, Melinda A., and Andrew J. Petto, eds. **Through the Looking Glass: Issues of Psychological Well-Being in Captive Nonhuman Primates.** Washington, DC: American Psychological Association, 1991. 285p. ISBN 1-55798-087-X.

The only rational reason for using nonhuman primates as surrogates for humans in biomedical or psychological research is because they resemble humans so closely. Chimpanzees, for example, have 99 percent of the same genetic material as humans.

Whether physically or psychologically ill, it is clear that an unhealthy primate will not provide an accurate model of a human. Therefore, scientists and clinicians sought methods and procedures to maintain the physical and psychological health of the primates in their charge long before the mandates outlined in the 1985 amendments to the Animal Welfare Act of 1966.

This book describes how to evaluate and promote psychological well-being in nonhuman primates. It also provides a brief overview of public (nonscientist) perception of primate research.

Reynolds, Vernon. **The Apes: The Gorilla, Chimpanzee, Orangutan, and Gibbon, Their History and Their World.** New York: E. P. Dutton, 1967.

Reynolds provides an excellent introduction to the behavior and natural life of the great apes. He describes the circumstances under which man first encountered these species as well as the natural environment of each species and their adaptations to that environment. Reynolds notes that all of the great apes are considered endangered species in their natural habitats. Although hunting or trapping these species has been illegal for several decades, poaching is still a problem, as is the loss of habitat because of land development.

Because of their similarity to humans, great apes have been used as surrogates for humans in medical and psychological experiments. The great apes, and particularly the chimpanzee, have made invaluable contributions to the study of the causes and development of methods to prevent or cure diseases such as malaria, poliomyelitis, diphtheria, syphilis, whooping cough, heart disease, and cancer. In the early 1960s, two chimpanzees, Ham and Enos, made important space flights that demonstrated that launching, acceleration, weightlessness, and reentry were safe for human beings. These early chimpanzee flights allowed manned space flight to develop.

Ruppenthal, Gerald C., ed. **Nursery Care of Nonhuman Primates.** New York: Plenum Press, 1979. ISBN 0-306-40150-9.

Ruppenthal says it is likely and essential that nonhuman primates will serve as surrogates for humans. His book is divided into the following five sections concerning these animals: pregnancy and prenatal development; early assessment procedures; the nursery care and management of three commonly used genera (*Papio, Saimuri,* and *Macaca*); housing and early social development; and more exotic species.

Schaller, George B. **The Mountain Gorilla: Ecology and Behavior.** Chicago: University of Chicago Press, 1988. 484p. ISBN 0-226-73649-0.

Schaller provides an overview of the scientific literature dealing with the ecology and behavior of the mountain gorilla. He supplements this information with his own observations of mountain gorillas in their native habitat.

Yerkes, Robert M. **Chimpanzees: A Laboratory Colony.** New Haven, CT: Yale University Press, 1943.

Yerkes was one of the pioneers in the study of the behavior of nonhuman primates. Most of his work focused on the study of the chimpanzee's abilities. This book offers an overview of his work. It describes the methods Yerkes and his colleagues used to set up one of the first laboratory colonies for the breeding and study of nonhuman primates.

Professional Societies

Most scientists and clinicians who work with animals are members of one or more professional societies. One of the functions of these societies is to provide a canon of ethics for professionals. Another is to provide a forum, typically at a national or international meeting, for the interchange of ideas and information. These organizations include the Federation of American Societies for Experimental Biology, the American Psychological Association, the American Physiological Society, the Society for Neuroscience, and the American Association for Laboratory Animal Science (a group that sets ethical standards for technicians who work with animals).

Animal Care and Experimentation Committee. **Sourcebook for the Use of Animals in Physiological Research and Teaching.** Bethesda, MD: American Physiological Society, 1993.

This book highlights the American Physiological Society's ethical standards and provides advice on how to deal with animal rights activists.

Vegetarianism

Many animal rights activists argue that animals have an equal natural right to life and, thus, vegetarianism is morally obligatory.

Akers, Keith. **A Vegetarian Sourcebook.** New York: Putman's, 1986. 246p. ISBN 0-931411-04-1.

Akers discusses the nutritional, ecological, and ethical aspects of vegetarianism.

Altman, Nathaniel. **Eating for Life: The Ultimate Diet.** New York: Vegetus Books, 1986.

Altman holds that humans are anatomically, physiologically, and instinctively suited to a diet of fruits, vegetables, nuts, and grains.

Braunstein, Mark M. **Radical Vegetarianism: A Dialectic of Diet and Ethics.** 2d ed. Los Angeles: Panjandrum Books, 1993. 160p. ISBN 0-9635663-1-8.

Braunstein discusses the advantages of eating fruits and avoiding consumption of flesh and milk.

Dyer, Judith C. **Vegetarianism: An Annotated Bibliography** Metuchen, NJ: Scarecrow Press, 1982. 292p. ISBN 0-8108-1532-X.

This annotated bibliography dealing with the vegetarian lifestyle covers the history of the movement, as well as the medical and philosophical aspects of vegetarianism. It also provides a list of more than 200 vegetarian cookbooks.

Hartbarger, Janie C., and J. Neil. **Eating for the Eighties: A Complete Guide to Vegetarian Nutrition.** Philadelphia: Saunders Press, 1981.

The authors maintain that meat is not good for you. They propose a vegetarian diet that they say is suitable for normal adults, as well as pregnant females, babies, children, and athletes.

Hur, Robin. **Food Reform: Our Desperate Need.** Austin, TX: Heidelberg Press, 1975.

Hur maintains that the vegan diet, which avoids animal fat and protein, sugar, salt, and processed foods, leads to a decrease in degenerative diseases.

Inglis, Jane. **Some People Don't Eat Meat.** Herts: Oakroyd Press, 1987.

This book is designed to describe the vegetarian lifestyle to primary and elementary school children.

Robbins, John. **Diet for a New America: How Your Food Choices Affect Your Health, Happiness and the Future of Life on Earth.** Walpole, NH: Stillpoint Publishing, 1987. 432p. ISBN 0-913299-54-5.

Robbins argues for the vegetarian lifestyle. He proposes that organizations such as the National Livestock and Meat Board, the National Dairy Council, and the National Commission on Egg Nutrition have fostered a false and harmful obsession with protein. Robbins argues that animal-based diets that are high in protein and fat are responsible for the increase in degenerative diseases such as arteriosclerosis and cancer.

Salt, Henry S. **The Logic of Vegetarianism: Essays and Dialogues.** London: George Bell, 1906.

Salt presents the moral, scientific, economic, health, social, and aesthetic arguments for vegetarianism. He provides a comprehensive critique for antivegetarianism. Many of the arguments that Salt refuted in this book are still used by people to argue against vegetarianism.

Tryon, Thomas. **The Way to Health, Long Life and Happiness.**
London: Andrew Sowle, 1683.

Tryon, who was born in 1634, decided in the mid-seventeenth century to
forbear eating any kind of meat. Instead, he confined himself to bread
and fruit, later adding butter and cheese. This is the first book in the
English language to use the term "rights" in regard to animals. Tryon
was widely read in both England and America. Benjamin Franklin was
greatly impressed on reading his books and reportedly became a *Tryonist*
for a time.

8

Selected Nonprint Resources

THERE ARE MANY NONPRINT SOURCES OF INFORMATION about the animal rights debate. This chapter lists computer databases and simulation programs on the subject, as well as a number of instructional videotapes.

Databases

Prior to 1966, the primary way to obtain recent information about a topic was to search through the printed (hard-copy) version of the appropriate indexing or abstracting service, such as *Index Medicus, Psychological Abstracts, Biological Abstracts,* or *Chemical Abstracts.* These printed databases are updated monthly or bimonthly and are typically cumulated at the end of the year.

Searching printed databases, which could be done by author or subject index, is tedious. The subject index is generally divided into major headings and subheadings. Each author or subject entry has one or more numbers associated with it referring to a specific abstract. The abstract contains a complete bibliographic entry (author's name, the title of the article, journal name, year, volume, and pages), as well as a brief description of the contents of the article.

In 1963, The National Library of Medicine introduced MEDLARS (Medical Literature Analysis and Retrieval System), a computer database based on *Index Medicus*. In 1966, MEDLINE (*MED*LARS On*line*) was introduced. With appropriate hardware and software, an individual can sit at a terminal or a personal computer and connect "online" via telephone lines to a large mainframe computer located at the National Library of Medicine and search the MEDLINE database.

There are many advantages to online searching. The most obvious is the speed with which the computer can select the appropriate items out of millions of citations. Another advantage is currency. MEDLINE is currently updated weekly from January to October and monthly in November and December. More than 30,000 citations are added each month.

With the computerized version, all elements of an entry are available when doing a search. This includes the author's name, title words, key words or subject terms, affiliations of the author(s), journal name, publication date, language, and format (e.g., article or literature review). Prior to the mid-1980s, when the text of the abstract or the full paper was present, it was in the form of an "image" of the page. This was because the text of the abstract or article was not typed into the database, but rather scanned in. In other words, when text of the abstract or paper was scanned into a database, it was treated as a "picture" of the text, rather than as text. Improvements in scanning technology have allowed database producers to scan an article into the database and treat it as text. That means that it is possible to search the text word by word and if you download the text of the abstract or paper to your computer, you can edit it in much the same manner as text you typed into the computer.

The items listed above (i.e., author's name, key words) or, when available, the entire text of the abstract or article, can be combined with Boolean logic operators: "and," "or," "and/or," "not." For example, if you search the database for "alcohol" "and" "review," you would get a list of all articles contained in the database that dealt with alcohol and were reviews. Or if you searched "alcohol" "not" "English," you would get a list of all articles that dealt with alcohol but were not in English.

MEDLINE can also be searched using 16,000 MeSH (medical subject headings) terms that are arranged hierarchically into one or more of 15 major categories called "trees." For example, "Anatomical Terms (A)" is a major tree heading under which the nervous system is represented by A8, the central nervous system by A8.186, the brain by A8.186.211, and the brain stem by A8.186.211.132. By using Boolean logic operators, the MeSH tree headings can be combined with subheadings or qualifiers. For example, the subheading "Abnormalities" could be combined using the Boolean logic operator "AND" with the MeSH heading A8.186.211.132 (brain stem) to yield a list of articles describing abnormalities of the brain stem.

Since 1966, a wide variety of databases have become available online either from the originator (e.g., MEDLINE comes from the National Library of Medicine) or from a database provider (e.g., DIALOG Information Services, Inc., of Palo Alto, California). Many of these databases provide bibliographic citations, abstracts, and/or the full text of the article.

In the mid-1980s, selected databases began to appear on CD-ROM (compact disk read only memory). SilverPlatter (Newton Lower Falls, Massachusetts) and Dialog OnDisc (Palo Alto, California) are database providers on CD-ROM. Like the familiar audio CD, the CD-ROM is made of durable plastic with a reflective metal coating and lacquered surface. A typical CD-ROM can hold the equivalent of 330,000 typewritten pages. With appropriate hardware and software, a database on CD-ROM can be searched in basically the same manner as an online database.

A Sample Literature Search

The U.S. Department of Agriculture regulations to implement the 1985 amendments to the Animal Welfare Act of 1966 (see chapter 5) require that principal investigator(s), when seeking to have an experimental protocol approved by their local Institutional Animal Care and Use Committee, must perform a series of literature searches. The goal of these searches is to minimize the number of animals that are used in research and testing.

In Phase I of the literature search (reduction and refinement), the goal is to determine if the proposed work is duplicating studies that have already been performed and/or to refine the experimental techniques. In Phase II (replacement), the goal is to determine if animals can be replaced with (1) *in vitro* tests (such as a product, enzyme, or tissue that can be grown and tested in culture); (2) computer or statistical models; or (3) alternate (lower) species, such as fish or invertebrates.

For example, BIOSIS Previews (see description below) would be searched under the following concept codes: "toxicology—general, methods, and experimental"; "pharmacological testing"; and "toxicology—environmental and industrial" to find references dealing with testing. Alternatives to whole animal testing could be found under the concept codes: "*in vitro* studies—cellular and subcellular"; "tissue culture—apparatus, methods and media"; and "mathematical biology and statistical methods."

The descriptor "animal testing alternatives" could be used to search MEDLINE for similar information, although this heading tends to cover legislative history and ethical issues. However, the MeSH terms "toxicology" and "models" could be coordinated with the descriptors "cell," "tissue," "organ culture," or *in vitro.* Other descriptors that might yield useful results include "drug screening," "mutagenicity tests," "teratogens," "toxins," "morphogenesis," "neurotoxins," "carcinogens," or "abnormalties, drug induced."

EMBASE (Excerpta Medica Online [see below]) would be searched under its "master list of medical terms" such as "toxicity testing," "toxicology," "*in vitro* study," and "nonbiological model."

The cost of doing a literature search varies widely, even when searching the same database, because they are available in different formats, from a number of different vendors. Normally, access to an "online" database is via one of the large vendors (e.g., Dialog, CompuServ). The cost of an online search depends on the time of day the search is done, which vendor is selected, how long the search takes, and whether the results of the search are collected online (i.e., downloaded directly to the searcher's computer) or printed offline and mailed to the searcher.

For example, it is possible to go online with one of the vendors and type in a search and then disconnect. The actual search may be done in the middle of the night and the results mailed to the searcher. On the other hand, it is possible to go online and conduct the search, modifying the search based on the results obtained and then downloading the results directly to the searcher's computer. Depending on the database and the vendor, the first search might cost an order of magnitude less than the second search. Some institutions, such as college or university libraries, public libraries, etc., subsidize the cost of the searches.

Databases available on CD-ROM are essentially free to the individual end user. But the cost of the database and the software to use it can be quite high—thousands of dollars per year.

Many databases might be consulted to complete the literature search. Following is a selection of the many possibilities.

AGRICOLA
Source: U.S. National Agricultural Library
            Beltsville, MD

AGRICOLA, which contains bibliographic data dating back to 1970, is updated monthly. It contains more than 2 million records and indexes, U.S. federal agencies' publications, FAO reports, publications of state agricultural experiment stations and extension services, as well as about 600 periodicals. It provides worldwide coverage of the literature of agricultural science and related topics, including the welfare of animals used for exhibition, education, and research.

Analytical Abstracts
Source: Royal Society of Chemistry
            Cambridge, England

The monthly, bibliographical Analytical Abstracts offers information from 1980 to present. It contains references from more than 1,300 journals that deal with all aspects of analytical chemistry, including pharmaceutical and environmental.

BIOBUSINESS
Source: BIOSIS
            Philadelphia, PA

BIOBUSINESS contains bibliographical references to more than 600 technical and business journals, magazines, newsletters, meeting proceedings, patents, and books. All deal with the business applications of biological and biomedical research, including those dealing with pharmaceuticals, medical devices, and toxicology. This database is updated weekly and contains listings from 1985 forward.

BIOETHICSLINE
Source: U.S. National Library of Medicine
            Bethesda, MD

The bimonthly updated BIOETHICSLINE provides bibliographic citations about human and animal experimentation. It also covers topics such as euthanasia, organ donation and transplantation, allocation of healthcare resources, patients' rights, codes of professional conduct, reproductive technologies, abortion, health therapies, and AIDS. More than 2,400 records are added each year to this database, which provides coverage from 1973 to present.

BIOSIS Previews
Source: BIOSIS
Philadelphia, PA

BIOSIS Previews, which provides listings from 1969 forward, provides weekly updates. It contains more than 8 million citations that provide worldwide coverage of biological and biomedical sciences. BIOSIS Previews offers abstracts from over 7,600 primary journals and monographs, which yield more than 280,000 citations each year. It also includes 260,000 citations a year from meeting abstracts, reviews, books, notes, letters, government reports, and research communications.

CA Search (CAS)
Source: Chemical Abstracts Service
Columbus, OH

CA Search contains more than 10 million bibliographic citations to the worldwide literature dealing with chemistry and its applications. It can be searched by the CAS Registry number system, which assigns a unique number to each specific chemical compound. This database, which is updated biweekly, offers coverage from 1967 to present.

CAB Abstracts
Source: CAB International
Slough, England

CAB Abstracts offers coverage from 1972 to present. It provides bibliographical coverage of more than 8,500 journals worldwide that contain information about agricultural and biological sciences. About 130,000 items are added each year with updates added monthly.

CANCERLIT
Source: U.S. National Cancer Institute
Bethesda, MD

CANCERLIT, which has listings from 1963, offers bibliographical listings covering all aspects of experimental and clinical studies dealing with cancer. It searches more than 3,500 biomedical journals, as well as meeting proceedings, books, reports, and doctoral theses, and is updated with more than 6,000 new references each month.

Chemical Industry Notes
Source: Chemical Abstracts Service
Columbus, OH

The bibliographical Chemical Industry Notes offers coverage from 1974 to present and provides weekly updates. It indexes more than 80 journals, newspapers, and trade magazines worldwide that deal with the business aspects of the chemical industry.

CHEMTOX ONLINE
Source: Resource Consultants, Inc.
            Brentwood, TN

This directory provides only current information. It offers updates quarterly concerning about 6,400 chemicals that are dangerous to individuals and/or the environment.

Conference Papers Index
Source: Cambridge Scientific Abstracts
            Bethesda, MD

This bibliographical source provides access to papers dating since 1973 that were presented at more than 1,000 major regional, national, and international scientific and technical meetings each year. It offers bimonthly updates.

Current Contents Search
Source: Institute for Scientific Information
            Philadelphia, PA

Current Contents Search offers, as its name suggests, only current bibliographical listings. It is a weekly updated resource that allows searches of the tables of contents of leading journals in the sciences. There is a time lag between when an article appears in a journal (or when a presentation from a professional meeting yields an abstract) and the time the citation to that article (or abstract) appears in any database. This lag time has been steadily decreasing over the last decade. Further, *Current Contents* provides virtually immediate access to articles that appear in journals. This is because the table of contents, which lists the articles that appear in an issue of a journal, is provided to *Current Contents* at or before publication. Thus, this database provides timely access.

DERWENT RINGDOC
Source: Derwent Publications, Inc.
            London, England

DERWENT RINGDOC, which offers coverage from 1964 to present, provides monthly updates of bibliographical information from 800 key worldwide journals dealing with the pharmaceutical industry. More than 4,000 records are added each month.

Dissertation Abstracts Online
Source: University Microfilms International
Ann Arbor, MI

Updated monthly, this bibliographic database provides an author, title, and subject guide to virtually every doctoral dissertation accepted by accredited educational institutions since 1861, when the first academic doctoral degree was granted.

EMBASE (Excerpta Medica)
Source: Elsevier Science Publishers
Amsterdam, Netherlands

EMBASE, which offers information from 1974 to present, contains bibliographical citations from over 3,500 pharmacological and biomedical journals worldwide. Over 350,000 records are added each year, with updates made weekly.

F-D-C Reports
Source: F-D-C Reports, Inc.
Chevy Chase, MD

F-D-C Reports provides the complete text from articles dealing with the healthcare industry, including pharmacology and toxicology. *F-D-C* has offerings dating from 1987 and is updated weekly.

Federal Research in Progress
Source: National Technical Information Service
Springfield, VA

This monthly updated resource provides access to bibliographical information about federally funded research projects dating from 1970 to present. For each project listed, Federal Research records the project's title, the name of the principal investigator, and the performing/sponsoring organization. It also offers a description of the research.

International Pharmaceutical Abstracts
Source: American Society of Hospital Pharmacists
Bethesda, MD

This bibliographic database, which offers information from 1970 to present, provides monthly updates. It covers more than 650 pharmaceutical, medical, and related journals, as well as state pharmacy journals.

Life Sciences Collection
Source: Cambridge Scientific Abstracts
Bethesda, MD

The Life Sciences Collection is a bibliographic resource that provides monthly updates and has information dating from 1978.

Magazine Index
Source: Information Access Co.
            Foster City, CA

This bibliographical resource, which offers coverage from 1973 to present, offers weekly updates on the contents of more than 500 popular magazines.

NEWSEARCH
Source: Information Access Co.
            Foster City, CA

Users of this bibliographical service, which provides listings for the current month only, can receive a daily index of news stories and articles from 1,700 newspapers, magazines, and periodicals.

NIOSHTIC (Occupational Safety and Health)
Source: National Institute for Occupational Safety and Health
            Cincinnati, OH

Offering information dating from 1973 to present, NIOSHTIC provides citations to more the 2,000 different journals, as well as more than 70,000 monographs and technical reports that deal with all aspects of occupation safety and health. It is updated quarterly.

NTIS (National Technical Information Service)
Source: National Technical Information Service
            Springfield, VA

The NTIS provides coverage dates from 1964 to present. This bibliographical resource lists the results of government-sponsored research, development, engineering, and analysis.

Pharmaceutical and Healthcare Industry News Database
Source: PJB Publications
            Surrey, England

This database is a complete-text resource. It provides coverage of worldwide pharmaceutical matters, medical devices, and animal health. It is updated daily.

Pharmaceutical News Index
Source: UMI/Data Courier
            Louisville, KY

The Pharmaceutical News Index is an online bibliographical source of information about pharmaceuticals, cosmetics, and medical devices. It is updated weekly and offers coverage from 1974 to present.

PHARMAPROJECTS
Source: PJB Publications
           Surrey, England

PHARMAPROJECTS is a monthly updated directory that provides information about the progress on new pharmaceutical products. It provides information dating from 1980 to present.

PsycINFO
Source: American Psychological Association
           Washington, DC

PsycINFO, which is updated monthly, provides a bibliography of worldwide literature in psychology and the behavioral sciences dating from 1967 to present.

Registry of Toxic Effects of Chemical Substances
Source: National Institute for Occupational Safety and Health
           Address not available

This quarterly updated registry provides a comprehensive dictionary of basic toxicological information on more than 100,000 chemical substances. Its information dates from 1971 to present.

SCISEARCH
Source: Institute for Scientific Information
           Philadelphia, PA

SCISEARCH, which is updated weekly, presents bibliographical information dating from 1974 to present. It allows retrieval of newly published articles based on an author's reference to prior articles. For example, if a search of MEDLINE, AGRICOLA, and other sources yielded information about an article written several years ago that described a particular *in vitro* test, then SCISEARCH can be searched for the author's name. Accessing SCISEARCH would yield a list of all papers that cited the original author's work. The list contains a complete bibliographic reference to the article(s) that cited the original author's work. SCISEARCH is valuable because it allows an investigator to follow the impact of a particular idea or technique forward in time. If no one cites a particular paper, it may mean that the paper had minimum or no impact. If many people cite it, that may mean it is having an impact.

  SCISEARCH also allows searches by test words via the PERMU-TEXT index. This is especially valuable for new terms, because they often appear as PERMUTEXT entries before they become available as text terms in other databases.

TOXLINE
Source: U.S. National Library of Medicine
            Bethesda, MD

The monthly updated TOXLINE offers bibliographical listings covering the adverse effects of chemicals, drugs, and physical agents on living systems.

TOXNET
Source: U.S. National Library of Medicine
            Bethesda, MD

TOXNET is updated monthly. It contains the Hazardous Substances Data Bank, the Toxicology Data Base, and the Chemical Carcinogenesis Research Information System. It also provides numerical toxicological and biochemical data.

Unlisted Drugs
Source: Pharmaco Medical Documentation, Inc.
            Madison, NJ

Unlisted Drugs is a complete-text database that is updated monthly. It provides online information about new drugs including the drug's name, the company code for the drug, the drug's pharmacological use, and its chemical and molecular formulas. It also provides bibliographical citations.

Computer Simulation Programs

Long before the 1985 regulations (see chapter 5) made it a formal requirement, scientists and clinicians were striving to limit the number of animals used in research, product testing, and, especially, teaching.

One method that is used to replace animals is to develop computer models or simulations. Prior to the 1980s, the output of computer simulations were graphs or simple line drawings. The continued development of powerful desktop computers, high density storage devices (e.g., CD-ROM, videodiscs), powerful software, and networking (i.e., connecting powerful desktop computers to even more powerful mainframe computers) has allowed simulation designers to add 3-D graphics, as well as digitized photographs to simulations.

Animated computer graphics, as well as audio and visual recordings, can also be used in simulations. Computer-based multimedia simulations, especially those using interactive videodiscs, provide a powerful teaching tool. These simulations aim at a wide range of users including laypeople; high school or college students learning subjects such as anatomy, physiology, and pharmacology; graduate or professional students learning more sophisticated subjects such as neuroanatomy or pharmakokinetics (the study of how drugs are absorbed, distributed, and eliminated from the body); and professionals, such as scientists and clinicians, who are trying to learn a new experimental or clinical technique. The following listings offer a variety of computer simulation programs, including ones that use animated graphics.

For the programs below, contact the source of the software for current price and availability. The National Agricultural Library (10301 Baltimore Blvd., Beltsville, MD 20705) acts as a clearinghouse for information about animal rights/animal welfare and can supply information about new software.

Anesthesia and Analgesia of Laboratory Animals
Source: Dr. R. T. Fosse
Laboratory Animal Veterinary Hospital University of Bergen
Armauer Hansen's House
Haukeland Hospital N-5021 Bergen, Norway

This program (MacIntosh SE/plus, SE30, MacII, or MacIIcs) is aimed at a graduate/professional audience. It teaches the user the principles of anesthesia and analgesia for rats, mice, and guinea pigs. It covers inhalation, injection, and local anesthesia. The program also details dose calculations for common drugs, and how to recognize pain and use analgesics to eliminate it.

Behavior on a Disk
Source: CMS Academic Software
Address not available

This program is designed for undergraduates, as well as graduate students. It simulates learning phenomena, such as the shaping of behavior and the effect of positive reinforcement.

Biology Dissection Guides
Source: Carolina Biological Supply Co.
2700 York Rd.
Burlington, NC 27215

This program (Apple II or IBM PC) for middle school and high school students simulates the dissection of a starfish, earthworm, clam, crayfish, grasshopper, perch, and frog.

Cardiac Electrophysiology and Pharmacology
Source: Dr. J. R. Walker
Integrated Functional Laboratory
University of Texas Medical Branch
Galveston, TX 77550

This IBM or compatible graduate/professional program presents five simultaneous electrophysiological traces that represent the electrical activity of the sino-atrial node, the atrio-ventricular node, the right and left ventricle, and the blood volume from the left ventricle. The traces demonstrate the recordings obtained from a normal heart and various pathological conditions. This simulation also allows the user to attempt to identify four anti-arrhythmic agents based on their effects on the model.

Cardiac Muscle Mechanics
Source: Compress
P.O. Box 102
Wentworth, NH 03282

This program (IBM or compatibles) for undergraduate and graduate students provides a simulation of the effects of stimulation of the heart muscle in response to changes in length, load, and contractility.

CARDIOLAB
Source: Elsevier-BIOSOFT
52 Vanderbilt Ave.
New York, NY 10017

This graduate/professional program (IBM, Apple II, BCC) simulates cardiovascular experiments that would normally be conducted on anesthetized or pithed animals. It allows students to determine the effects of drugs on simulated heart rate and blood pressure traces.

Cardiovascular Lab Videodisc Simulation
Source: Dr. C. E. Branch
Department of Physiology and Pharmacology
College of Veterinary Medicine, Auburn University
Auburn, AL 36849

This program, which is for professionals, simulates cardiovascular and respiratory physiology experiments using a videodisc with 28 minutes of motion sequences and 400 still frames. (May be used with IBM compatibles with IBM Infowindows, Matrox Overlay, Custom Overlay, Dual Monitor, Dummy Videodisc, Pioneer LD-V6000, or LD-V4200 videodisc player and CGA, EGA, or VGA graphic adapters.) The disk shows an anesthetized dog that is prepared for recording the electrocardiogram, carotid blood flow, venous and arterial blood pressure, and heart rate. The program shows how this preparation would be used for experiments, such as the effect of positive pressure ventilation on circulatory function.

Cardiovascular Pharmacology
Source: Dr. J. R. Walker
Integrated Functional Laboratory
University of Texas Medical Branch
Galveston, TX 77550

This simulation, which is aimed at graduate students and professionals, produces tracings that represent arterial pressure, cardiac output, total peripheral resistance, and contractility on IBMs or IBM compatibles. It shows the effects on these tracings of drugs such as acetylcholine, epinephrine, norephineprine, isoproterenol, angiotensis, and atropine.

Cat Superior Cervical Ganglion-Nictitating Membrane
Source: Dr. D. Dewhurst
Department of Applied Science
Leeds Polytechnic
Calverley St.
Leeds, LS1 3HE
England

This program (IBM or compatibles) for undergraduates simulates an *in vivo* cat superior cervical ganglion-nictitating membrane preparation that is commonly used in physiology and pharmacology laboratory exercises. Muscle contractions are displayed on a chart recorder. The effects of selected drugs, applied to the ganglion or the nictitating membrane, can be simulated as can the effects of pre-ganglionic nerve stimulation.

The Digestion Simulator
Source: Carolina Biological Supply Co.
2700 York Rd.
Burlington, NC 27215

This Apple II program for middle school and high school students uses color graphics to depict the human digestive process.

Effects of Drugs on the Uterus and the Intestine
Source: Dr. J. R. Walker
University of Texas Medical Branch
Galveston, TX 77550

This program (IBM or compatibles) for undergraduate and graduate students simulates the effects of estrogen on uterine contractions and the effects of drugs on the contractions of the intestine.

Exercises in Muscle Contraction
Source: Educational Images, Ltd.
P.O. Box 3456
West Side Elmira, NY 14905

This Apple II program for high school and undergraduate students uses animated exercises to define the structure and functions of a muscle motor unit. It uses a simulated electromyographic recording to show a single twitch, summation (the effects of multiple, low-level stimulations, each delivered before the effects of the last has gone away), treppe (when the heart is stimulated to beat after it has been quiescent for a period of time, the initial contractions will increase in amplitude, like a staircase, until a maximum steady level is reached), and tetanus.

Experiments in Metabolism
Source: Educational Images, Ltd.
P.O. Box 3456
West Side Elmira, NY 14905

This Apple II program for high school students simulates the metabolism of a mouse. It shows how the basal metabolism rate is determined and the factors that affect it.

Frog Heart
Source: Dr. D. Dewhurst
Department of Applied Science
Leeds Polytechnic
Calverley St.
Leeds LS1 3HE
England

This IBM or compatible program for high school and undergraduate students simulates the experiments performed on the heart of a pithed frog. These experiments are commonly used in physiology and pharmacology laboratory exercises. The frog's simulated heart rate is shown on a scrolling chart recorder. The effects of various drugs, environmental conditions, and experimental manipulations can also be simulated.

Ileum
Source: Elsevier-BIOSOFT
52 Vanderbilt Ave.
New York, NY 10017

This program for graduate students and professionals simulates the isolated guinea pig ileum. (IBM PCs or Apple II may be used.) The simulation offers a preparation commonly used in physiology and pharmacology laboratory exercises. The program can simulate the effects of a variety of drugs on the ileum.

MacDope; MacMan; MacPee; MacPuff

Source: Oxford Electronic Publishing Co.
Oxford University Press
200 Madison Ave.
New York, NY 10016

The *Mac* refers to McMaster University, not to the MacIntosh computer (IBM PC and compatibles with CGA or EGA graphics adapter are necessary). This simulation is designed for graduate students and professionals. The *MacDope* program allows the user to "administer" up to four common drugs to a variety of human patients and to monitor the effects of these drugs. *MacMan* presents information about the anatomy and physiology of the cardiovascular system in graphic displays and tables. It allows the user to simulate a variety of pathological conditions and to evaluate the effects of drugs. *MacPee* demonstrates the interactions between the circulatory system, kidneys, body fluids, and electrolyte compartments. It reports on plasma sodium, potassium, urea, creatinin, albumin, hemoglobin, packed cell volume, right arterial pressure, body weight, and level of excretion of water and solutes. *MacPee* can simulate the effects of diabetes *insipidus* and other pathological conditions. Finally, *MacPuff* models the lungs, airways, pulmonary circulation, and gas exchange.

MAXSIM

Source: Dr. J. L. Gabrielsson
Firma Biopharmacon
Geijersgatan 42, S-75226
Sweden

This program, designed for IBMs and compatibles and Apple MacIntosh SE and II, teaches graduate students and professionals pharmacokinetics and clinical pharmacology. It simulates linear and nonlinear physiological, compartmental, pulmonary, and placental models.

Mechanical Properties of Active Muscle

Source: Compress
P.O. Box 102
Wentworth, NH 03282

Undergraduates are the audience for this IBM or compatible program, which simulates the contraction of skeletal muscle. It demonstrates isometric and isotonic contractions.

Neuromuscular Pharmacology
Source: Dr. D. Dewhurst
             Department of Applied Science
             Leeds Polytechnic
             Calverley St.
             Leeds, LS1 3HE
             England

This program for undergraduates simulates experiments performed on the sciatic nerve-tibialis anterior muscle of the cat. In this preparation, the simulation illustrates the action of depolarizing and non-depolarizing neuromuscular blocking agents. It was designed for the IBM or compatibles.

Physiological Simulation Software
Source: Dr. J. E. Randall
             609 So. Jordan St.
             Bloomington, IN 47401

This IBM series of five simulations is aimed at undergraduate and graduate students as well as professionals. It teaches the basic concepts of physiology and pharmacology using tabular and graphic displays.

Sarimner
Source: Department of Pediatrics
             Faculty of Health Sciences
             Linkoping
             Sweden

Designed for the general public as well as the professional, this program (for IBM compatibles with Hercules, EGA, or VGA graphics) simulates how blood glucose levels are affected by changes in eating, exercise, and insulin injections.

Virtual Reality

While still in its infancy, virtual reality holds much promise as a simulation for research, testing, and education that has traditionally involved animals. Virtual reality technology (hardware and software) allows you to "step into" a computer-generated world, where you can look around, move around, and interact with the components. Special goggles allow you to "see" this artificial world. Sound is provided by earphones or speakers. However, tactile sensations (those acting on your skin and its senses) and force sensations (feedback from your muscles, tendons, and joints) are more difficult to model. Because of the complexity of these sensory systems, it is unlikely that virtual reality technology will achieve the same level of realism with these senses as with the visual and auditory senses.

In virtual reality simulations, tracking devices, such as wired gloves and clothing and motion detectors, passively monitor various body parts to create a feeling of being physically present in the virtual world. Interaction devices allow the user to manipulate virtual objects. It is likely that improvements in hardware—especially high density storage devices such as CD-ROM and videodisc technology—and powerful software for manipulating images will continue. It is also likely that costs will continue to decrease. So virtual reality technology promises to provide more and more powerful tools to teach anatomy, physiology, pharmacology, and toxicology.

It is likely that new computer simulation programs and virtual reality systems will continue to appear and improve. The Animal Welfare Information Center of the National Agricultural Library (10301 Baltimore Blvd., Beltsville, MD 20705) is an excellent source of information about these topics as they relate to the use of animals in research and teaching. Another source is the National Library of Medicine (8600 Rockville Pike, Bethesda, MD 20894).

Modeling a Simulation

To develop a model or simulation, modelers must understand the topic they are attempting to model. Although amazing strides have been made in neurobiology during the last few decades, it is unlikely that computer simulations will replace basic (experimental) research in these areas. This is because many basic facts are still unknown about the functions of the nervous system and the interfaces between it, the environment, and behavior.

Computer simulations can be used to teach developmental biology, as well as the methods and procedures used in the testing of new environmental chemicals, physical agents (ionizing and non-ionizing radiation), and drugs. However, until we have a better understanding of these topics, it is unlikely that computer simulations can replace experimental research in these areas.

Finally, computer and virtual reality simulations are unlikely to replace actual hands-on experience in training surgeons and other operating room personnel to perform standard procedures. Developing new surgical procedures will also require hands-on experience.

Noncomputer Models: Mannequins

Obstetrical mannequins were first introduced in Paris around 1700 for the instruction of midwives. Mannequins allow practical training without any inconvenience for patients or the use of animal models.

BIOLIKE Partial Body Mannequins
Source: HEALTH EDCO
P.O. Box 21207
Waco, TX 76702

Partial body mannequins, such as arms or hands, covered with BIO-LIKE—a synthetic tissue that has the same feel and characteristics as skin—are available to allow students to practice venipuncture, arterial puncture, and suturing.

CP-Arlene
Source: NASCO
1534 Princeton Ave.
Modesto, CA 95352

CP-Arlene is one of the most famous and well-known mannequins. It is used for training people how to do cardiopulmonary resuscitation (CPR). It is available in a variety of configurations (torso and head, with or without arms, legs, and/or electronic monitoring). Mannequins that simulate infants and children are also available for CPR training.

Harvey Cardiology Simulator
Source: Medical Training and Simulation Laboratory
University of Miami School of Medicine
Miami, FL 33101

Harvey is a life-size cardiology patient mannequin and a computer-based interactive laserdisk system. The mannequin was developed by M. S. Gordon, M.D., and his colleagues at the University of Miami's Medical

Training and Simulation Laboratory. Harvey has carotid, brachial, radial, and femoral pulses, venous pulsations, precordial movements, respiration, and blood pressure. The mannequin can be auscultated. Electrocardiograms, X rays, and laboratory data are supplied by the computer.

Electronic Bulletin Boards

Computer users who have the appropriate hardware (a computer and modem) and software can exchange information via centralized electronic locations called electronic bulletin boards.

ALF (Agricultural Library Forum)
Source: Capital PC User's Group
          P.O. Box 6128
          Silver Spring, MD 20906
          (301) 504-6510; (301) 504-5111; (301) 504-5496; or
          (301) 504-5497

ALF is an electronic bulletin board for accessing information about the National Agricultural Library's programs, products, and services. It is also used for exchanging information with others interested in agriculture and animal welfare. ALF is open 24 hours per day, seven days per week. It runs on a stand-alone microcomputer with a remote bulletin board system for personal computers (RBBS-PC). ALF is a "user ware" (public domain) program. ALF currently supports four types of electronic communications: *messages,* which allow participants to electronically exchange information; *bulletins,* which are brief announcements about the products and services of the National Agricultural Library; *conferences,* which allow callers to participate in roundtable discussions of items of mutual interest; and *file transfers,* which allow agriculture-related software and uncopyrighted text files to be uploaded (sent) and downloaded (received) from ALF. A brief hard-copy guide to ALF is available from the National Agricultural Library, Beltsville, Maryland 20705-2351.

The equipment required to be connected with ALF is a computer or terminal that can be connected to a telephone line via a modem. ALF accepts modem speeds of 300, 1200, 2400, or 9600 BAUD. Communications software such as CrossTalk, Qmodem, PC-Talk, Procomm, Smart-Com, and Telix will work.

Approximately five seconds after connecting with ALF, a welcome message appears on the computer screen. At the prompts, enter your first name, your last name, and your city and state. If you are a new user, the computer will prompt you to enter a password for future access. Follow computer prompts to "log on" (use) ALF.

Audiocassettes and Videotapes

About Animals: The Question Is . . .
Format: VHS videotape
Length: 22 min.
Source: Progressive Animal Welfare Society
Lynnwood, WA

This tape provides a historical review of beliefs about the use of animals for food and experimentation. The viewpoints of supporters and critics are presented.

Alternatives in Animal Research
Format: VHS and U-Matic videotape
Length: 60 min.
Source: Texas Tech University Health Sciences Center
Lubbock, TX

An overview of man's use of animals is provided, including the use of animals in research and the benefits obtained from this use. This tape discusses the current U.S. federal guidelines and regulations concerning animal welfare, as well as the impact of the animal rights movement. The concepts of refinement, reduction, and replacement are discussed.

The America's View of Animals
Format: VHS videotape
Length: 45 min.
Source: University of Minnesota
Minneapolis, MN

This is a discussion of how current attitudes toward animals and human-animal relationships are influenced by religious beliefs (Jewish, Catholic, Protestant, and Native American) and historical conventions.

Amphibians: Medicine and Husbandry
Format: Audiocassette with 64 slides
Length: 23 min.
Source: University of Michigan
Ann Arbor, MI

This program covers the historical use of amphibians in laboratory work; their taxonomy and husbandry; and sources of frogs, salamanders, newts, and tadpoles. Water quality parameters are discussed, as are selected diseases, such as *red leg syndrome,* Lucke renal adenocarcinoma, mycobacterial and pigmented fungal infections, and parasites.

Animal Behavior in the Wild
Format: VHS videotape
Length: 45 min.
Source: University of Minnesota
             Minneapolis, MN

In this video, University of Minnesota Drs. Richard Phillips and David Smith illustrate aspects of animal behavior and communication.

Animal Research: The Cost of Hope
Format: VHS and U-Matic videotape
Length: 20 min.
Source: Michael Criley
             Tucson, AZ

This video illustrates the contributions of animal research to the advancement of human health care. It discusses the animal research versus animal rights debate, as well as the acquisition of dogs from pounds for biomedical research.

Animal Rights/Animal Welfare
Format: VHS videotape
Length: 20 min.
Source: National Pork Producers Council

The relationship between factory farming and the animal rights/welfare controversy is discussed here. This video provides advice for factory farmers on how to deal with the issues and animal rights groups.

Animal Rights: The Issues, the Movement
Format: 35 mm film with script
Length: 17 min.
Source: Animal Rights Network, Inc.
             Westport, CT

This film provides an introduction to the animal rights philosophy with respect to the use of animals for food and experimentation.

Animal Welfare Information Center:
Resources Today for the Research of Tomorrow
Format: VHS videotape
Length: 11 min.
Source: Video and Teleconference Division
             U.S. Department of Agriculture
             Washington, DC

This video describes the products and services of the Animal Welfare Information Center of the National Agricultural Library.

Animal Welfare: The Farmer's Story
Format: VHS and U-Matic videotape
Length: 28 min.
Source: The American Farm Bureau Federation
Park Ridge, IL

This video uses on-site interviews with farmers to explore animal farming practices.

The Animals Are Crying
Format: 16 mm film
Length: 28 min.
Source: Learning Corporation of America
New York, NY

Dog and cat overpopulation is illustrated in this film about a young family's visit to an animal shelter.

The Animals Film
Format: VHS videotape
Length: 136 min.
Source: Cinema Guild
New York, NY

This is an examination of animal rights philosophy and activities. It contains interviews with activists about animal population control, intensive livestock farming, hunting, animal products, and animal experimentation and testing.

Animals in Biomedical Research
Format: VHS videotape
Length: 45 min.
Source: University of Minnesota
Minneapolis, MN

This video examines alternatives to animal research, methods of reducing the use of animals in research, and the use of animals in teaching. It also covers advances in medicine that have been made via animal research.

Animals in Research: A Complex Issue
Format: U-Matic video
Length: 6 min.
Source: Southern Illinois University
School of Medicine
Springfield, IL

This video discusses why the need for regulating animal research should be weighed against the costs and benefits to all of society. It covers the benefits of animal research and discusses painful procedures performed by biomedical researchers.

Animals in Zoos: Issues and Concerns
Format: VHS videotape
Length: 45 min.
Source: University of Minnesota
            Minneapolis, MN

The role of zoos in maintaining genetic diversity in captive animal populations is discussed by a panel of experts.

Animals, Nature and Religion
Format: VHS videotape
Length: 38 min.
Source: Connecticut Video Productions
            Old Saybrook, CT

In this video, veterinarian Michael W. Fox discusses why he thinks humankind's world view should shift from one of self-centered domination to a more holistic view of nature and animals.

Aseptic Surgery of Rodents
Format: VHS videotape
Length: 30 min.
Source: Laboratory Animal Training Association
            Raleigh, NC

This video provides instruction on how to perform aseptic surgery on common laboratory rodents following the guidelines and policies of the Public Health Service and regulations of the U.S. Department of Agriculture.

Bandaging and Splinting
Format: U-Matic videotape
Length: 55 min.
Source: University of California at Davis
            Davis, CA

Using the dog as a model, the veterinarian in this video demonstrates proper methods of making and applying bandages and splints using a variety of materials.

Biomethodology of the Cat
Format: VHS videotape
Length: 14 min.
Source: MTM Associates, Inc.
            Manassas, VA

This video demonstrates how to handle, restrain, and manipulate cats for research, including giving injections, collecting blood, and performing euthanasia. This is part of a series including tapes about the methods used with dogs, guinea pigs, mice, and rabbits.

Biomethodology of the Primate
Format: VHS videotape
Length: 15 min.
Source: MTM Associates, Inc.
            Manassas, VA

Techniques for manipulating primates for research are demonstrated in this video as are manual and chemical restraint, identification, injection routes, blood collection, and euthanasia.

Biomethodology of the Rat
Format: VHS videotape
Length: 16 min.
Source: MTM Associates
            Silver Spring, MD

This video offers a demonstration of basic techniques involving laboratory rats including identification, restraint, injection, blood collection, and euthanasia.

Breaking Barriers
Format: VHS videotape
Length: 16 min.
Source: People for the Ethical Treatment of Animals (PETA)
            Washington, DC

This video illustrates the stereotypic behaviors and unusual vocalizations exhibited by primates that are infected with human pathogens and are housed in isolated or in stimuli-deprived environments.

Britches
Format: VHS videotape
Length: 16 min.
Source: People for the Ethical Treatment of Animals (PETA)
            Washington, DC

This video documents the Animal Liberation Front's break-in at a research facility 20 April 1985 at the University of California, Riverside. The activists removed cats, rabbits, pigeons, mice, opossums, and a young macaque identified as "Britches."

BST: Continuing a Dairy Tradition
Format: VHS videotape

Length: 11 min.
Source: Monsanto Company
St. Louis, MO

This video discusses bovine somatotropin, including its use and safety by experts in animal science, human health, and agricultural economics.

Caging Systems, Bedding Materials & Environmental Considerations for Laboratory Rodents
Format: 53 slides, audiocassette
Length: 22 min.
Source: University of Washington
Seattle, WA

This program discusses the selection of cage styles and bedding materials for laboratory rodents. It talks about the importance of controlling temperature, humidity, light cycles, and noise.

Carnivore Restraint and Handling
Format: Audiocassette with 112 slides
Length: 25 min.
Source: San Diego Zoological Society
San Diego, CA

University of California
Davis, CA

This slide set demonstrates techniques for restraining various species of wild carnivores, such as chemical immobilization. It also covers proper techniques for cleaning, feeding, and administering medicines.

Cat Care: A Video Guide to Successful Cat Care
Format: VHS videotape
Length: 43 min.
Source: United Media Productions
New York, NY

Veterinarian Michael W. Fox talks about adopting, owning, and caring for pet cats in this video. The information includes how to eliminate fleas, vaccinations, illness, spaying/neutering, and behavior.

Cattle Handling and Transportation
Format: VHS videotape
Length: 16 min.
Source: Livestock Conservation Institute
Madison, WI

This video demonstrates how to move and transport livestock humanely and efficiently. Factors such as vision, reaction to noise, flight zones, following behaviors, and circling behaviors are discussed. The proper uses of squeeze chutes, driving techniques, and loading and unloading procedures are also described.

The Challenge of Animals in Research
Format: VHS videotape
Length: 30 min.
Source: Texas Tech University Health Sciences Center
            Lubbock, TX

This video discusses different attitudes and ethics concerning the use of animals in biomedical research.

Changing Relationship between Humans and Animals
Format: VHS videotape
Length: 45 min.
Source: University of Minnesota
            Minneapolis, MN

This program offers a panel discussion in which the participants address questions such as: What would a world without animals be like? Do we need animals anymore? Why do we have animals if we do not need them?

Cleveland City Club Forum Debate: Animals in Medical Research
Format: VHS videotape
Length: 60 min.
Source: Cuyahoga Community College
            Cleveland, OH

In this video, Robert J. White, M.D., debates Ingrid Newkirk of People for the Ethical Treatment of Animals concerning the use of animals in medical research.

Development and Reproduction of Mice in a Laboratory Setting
Format: Audiocassete with 39 slides
Length: 15 min.
Source: University of Washington
            Seattle, WA

This is an interactive program in which the viewer, after being provided with facts about normal mouse development and reproduction, is asked to apply these facts to animal care situations. The tape set recommends supervised practice with live animals at the time of presentation to reinforce the learning experience and encourage skill-building confidence.

Diseases of Laboratory Animals as Complications of Biomedical Research

Format: Audiocassette with 39 slides
Length: 21 min.
Source: Washington State University
Pullman, WA

This program presents basic information about laboratory animal diseases and the medicines with which to treat them. It is aimed at veterinary and other biomedical science students.

Dissection and Anatomy of the Brain

Format: VHS videotape
Length: 23 min.
Source: Nebraska Scientific
Omaha, NE

This video demonstrates the dissection of a sheep's brain. It discusses brain development and function.

Dissection and Anatomy of the Cat

Format: VHS videotape
Length: 25 min.
Source: Nebraska Scientific
Omaha, NE

This video covers the external and internal anatomy of the cat. Mammalian characteristics are discussed.

Dissection and Anatomy of the Eye

Format: VHS videotape
Length: 16 min.
Source: Nebraska Scientific
Omaha, NE

A bovine eye and a plastic model are used in this discussion about the dissection and anatomy of the eye.

Dissection and Anatomy of the Heart

Format: VHS videotape
Length: 15 min.
Source: Nebraska Scientific
Omaha, NE

This video covers the characteristics of the mammalian heart. It uses a plastic model of a human heart and the heart of a fetal pig to demonstrate dissection.

Dissection and Anatomy of the Shark

Format: VHS videotape
Length: 26 min.
Source: Nebraska Scientific
Omaha, NE

This video gives a brief history and other information about sharks. It uses a dogfish shark to demonstrate dissection of the internal and external anatomy.

Do Animals Reason?

Format: 16mm film
Length: 14 min.
Source: National Geographic Society
Washington, DC

This film introduces students to the learning abilities of animals, using classic and contemporary animal behavior experiments with fish, birds, and mammals.

Do Animals Think and Feel?

Format: VHS videotape
Length: 45 min.
Source: University of Minnesota
Minneapolis, MN

This video contains a panel discussion in which the participants compare and contrast the mental and emotional processes of animals and humans. They discuss animal behavior, consciousness, learning, intelligence, and emotions.

The Dog and Cat

Format: VHS videotape
Length: 35 min.
Source: Laboratory Animal Training Association
Raleigh, NC

This program provides information on the housing, nutrition, health care, restraint, and euthanasia of laboratory dogs and cats in accord with U.S. Department of Agriculture regulations and the Public Health Services' *Guide for the Care and Use of Laboratory Animals*. It also discusses required record keeping.

The Dog and Cat in Research

Format: Audiocassette with 72 slides
Length: 25 min.

Source: University of Washington
Seattle, WA

This program covers the acquisition, physical examination, conditioning, health maintenance, housing, and care of cats and dogs used in research and teaching.

Dog Lab: An Unnecessary Exercise
Format: VHS videotape
Length: 16 min.
Source: People for the Ethical Treatment of Animals (PETA)
Washington, DC

This video's taped segments of surgical training involving animals were obtained by PETA in 1987 from East Carolina University. PETA maintains that these segments highlight questionable surgical techniques performed on a dog. The narrator asserts that the instructor was callous, unprofessional, and inept.

Don't Kill the Animals
Format: VHS videotape
Length: 7 min.
Source: People for the Ethical Treatment of Animals (PETA)
Washington, DC

This video sets to music footage of an animal research lab break-in. It promotes vegetarianism while speaking against animal research, factory farming, fur production, and hunting.

Elephant Care and Handling
Format: Audiocassette with 75 slides
Length: 20 min.
Source: San Diego Zoological Society
San Diego, CA

University of California
Davis, CA

The taxonomy, anatomy, cleaning, feeding, handling, and restraint of captive Asian and African elephants are discussed and demonstrated in this training film for zoo caretakers.

Exodus at Yellowstone: The Second Catastrophe
Format: VHS videotape
Length: 30 min.

Source: Animal Protection Institute of America
Sacramento, CA

In this video, animal protection advocates voice their protests over bison hunting. In particular, they focus on the bison that were shot after straying beyond Yellowstone National Park boundaries in the winter of 1989, following a severe drought and fire that destroyed food supplies within the park.

Facing the Animal Rights Challenge
Format: Audiocassete with 49 slides
Length: 7 min.
Source: Animal Health Institute
Alexandria, VA

This program provides livestock producers with tips on how to deal with animal rights demonstrators and influence legislation affecting them. It also addresses the questions: What are animal rights groups? What are their origins? What do they want to accomplish?

The Family of Chimps
Format: U-Matic videotape
Length: 55 min.
Source: Filmmakers Library
New York, NY

This video illustrates how ethologists use the 2.5-acre wooded exhibit at the Burgers Zoo in Arnhem, Holland, to study chimpanzee behavior, such as social play, aggression, mating, and the development of social hierarchies.

Farm Animal Behavior Research
Format: VHS videotape
Length: 100 min.
Source: National Program Staff
Agricultural Research Service, USDA
Beltsville, MD

This program, which focuses on swine behavioral research, discusses farm animal welfare, the psychological well-being of farm animals, and animal awareness.

A Feminist View of Human-Animal Relations
Format: VHS videotape
Length: 45 min.
Source: University of Minnesota
Minneapolis, MN

The concepts of "victim" and "distribution of power" are discussed in reference to interactions between males and females and humans and animals.

The Frog Inside-Out
Format: VHS videotape
Length: 67 min.
Source: Instructivision, Inc.
Livingston, NJ

This program for high school or college biology students uses live animals, animations, diagrams, and micrographs of tissue cells to illustrate proper and humane dissection techniques. These tools demonstrate how the frog's anatomy allows it to adapt to life on land and in water. The video focuses on the anatomy and physiology of vision, reproduction, locomotion, respiration, vocalization, hibernation, and skin pigmentation. The narrator states that the video is intended to reduce the number of frogs used for experimental purposes.

The Future of Human-Animal Relations
Format: VHS videotape
Length: 45 min.
Source: University of Minnesota
Minneapolis, MN

This tape presents a panel discussion that addresses our changing expectations concerning pets, as well as the future of animals raised for food.

Gnotobiotic Pig Production
Format: VHS videotape
Length: 22 min.
Source: Purdue Research
West Lafayette, IN

This video details the equipment and methods of surgery, transfer, and rearing required for the production of gnotobiotic (germ-free) pigs, which are important research models.

Gnotobiotics in Production of Experimental Animals
Format: Audiocassette with 47 slides
Length: 22 min.
Source: University of Washington
Seattle, WA

This video describes the development, maintenance, and use of the isolator (a device that cleans the air to prevent airborne microbes from reaching animals) for production of experimental animals, the sterilization of isolators and supplies, and microbiologic monitoring techniques.

Granby's Primates
Format: VHS videotape
Length: 28 min.
Source: Filmmakers Library
New York, NY

Climbing structures were introduced into the primate housing facility at Granby Zoo in Quebec to relieve boredom and to stimulate more natural behavior. This tape documents how the behaviors of captive primates are modified by changes in their environment.

The Guinea Pig and Rabbit
Format: VHS videotape
Length: 28 min.
Source: Laboratory Animal Training Association
Raleigh, NC

The housing, nutrition, health care, safe handling, and restraint of laboratory guinea pigs and rabbits are considered in this video. It also covers record keeping for animal research, experimental techniques, and euthanasia. The standards described in this tape are consistent with the recommendations of the Public Health Services' *Guide for the Care and Use of Laboratory Animals* and U.S. Department of Agriculture regulations.

The Guinea Pig: Biology
Format: Audiocassette with 51 slides
Length: 20 min.
Source: University of Washington
Seattle, WA

The vital signs, growth, and hematological uniqueness of guinea pigs are highlighted in this tape, as are their reactions to antibiotics and anesthesia. Anatomy, physiology, reproduction, nutrition, and pharmacology of the guinea pig are presented.

The Guinea Pig: Diseases
Format: Audiocassette with 53 slides
Length: 18 min.
Source: University of Washington
Seattle, WA

Illnesses that affect guinea pigs are discussed in this video. These include bacterial, viral, and chlamydial infections; parasitic and neoplastic diseases; and nutritional and metabolic diseases.

The Guinea Pig: Introduction and Husbandry
Format: Audiocassette with 55 slides
Length: 25 min.

Source: University of Washington
            Seattle, WA

This program covers guinea pig taxonomy, history, uses, husbandry, behavior, and reproduction.

The Guns of Autumn
Format: U-Matic videotape
Length: 78 min.
Source: Carousel Films, Inc.
            New York, NY

This program unfavorably portrays hunting in its presentation of the thoughts and actions of hunters as they stalk bear, deer, bison, and waterfowl.

The Hamster: Biology and Diseases
Format: Audicassette with 62 slides
Length: 24 min.
Source: University of Washington
            Seattle, WA

This tape presents the anatomy, physiology, and pharmacology of hamsters. It also covers the various illnesses that affect them including enteritis, parasites, neoplasms, amyloidosis, and bacterial and viral diseases.

The Hamster: Introduction and Husbandry
Format: Audiocassette with 59 slides
Length: 25 min.
Source: University of Washington
            Seattle, WA

This program discusses the taxonomy, history, uses, husbandry, behavior, and reproduction of the hamster.

Handling and Restraining Laboratory Rodents
Format: Audiocassette with 40 slides
Length: 10 min.
Sources: Northwest Committee for Training in Laboratory Animal Care
            Health Sciences Center for Educational Resources
            Seattle, WA

Safe, effective methods of restraint (mechanical and by hand) for use with common laboratory rodents are described in this program. It also covers appropriate techniques for transferring animals between cages and from a cage to a restraining device.

Handling Hoofed Stock
Format: Audiocassette with 165 slides
Length: 50 min.
Sources: San Diego Zoological Society
San Diego, CA

University of California
Davis, CA

This program discusses general principles concerning safe handling of large exotic hoofed stock. It covers their cleaning, feeding, and transportation, as well as chemical and mechanical methods of restraint.

Heart Sounds and Murmurs: A Practical Guide
Format: Audiocassette and book
Length: N/A
Source: NASCO
Fort Atkinson, WI

This audiocassette and its accompanying book are designed to teach beginning auscultators the basics of listening to and interpreting heart sounds. It discusses how to distinguish normal sounds from abnormal ones.

Humane Care and Use of Laboratory Animals
Format: VHS videotape
Length: 32 min.
Source: Laboratory Animal Training Association
Raleigh, NC

This tape reviews the roles and responsibilities of research staff and institutional animal care and use committee members under the Animal Welfare Act and other U.S. legislation. It discusses humane laboratory animal care and use, focusing on ethical viewpoints, alternatives, and information resources.

Humane Educator/Obedience Trainer
Format: 35 mm film
Length: 7 min.
Source: Troll Associates
Mahwah, NJ

Made for the Humane Society of the United States, this film focuses on careers related to the care and training of animals. It is intended for the elementary grades.

The Image of Animals Today
Format: VHS videotape

Length: 45 min.
Source: University of Minnesota
Minneapolis, MN

In this video, a panel discusses the portrayal of animals in contemporary American mass media, such as cartoons, books, poems, and television. The panel formulates a general concept of what it perceives to be America's image of animals.

Inspection and Labeling Aspects of Genetically Engineered Food Animals
Format: VHS videotape
Length: 53 min.
Source: USDA Food Safety and Inspection Service
Washington, DC

In this video, Daniel Jones, of the USDA Office of Biotechnology, examines some of the legal and regulatory questions of labeling the meat of genetically engineered animals.

Intercultural Views of Animals
Format: VHS videotape
Length: 45 min.
Source: University of Minnesota
Minneapolis, MN

The human-animal relationship is discussed relative to the cultural habits, beliefs, and social conventions of the Hindus, Moslems, East Africans, and Buddhists, which are compared to American views.

Introduction of Foreign Genes into Livestock
Format: VHS videotape
Length: 53 min.
Source: Food Safety and Inspection Service
Washington, DC

Robert Wall, of the USDA Agricultural Research Service Reproduction Physiology Laboratory, is featured in this video. He discusses the introduction of foreign genes into sheep and pigs to increase feed efficiency.

Kiss the Animals Goodbye
Format: VHS videotape
Length: 20 min.
Source: Pyramid Film and Video
Santa Monica, CA

This video talks about animal population control, including euthanasia and adoption.

Laboratory Animal Medicine: What It Is and How It Relates to Veterinary Medicine

Format: Audiocassette with 61 slides
Length: 25 min.
Source: University of Washington
Seattle, WA

This program is designed to stimulate interest in laboratory animal medicine and science.

Laboratory Dogs

Format: VHS videotape
Length: 16 min.
Source: Animal Welfare Institute of New York
New York, NY

This tape describes the methods used to maintain a canine research facility and to ensure a supply of healthy, manageable dogs.

The Laboratory Rat: Biology, Husbandry, and Research Methodology

Format: Audiocassette with 59 slides
Length: 15 min.
Source: University of Washington
Seattle, WA

This program concerns methodology for research involving rats. It covers handling, restraint, blood collection, anesthesia, and euthanasia, as well as the basic anatomy and physiology of laboratory rats. Procedures for housing rats and manipulating them are also discussed.

The Laboratory Rat: Diseases

Format: Audiocassette with 48 slides
Length: 16 min.
Source: University of Washington
Seattle, WA

This program details the etiology, pathogenesis, diagnosis, prevention, and treatment of infections that attack laboratory rats.

The Laboratory Rat: Introduction

Format: Audiocassette with 46 slides
Length: 15 min.
Source: University of Washington
Seattle, WA

The topic of this video is the history of the domesticated rat. It looks at the rat's use in physiological, oncological, dental, nutritional, and behavioral research, as well as in evaluations of drugs. The video highlights the specific attributes that make this species particularly valuable as an experimental subject.

Life Force: Animal Welfare
Format: U-Matic videotape
Length: 27 min.
Source: Iowa State University Extension Service
            Ames, IA

This tape presents a panel discussion of views on the animal welfare movement and professional ethics.

Lung Sounds: A Practical Guide
Format: Audiocassette
Length: N/A
Source: NASCO
            Fort Atkinson, WI

This tape provides the auscultator with normal and abnormal lung sounds and discusses how to distinguish between them.

Manipulation of Mouse Embryos
Format: VHS videotape
Length: 12 min.
Source: Central Institute for Experimental Animals
            Tokyo, Japan

This tape describes techniques that will one day lead to the development of new animal models for human diseases by genetically manipulating laboratory rodents. Invasion of sperm into an ovum, cell development *in vitro,* and the effects of rat growth hormone on mice are illustrated. The video also details the methods used in enucleation (removing the nucleus), DNA injection into ova, *in vitro* fertilization, embryo implantation, and the development of aggregation chimeras (grafting a part of one embryo to another embryo).

Man's Best Friends
Format: VHS videotape
Length: 60 min.
Source: Cinema Guild
            New York, NY

This tape provides comprehensive, balanced coverage of the controversy surrounding the use of animals for research and testing. Its topics include the benefits of animal research, the Draize and LD50 tests, the laboratory animal industry, use of pound animals for research, animal dealers, animal auctions, and legislation.

Modern Veal Production: A Mixture of Technology and the Family Farm

Format: VHS videotape
Length: 9 min.
Source: American Veal Association
Freemont, WI

This video shows specially fed veal calves living in individual pens that reduce stress, decrease health risks, and increase feed efficiency. It is intended to show how farmers utilize modern technology and proper management practices to raise veal calves.

The Mongolian Gerbil

Format: Audiocassette with 60 slides
Length: 20 min.
Source: University of Washington
Seattle, WA

This program discusses the husbandry, reproduction, diseases, and research uses of gerbils.

The Mouse: Biology and Use in Research

Format: Audiocassette with 77 slides
Length: 25 min.
Source: University of Washington
Seattle, WA

The history of the research mouse—as well as its taxonomy, nomenclature, anatomy, reproduction, physiology, genetics, behavior, growth, nutrition, and life span—are highlighted in this program. Sources and costs of research mice are also covered.

The Mouse: Handling, Restraint, and Other Techniques

Format: Audiocassette with 48 slides
Length: 12 min.
Source: University of Washington
Seattle, WA

This program demonstrates how to sex mice, how to handle and restrain them, and how to administer drugs orally or by injection. Blood and urine collection, anesthesia, and euthanasia are discussed.

The Mouse: Neoplastic, Non-Infectious and Miscellaneous Diseases

Format: Audiocassette with 44 slides
Length: 14 min.
Source: University of Washington
Seattle, WA

This slide program illustrates the role of mice in cancer research. It also discusses noninfectious diseases and miscellaneous causes of disease (*hexamitiasis, encephalito-zoonosis eperythrozoonosis,* and *dermatomycosis*) in mice.

The Nature of Change
Format: VHS and U-Matic videotape
Length: 17 min.
Source: Monsanto Company
           St. Louis, MO

This video discusses the possible use of recombinant DNA technology to overcome the limitations of traditional animal and plant breeding. It highlights the use of bovine growth hormone to increase milk production in cows and *Agrobacterium tumefaciens* to improve crops.

Neuromuscular Blocking Agents
Format: U-Matic videotape
Length: 52 min.
Source: University of California
           Davis, CA

This video examines the mode of action of various neuromuscular blocking agents by demonstrating their effects on a cat and a chicken.

A New Leash on Life
Format: VHS videotape
Length: 15 min.
Source: W. J. Klein Company
           Charlotte, NC

This video presents the benefits and costs of owning a dog. It addresses the issues of pet abandonment, pound adoption, pet care, and living with pets in apartments.

The New Research Environment
Format: VHS videotape
Length: 14 min. (tape 1), 30 min. (tape 2)
Source: Foundation for Biomedical Research
           Washington, DC

This program consists of two videotapes. The *first* one provides a brief history of the anti-animal research movement. It explains how media coverage of a few instances of research animal abuse has significantly disrupted biomedical research. The *second* tape provides a dramatization of an Institutional Animal Care and Use Committee (IACUC) conducting a protocol review. It gives an overview of the role of the IACUC in ensuring humane laboratory animal treatment. It also demonstrates recommended procedures involved in survival surgery, including presurgical scrubbing and instrument sterilization, and postsurgical care. It covers the handling, identification, administration of injections and anesthesia, gavaging, blood collection, and euthanasia of laboratory animals. Rats and rabbits are used as the research subjects.

Nonhuman Primates
Format: 6 audiocassettes with 392 slides
Length: 145 min.
Source: University of Washington
Seattle, WA

This six-part program covers the taxonomy of primates, their biology, and their use in research and teaching. It also details the husbandry and breeding of primates, as well as their diseases (viral, bacterial, parasitic, and noninfectious).

The Nonhuman Primates
Format: VHS videotape
Length: 29 min.
Source: Laboratory Animal Training Association
Raleigh, NC

Following the recommendations of the U.S. Public Health Services' *Guide for the Care and Use of Laboratory Animals* and USDA regulations, this program describes the humane care and use of laboratory primates. Its topics include housing nutrition, environment, record keeping, animal health care, handling and restraint, experimental techniques, and euthanasia.

Nutrition and Feeding Methods for Laboratory Animals
Format: Audiocassette with 58 slides
Length: 25 min.
Source: University of Washington
Seattle, WA

This program examines the nutritional requirements of rodents, guinea pigs, rabbits, dogs, and cats. Feeding behaviors, typical feeding methods, and risks associated with improper feeding are discussed. A guide accompanies this slide set.

Orientation to Small Animal ICU
Format: U-Matic videotape
Length: 22 min.
Source: University of California at Davis
Davis, CA

This tape describes a variety of small animal ICU equipment, including the oxygen therapy unit, the DC defibrillator, the IVAC constant fluid infusion pump, the ultrasonic nebulizer, and the wall-mounted anesthetic machine and ventilator. It provides an introduction to their operation and maintenance that includes troubleshooting information.

The Other Side of the Fence
Format: VHS videotape
Length: 10 1/2 min.
Sources: American Society for the Prevention of Cruelty to Animals
            Varied Directions, Inc.
            Camden, ME

This video's still pictures and its footage of actual veal calf operations provide the viewer with a realistic depiction of modern veal production. Questions are raised about whether veal calves are provided with their fundamental needs of adequate shelter, nutrition, and companionship.

Our Side of the Fence
Format: VHS videotape
Length: 9 min.
Source: National Cattleman's Association
            Englewood, CO

This video promotes unification of agricultural groups to defeat the Massachusetts Referendum of November 1988. It discusses the importance of communicating with and educating the public on animal agriculture.

Practical Methodology: Humane Handling and Laboratory Techniques for the Guinea Pig
Format: VHS videotape
Length: 19 min.
Source: University of California at Davis
            Davis, CA

This video provides instruction on the proper restraint and handling of guinea pigs. which it uses to demonstrate common laboratory techniques, such as administering injections and oral dosages. Other tapes in the same series provide information about the hamster (22 min.), the mouse (18 min.), the rabbit (25 min.), and the rat (21 min.).

Practical Methodology—Nonhuman Primates:
Tape 1 Personnel Safety, Primate Handling and Restraint;
Tape 2 Special Laboratory Techniques
Format: VHS videotape
Length: 18 1/2 min.; 15 min.

Source: University of California at Davis
Davis, CA

This program contains two videos. The *first* tape covers Herpes B virus prevention, protective clothing, personal hygiene, and safe handling practices. It stresses the goal of minimizing stress to the animals and maximizing safety for the handler. The *second* tape describes and demonstrates laboratory techniques, such as gavaging, giving injections, and collecting blood.

Practical Methodology—Reptiles:
Tape 1 Humane Handling, Restraint and Husbandry;
Tape 2 Special Laboratory Techniques
Format: VHS videotape
Length: 17 min.; 17 min.
Source: University of California at Davis
Davis, CA

The *first* video discusses the basics of handling, restraining, and practicing husbandry of snakes, lizards, tortoises, and terrapins. The *second* discusses sexing and performing the following procedures on reptiles: sampling blood, placing catheters, selecting injection sites, gavaging orally, intubating, restraining, anesthetizing, and performing euthanasia.

Primates
Format: Audiocassette with 125 slides
Length: 25 min.
Sources: San Diego Zoological Society
San Diego, CA

University of California at Davis
Davis, CA

This program covers various aspects of working with nonhuman primates in research. It covers protective clothing; restraint devices; capture methods; methods for collecting blood, urine, and fecal samples; tuberculin testing; injections; gavaging; and administering medicines.

Progress without Pain
Format: VHS videotape
Length: 55 min.
Source: Lord Dowdling Fund for Humane Research
London, England

Rather than modern medicine, this program suggests that better nutrition, sanitation, hygiene, living conditions, and working conditions are the major factors responsible for improvements in health and increased life span in the West. The program further suggests that instead of animal models, chromatography, chemical analysis, cell and organ culture, theoretical techniques, clinical observations, and research with patients are more reliable indicators of the effects of disease and drugs on humans.

A Question of Life
Format: VHS videotape
Length: 15 min.
Source: California Biomedical Research Association
Berkeley, CA

The role of laboratory animals in the advancement of medicine is examined in this video. The program lists the medical benefits for humans and animals that have resulted from animal research.

A Question of Respect
Format: VHS videotape
Length: 12 min.
Source: American Society for the Prevention of Cruelty to Animals
New York, NY

The ASPCA looks at the relationship between earth, animals, and humans in this video, which discusses our responsibility toward animals with respect to research, product testing, and pets.

A Question of Safety: Importance of Product Safety Testing
Format: VHS videotape
Length: 14 1/2 min.
Source: Foundation for Biomedical Research
Washington, DC

This video discusses the concept of "acceptable risk." It stresses the importance of data from toxicity studies using animals to determine product safety under normal conditions and when treating for toxicity in cases of accidental poisoning. The program examines the use of alternatives to live animals.

Research Animals: A Realistic View
Format: VHS videotape
Length: 13 1/2 min.
Source: Southern Illinois University
Springfield, IL

This program discusses what the quality of animal care and equipment should be in a model animal research facility. A visual tour through an actual research facility serves to illustrate proper laboratory animal care.

Research Methods for Studying Animal Behavior in a Zoo Setting
Format: U-Matic videotape
Length: 19 min. (part 1), 60 min. (part 2)
Sources: Minnesota Zoological Garden
          Apple Valley, MN

          Washington Park Zoo
          Portland, OR

This program describes how a researcher formulates a research question, does reconnaissance observations, constructs an ethogram, develops sampling and data collection methods, performs data reduction and statistical analysis, and interprets the results of a study of animal behavior. The program demonstrates five different sampling methods. It allows the viewer to practice each method by watching and scoring samples of behavior presented in the tape.

Restraint and Handling of the Bird
Format: VHS videotape
Length: 34 min.
Source: University of California at Davis
          Davis, CA

This program demonstrates safe physical restraint techniques for the following groups of birds: flightless birds, waterfowl, shorebirds, galliformes, long-billed/long-legged birds, large-billed birds, psittacines, hummingbirds, and swifts.

Reverence for Life: Rights and Responsibilities
Format: VHS videotape
Length: 45 min.
Source: University of Minnesota
          Minneapolis, MN

This video shows a panel discussion on how people value and treat animals. The equality of different life forms, the rights of animals, and human responsibility toward animals are discussed.

Share the Care: Humane Education
Format: VHS videotape
Length: 45 min.
Source: University of Minnesota
          Minneapolis, MN

In this video, panelists from the Minnesota Humane Society and the University of Minnesota discuss Share the Care, a project designed to teach elementary and secondary students humane treatment of animals. The aim of Share the Care is to develop ideas and opinions about animals rather than just providing information. Share the Care hopes to impart to participants a respect and fondness for animals.

Signs of Enrichment
Format: VHS videotape
Length: 41 min.
Source: Friends of Washoe Foundation
         Ellensburg, WA

This video demonstrates techniques for enriching the environment of chimpanzees. These include giving the chimpanzees balloons, crayons, and other toys, as well as varying their diet.

Silent World: Genetic Engineering—Ethical, Environmental and Animal Welfare Concerns
Format: VHS videotape
Length: 39 min.
Source: Center for Respect of Life and Environment
         Washington, DC

This video examines the potential impact of recent genetic manipulations on animal welfare. These manipulations include producing monoclonal antibodies using mice, inserting the avian leukosis virus into poultry and the AIDS virus into mice, genetically engineering bacteria for bacterial pesticides, and endowing pigs with the human growth gene. Veterinarian Michael W. Fox warns that the production of genetically altered organisms could lead to environmental devastation, reduced biological diversity, and increased suffering of research animals. The program concludes with a plea for greater respect for the sanctity of life and possible alternatives to genetic engineering.

Silver Spring Monkeys
Format: VHS videotape
Length: 17 min.
Source: People for the Ethical Treatment of Animals (PETA)
         Washington, DC

This video recording consists of a series of photographs taken by PETA member Alex Pacheco while working at the National Institutes of Health's Institute of Behavioral Research in Silver Spring, Maryland. The photographs document the alleged poor care and treatment of primates that were held at the laboratory of Dr. Edward Taub. They were used by Pacheco to testify on animal abuse before the U.S. House Subcommittee on Science Research and Technology.

Sorry, Charlie
Format: VHS videotape
Length: 14 min.
Source: Arizona Humane Society
Phoenix, AZ

This tape dramatizes the plight of an abandoned dog that is picked up by an animal control worker and brought to a shelter. It is designed to help educate children about the plight of stray animals and to foster responsible pet ownership.

Speaking of Harvey
Format: 16 mm film
Length: 9 min.
Source: Pyramid Film & Video
Santa Monica, CA

This film shows a young physiologist de-arterializing a rabbit's liver. While performing the surgery, the researcher shares his thoughts and feelings about his work and the emotional difficulties he and other researchers experience working with live animals. The tape is for biology students from junior high through college. It introduces the concept of scientific ethics in relation to animal experimentation.

Suffer the Animals
Format: 16 mm film
Length: 25 min.
Source: British Films, Ltd.
London, England

This film, which is suitable for students high school age and older, is a graphic depiction of experimental animals undergoing stressful and/or painful procedures. The film expresses the view that the use of animals for research and testing is unnecessary. It briefly discusses possible alternatives to animal experimentation.

Terrorism in Dixon
Format: VHS videotape
Length: 10 min.
Source: AgriBase
Kansas City, MO

On 29 January 1989, a fire gutted the Dixon livestock auction in Dixon, CA. The environmentalist group, Earth First, claimed responsibility for the blaze. This video examines the aftermath of the fire that destroyed an estimated $400,000 worth of property.

To Hunt or Not To Hunt
Format: VHS videotape
Length: 45 min.
Source: University of Minnesota
            Minneapolis, MN

This tape presents a panel discussion on why people hunt and whether hunting should be permitted.

Tools for Research: Questions about Animal Rights
Format: VHS videotape
Length: 37 min.
Source: Bullfrog Films
            Oley, PA

This video includes old footage from the U.S. Department of Defense animal experiments and from cosmetic and pharmaceutical laboratory animal testing. A panel of animal rights activists discusses the basic assumptions about animal research, such as: (1) Do existing laws actually protect laboratory animals? (2) Is all animal research of value to humans? (3) Is most current research repetitive and wasteful? (4) Can experimental results from animals be accurately extrapolated to humans? and (5) Do lab animals suffer?

Transgenic Farm Animals
Format: VHS videotape
Length: 53 min.
Source: USDA Food Safety and Inspection Service
            Washington, DC

This is a videotaped seminar given by physiologist Douglas Bold of the USDA Agricultural Research Service Reproduction Physiology Lab. Bold describes the methodology and results of a research project in which a foreign growth gene was transferred by microinjection into the pronuclei of a pig's ovum.

The Ultimate Test Animal
Format: VHS videotape
Length: 41 min.
Source: Cinema Guild
            New York, NY

The validity of data from animal studies is called into question in this program. It examines the controversy about the safety and side effects of Depo Provera, a contraceptive drug produced by Upjohn Company and currently available in the United States and some Third World countries.

Understanding Farm Animal Behavior
Format: VHS videotape
Length: 45 min.
Source: University of Minnesota
Minneapolis, MN

This tape presents a panel discussion of farm animal behavior and animal rights in relation to factory farming.

Unnecessary Fuss
Format: VHS videotape
Length: 29 min.
Source: People for the Ethical Treatment of Animals (PETA)
Washington, DC

This video has segments highlighting neurological procedures on baboons and critiquing research methodologies by scientists. The segments were taken from videotape removed from the University of Pennsylvania Head Injury Clinic by the Animal Liberation Front in June 1984.

Using Animals in Research: Guidelines for Investigators
Format: U-Matic videotape
Length: 240 min. (six videotapes)
Source: U.S. Department of Agriculture
Agricultural Research Service
Beltsville, MD

This video records in its entirety a course sponsored by the USDA/Agricultural Research Service. The course included speakers from the Animal and Plant Health Inspection Service, the National Institutes of Health, the Public Health Service, and the Agricultural Research Service. They discussed information on laws, policies, and practices that affect the use of research animals, and techniques that are commonly used in an animal laboratory. The videos also provide references for those who want to learn more about specific procedures.

The Value of Animal Research in the Betterment of Health
Format: VHS videotape
Length: 17 min.
Source: University of Florida
Gainesville, FL

An overview of animal use in research, this program emphasizes the role of animal experimentation in the advancement of human health care.

Voices I Have Heard
Format: VHS videotape

Length: 60 min.
Source: Culture and Animals Foundation
Raleigh, NC

Older activists tell how they are improving the welfare of animals. Among the activities undertaken by these individuals are: caring for injured wildlife, protesting animal research, maintaining a private wildlife refuge, preventing carriage horse abuse, promoting alternatives to the use of live animals for experimentation, protecting Canadian seal pups, and rescuing burros in the Grand Canyon.

We Are All Noah
Format: VHS videotape
Length: 25 min.
Source: American Fund for Alternatives to Animal Research

In this video, representatives from the Jewish and Christian faiths call for a more compassionate relationship between humans and animals. Painful research and testing procedures, fur trapping, intensive animal agriculture, and pound animal euthanasia are discussed.

Who Cares Anyway
Format: VHS videotape
Length: 30 min.
Source: Lynx Film Production
Toronto, Ontario
Canada

This video discusses the abuses of puppy-mill breeding, what happens when animals are no longer desirable as pets, and what happens to animals in shelters.

Who Speaks for the Animals?
Format: Audiocassette with 80 slides
Length: 15 min.
Source: U.S. Department of Agriculture
Animal and Plant Health Inspection Service
Hyattsville, MD

This slide set presents an overview of animal welfare issues. It discusses the role of the Animal and Plant Health Inspection Service (APHIS) in enforcing legislation designed to protect animals from abuse.

Will I Be Alright Doctor?
Format: VHS videotape
Length: 14 min.

Source: Foundation for Biomedical Research
Washington, DC

In this video, surgeons and patients discuss the contribution of animal research to the advancement of human health care, such as organ transplants, correcting congenital birth defects, and improving chemotherapy treatments for leukemia patients.

Index

Dr. Clifford Sherry is a senior scientist and principal investigator with Systems Research Laboratories. He has taught human physiology and psychopharmacology to more than 2,000 students with widely varying backgrounds and abilities. He has professional publications in more than 30 different scientific journals. His scientific interests include neurophysiology, psychopharmacology, reproductive behavior/physiology, teratology (the study of birth defects), and the bio-behavioral effects of electromagnetic fields and potentials. He has an ever-increasing number of articles and magazines that focus on, but are not limited to, making science, medicine, computers, and the law understandable to nonspecialists.

His first book, *Mathematics of Technical Analysts: Applying Statistics to Trading Stocks, Options, and Futures,* was published by Probus Publishing Company in 1992. He has recently completed a second book for Probus, *Randomness and the Financial Markets: A Scientific Approach to Trading,* and is working on a third. He has written two books for the Rosen Publishing Group that are included in the Drug Abuse Prevention Library: *Drugs and Eating Disorders* and *Inhalants.* He has also written another book for young adults, *Opportunities in Medical Imaging Careers,* published by VGM Career Horizons.